MILAN 2015
GUIDE TO THE EXPO IN
WORLD'S
AND AROUND THE CITY
FAIR

MILAN 2015

GUIDE TO THE EXPO IN

WORLD'S

AND AROUND THE CITY

FAIR

RIZZOLI
NEW YORK

New York · Paris · London · Milan

Concept and coordination
Armando Peres

Texts
Massimiliano Bagioli
and Manuela Villani

Art direction and graphic design
CReE

Editorial coordination
Cristina Scalabrini

Translation
AG Studio

Iconography
© Centimetri (infographics)
© Shutterstock (Photos)
© Nasa Images (Photos pp. 28–29)
© Danilo Donadoni/Marka (Cover)

The publishers are available
to anyone holding rights
to any iconographic sources
not acknowledged.

Any data regarding the Expo is
up-to-date as of October 2013.

First published in the United States
of America in 2014 by Rizzoli
International Publications, Inc.
300 Park Avenue South
New York, NY 10010
www.rizzoliusa.com

Originally published in Italian
in 2013 by RCS Libri S.p.A.

© 2013 RCS Libri SpA, Milan
All rights reserved
www.rizzoli.eu

2014 2015 2016 2017 /
10 9 8 7 6 5 4 3 2 1

ISBN: 978-0-8478-4285-8

Library of Congress Control
Number: 2013950260

Printed in Italy

With the Support of:

 FEDERTURISMO
CONFINDUSTRIA

Exclusive Dealers
for national advertising
RCS MediaGroup SpA
Advertising Department
Via A. Rizzoli, 8 - 20132 Milano
Phone: 02 25846543
www.rcspubblicita.it
rcspubblicita@rcs.it

For local advertising
Guido Coppola
rizzoli.illustrati@rcs.it

PREFACE

There is just over a year to go before the start of the incredible event that is going to be Expo 2015. It is a one-off occasion and exceptional, but not only as a truly global debate dealing with one of the hottest topics for the future of mankind, "Feeding the Planet, Energy for Life," also as a chance to show over twenty million visitors who are expected to attend, many of them foreigners and visiting Milan for the first time, the many and the new faces of our city and its surroundings.

So we thought it was a good idea to offer a new guide, a useful tool of knowledge, specially prepared for them. Something that can give answers to all those questions we are still asking as to what Expo 2015 is really going to be: an universal exhibition, not a trade fair—an immense workshop of innovation and research, with the ambitious aim of laying down guidelines for the world that can guarantee a future for humanity with healthy, safe, and sufficient food for all.

A large part of our guide, though, is dedicated to providing all that practical, essential information that is so handy for a visit or a stay. That is, how to get there, how to get organized, what to see and how to move amid all the attractions, starting from what the Expo offers. What countries are on show? What pavilions will we see? And so on.

Then Milan and its surroundings. A lot of ideas on where to eat and sleep and especially what to do; out of all the cultural attractions, events and opportunities for entertainment and shopping that will be available in the city and the whole area around it.

Milan already boasts over five million visitors and is an important tourist destination, both for Italians and especially people from abroad. The main reason for a visit is business, and unfortunately it's a short stay. We would like this new guide to make a contribution, tacking advantage of the pulling power of Expo 2015, toward helping people to get to know our country better, starting from Milan, its metropolitan area, the region with its lakes and mountains, right down to the sea, as far as Venice and even farther on. Anyone who has the time and the desire can discover and appreciate our artistic and cultural heritage, the many typical products of our identity, from fashion to design, from enogastronomy to much more. Many of those who come to visit may thus feel the need to stay a little longer and, above all, to come back and visit us again after Expo 2015.

Armando Peres

MILAN EXPO

CONTENTS

HEADING TO THE EXPO

THE WORLD AT A CONVENTION

States from the five continents, major world organizations, millions of visitors from all corners: everybody in Milan for six months

- Afghanistan
- Albania
- Algeria
- Angola
- Argentina
- Armenia
- Austria
- Azerbaijan
- Bahrain
- Bangladesh
- Benin
- Belarus
- Belgium
- Bolivia
- Brazil
- Brunei
- Bulgaria
- Burundi
- Cambodia
- Cameroon
- Cape Verde
- Central African Republic

Expo Participating Countries

- CERN
- Chile
- China
- Colombia
- Congo-Brazzaville
- Congo-Kinshasa
- Costa Rica
- Croatia
- Cuba
- Czech Republic
- Dominica
- Dominican Republic
- Ecuador
- Egypt
- El Salvador
- Equatorial Guinea
- Eritrea
- Estonia
- Ethiopia

- European Commission
- France
- Gabon
- Gambia
- Georgia
- Germany
- Ghana
- Greece
- Guatemala
- Guinea-Bissau
- Guinea-Conakry
- Haiti
- Honduras
- Hungary
- India
- Indonesia
- Iran
- Iraq
- Israel
- Italy
- Japan
- Jordan
- Kazakhstan
- Kenya
- Kuwait
- Kyrgyzstan
- Laos
- Latvia
- Leban
- Lithuania
- Malaysia
- Maldives
- Mali
- Malta
- Mauritania
- Mexico
- Micronesia
- Moldova
- Mongolia
- Montenegro
- Mozambique
- Myanmar
- Nepal
- Niger
- Nigeria
- Oman
- Pakistan
- Palestine
- Paraguay
- Peru
- Principality of Monaco

- Qatar
- Republic of Côte d'Ivoire
- Republic of Palau
- Republic of Panama
- Romania
- Russia
- Rwanda
- Saint Vincent and the Grenadines
- San Marino
- Santa Lucia
- São Tomé and Principe
- Saudi Arabia
- Senegal
- Serbia
- Seychelles
- Sierra Leone
- Slovakia
- Slovenia
- South Korea
- Sovereign Order of Malta
- Spain
- Sri Lanka
- Switzerland
- Syria
- Tajikistan
- Tanzania
- Thailand
- Togo
- Tunisia
- Turkey
- Turkmenistan
- Ukraine
- Uganda
- Union of the Comoros
- United Arab Emirates
- United Kingdom
- UNO
- Uruguay
- Uzbekistan
- Vanuatu
- Vatican City
- Vietnam
- Yemen
- Zambia
- Zimbabwe

EUROPE 34

AFRICA 37

ASIA 38

SOUTH AMERICA 9

CENTRAL AND NORTH AMERICA 12

OCEANIA 3

Origins of the

20 million

Expo visitors

Type of Italian visitor

Young and dynamic

City man 19.9%

Interested woman 13,7%

Static type man 11.8%

Casual youth 10.6%

Retiree 5.1%

rticipants of Expo Milano 2015

4 INTERNATIONAL ORGANIZATIONS

1

1. Participating countries and organizations

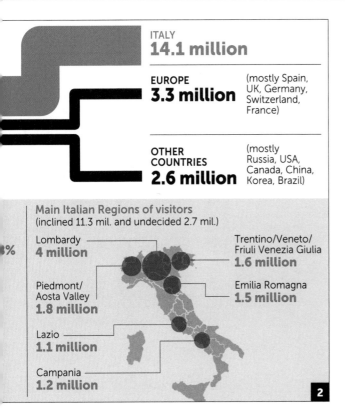

ITALY
14.1 million

EUROPE
3.3 million (mostly Spain, UK, Germany, Switzerland, France)

OTHER COUNTRIES
2.6 million (mostly Russia, USA, Canada, China, Korea, Brazil)

Main Italian Regions of visitors
(inclined 11.3 mil. and undecided 2.7 mil.)

Lombardy
4 million

Trentino/Veneto/ Friuli Venezia Giulia
1.6 million

Piedmont/ Aosta Valley
1.8 million

Emilia Romagna
1.5 million

Lazio
1.1 million

Campania
1.2 million

2

2. Identikit of the visitors expected at Expo 2015

HOW AN EVENT IS BORN

Milan is getting itself ready for the oldest and most prestigious international exhibition with a fresh purpose and material for its planned theme, focusing on the visitor and his/her needs.

What is the expo?

This is the most important international-level exhibition dealing with noncommercial matters of worldwide interest. It is held once every five years and lasts for six months. The host city is chosen by a special committee, following a bidding process by various candidates, similar to the system used for major international sporting events. Between each expo, smaller international exhibitions are held, usually lasting three months and dealing with more specific themes.

The idea of an international exhibition arose in the mid-1800s, the era of the positivist mentality and the notion that technological progress was the key to improving the human condition. During the 1900s, this spirit waned a little and the grand events lost some of their celebratory connotations and that aspect of large-scale trade fairs. In recent decades, they have been reconfigured more and more as moments for reflection and international debate; a sociocultural planning workshop that is unrivaled on the world's stage.

The International Committee

The BIE (Bureau International des Expositions), the International Exhibitions Bureau, was set up in 1931, with headquarters in Paris, France, as the organizing body for the universal exhibitions. The aim was to encourage themes that educated the public and tried to find ways (using models that had already been tried out or other viable ideas) of catering to the needs of civilization and sustainable growth.

While the main aim, as stated by the BIE's convention, is to "create a platform for international dialogue" and to help reinforce international relations in numerous areas—

"Feeding the Planet, Energy for Life" is the theme, a decisive one for the fate of humanity, and the reason Milan was chosen as the site of the Expo in 2015.

Thematic areas

Thematic clusters

Pavilions of single participants

Event areas

Companies

Service area

Children's park

Civil society (Cascina Triulza)

Expo Center

Pavilion Zero

3

12

economical, cultural, political, scientific, and educational—the opportunities for development available to the organizing cities have taken on a more than marginal role.

A simple master plan with high symbolic value

The overall structure that the various pavilions are built on is very simple and basic, so as not to come into conflict with the architectural multiplicity of the various participants. The master plan grid is formed by two perpendicular axes, called Cardo and Decumanus, the titles of the two principal arteries of the city of Rome. The Decumanus, 1.5 kms long, makes a symbolic connection between the point of consumption and the point of production of food (city–country). The pavilions of the various participating countries are set up along it and clearly visible. The Cardo, on the other hand, is 400 meters long and flanked by the exhibition stands of the host country, the regional and city authorities, as well as businesses and associations. At one end there is the Italian Pavilion.

The intersection between the two axes will feature a plaza, the main meeting point, that's the same size as the square in front of La Scala Opera House, while the cardinal points of this remarkable layout will be identified by symbolic places, major landmarks where the exhibition's main events will be held: the Hills, the Open Air Theatre, the Piazza d'Acqua (Water Plaza), and the Expo Center. The whole site will be encircled by a canal, as a symbol of the role water plays in the balance of this planet, but also as an ideal link with the canals of Milan, known as the Navigli.

3. Division of the areas and spaces occupied by Expo 2015

6 months

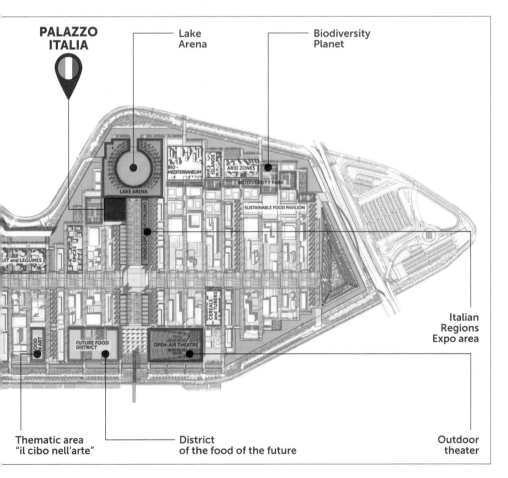

PALAZZO ITALIA

Lake Arena

Biodiversity Planet

Italian Regions Expo area

Thematic area "il cibo nell'arte"

District of the food of the future

Outdoor theater

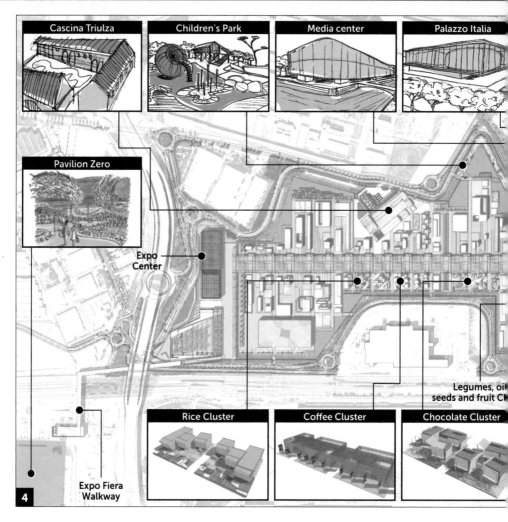

Cascina Triulza | Children's Park | Media center | Palazzo Italia

Pavilion Zero

Expo Center

Legumes, oil seeds and fruit Cl

Rice Cluster | Coffee Cluster | Chocolate Cluster

4

Expo Fiera Walkway

Digital Smart City and Cyber Expo—digital identity: leading-edge technology

The event will have leading-edge technology at its disposal, with innovative solutions tested and put into operation for the occasion, capable of providing a uniquely intelligent framework for tourism and for the cultural and commercial aims of the exhibition.

The creation of the Digital Smart City will be particularly useful to visitors who can use it to become key-citizens and create their own tours according to their interests and available time. It is a system that will put information about events and places in the fair at a visitor's fingertips at any time, making it easier to move around the whole metropolitan area. At the same time, visitors will be able to try out more engaging forms of visits, going deeper into the themes through multimedia material or using greater social interaction to create tours that they can share with friends or establishing new, efficient relationships.

Cyber Expo, a multiplatform multimedia system, will enable anyone who can't go to the exhibition to get a first-hand view of everything, a virtual expo that is a complete reproduction of the real one. This tool will become even more valuable once the event itself has finished, since it will extend its duration and help keep the debate about the themes of Expo 2015 running.

1 billion contacts

Italian Pavilion

On April 19, 2013, the winning design was announced

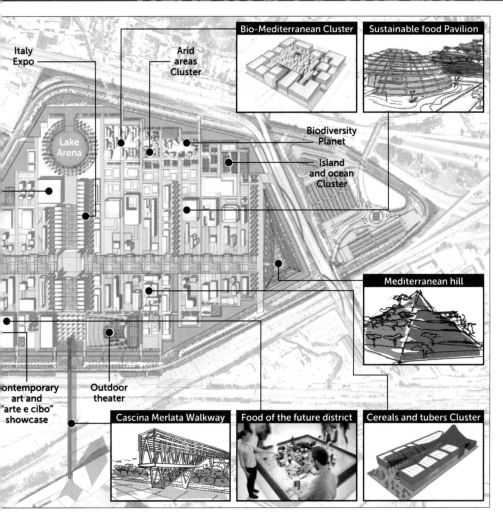

Italy Expo

Arid areas Cluster

Bio-Mediterranean Cluster

Sustainable food Pavilion

Lake Arena

Biodiversity Planet

Island and ocean Cluster

Mediterranean hill

contemporary art and "arte e cibo" showcase

Outdoor theater

Cascina Merlata Walkway

Food of the future district

Cereals and tubers Cluster

for the Italian Pavilion, the main center for the institutions and representative bodies of the host country of Expo 2015. Of the 68 designs presented to the international selection process, the jury selected the one created by the Italian firms Nemesis & Partners Srl from Rome, Proger SpA from Pescara, and BMS Progetti Srl from Milan.

Their design is an innovative, original interpretation of the guidelines for the pavilion that were mapped out by Marco Balich, the world-famous Olympic master of ceremonies. It features transparency, energy, water, technology, and environmental compatibility and is built around the essential iconic elements of the Nursery and the Tree of Life, as expressions of Original Nature, the generator of all living things.

The winning design also features an ultralight structure, which can interact with its surrounding environment and has sustainable energy, organized around a plaza where the Tree of Life stands. The spaces in this sort of "green Beaubourg," reminiscent also of Crystal Palace (the transparent pavilion built for the London Exhibition 1851) are made up of four main blocks, for the same number of functions: Exhibition Area, Auditorium, Administration Offices, and Meeting Rooms. According to Diana Bracco, president of Expo 2015 and general commissioner for the Italian Pavilion, these quite emblematic spaces "will offer our visitors from all over the world the magic of a trip through the typical experiences peculiar to our country and bring back to life the legendary Grand Tour."

4. The main pavilions and their locations

15

A HARD-WORKING WAIT

Infrastructural work is being carried out to improve accessibility, while events are held on the subject of food and nutrition, as Milan and its citizens head toward the great event of 2015.

A concrete route to Expo 2015

Since 2012 the preparations for the great event have started to light up the lives of Milan's population, especially during the so-called Expo Days, a kind of general rehearsal organized together with the Milan City Council. These are days (one whole week in the first year and the month of May in 2013) with a long list of appointments: conferences, exhibitions, shows, book launches, kids' workshops, workshops, and wine and food tasting going on all over the city. The aim of this is to create more aware-ness of the Expo themes, food and nutrition, sustainable growth and the environment, and at the same time bring the city's population and its tourists into closer contact with the atmosphere of a universal exhibition. The Expo Days already include some major events of symbolic importance, such as the unfurling of the flags of the countries that have, one by one, confirmed their presence, or the Planetary Table, organized on May 5, 2012 in the cathedral square, Piazza Duomo. This was an enormous table, stretching for 200 meters, laid by 12 of the 150 or so foreign communi-ties living in Milan, to provide a free taste of their ethnic food. It was a unique occasion for cross-cultural exchange and discussion, as a precursor to the full-scale Expo scenario. More than twenty farms, from Milan and Monza, also play an important part on these occasions, opening to the public for the day to show that certain important themes of the exhibition, such as urban agriculture and territorial cohesion, are already a reality in these parts, which we can get to know and make use of.

5. Diagram of improvements to the road network in Lombardy for Expo 2015

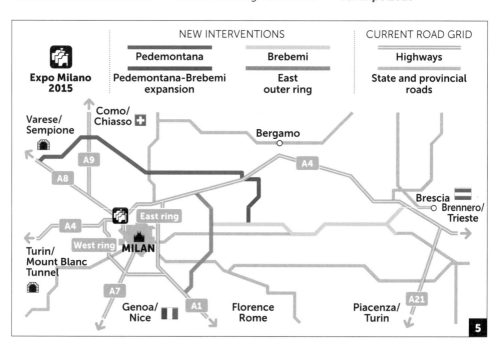

EDUCATING WITH ENJOYMENT

**Facing sustainable nutrition and the risks
of sophistication as recreation, without forgetting that a visit
to the Expo is, above all, a moment of leisure.**

The challenge of Expo 2015: an exhibition focusing on the visitor

At the heart of the organization of Expo 2015, there is, above all, the person, both as principal beneficiary of sustainable development and as the main figure in a learning curve. One of the cardinal concepts of this exhibition is the visitor experience: every aspec—from the site, the pavilions, the stands, eateries, shows, right down to the dynamics of the visit itself—has to take the visitor into consideration, to ensure that he/she is really involved in the questions being dealt with. Even if it just creates interest, or, beyond that, becomes an experience of research and knowledge, the event will achieve its objective and have a real influence on the relationship between the world community and the planet and its resources, encouraging constructive debate on an international level about food and nutrition; to bring about a beneficial improvement. The main instrument in this education will be dialogue, something that is tied to with the very nature of international exhibitions; not only will the pavilions be designed to try and facilitate a grasp of a new outlook, but everyone will be given the chance to talk to organizers and participants of the Expo—in line with a true concept of engagement with the visitor.

Making the Expo a path of awareness and knowledge

Even though it is defined in the theme—with its possible variations, and partly conditioned by the main guidelines drawn up by the organizing committee—the outcome of Expo 2015 will depend, in the long run, on how much the participants are prepared to let themselves be affected by the problems raised. The invitation offered to the various delegations is to tackle this theme with suitable structures and ideas that can transmit awareness of good, healthy nutrition, which responds to the real needs of people and, at the same time, respects the system of nature that we are all part of. The challenge is, first of all, to ask ourselves certain cogent questions about the development of the planet, concerning the robustness of food production systems, the possibility of passing technological means and natural resources down to the future, safeguards for biodiversity, the very concept of nutrition; to set out on a path of awareness and knowledge through exhibitions, conventions, and teaching. A real commitment to face these questions will truly lead to the establishment of a platform for dialogue that can be heard around the world and would be capable of tapping into the great millennium goals declared by the United Nations and making new, constructive contributions to the development of the planet.

CROSSROADS OF EUROPE

With Expo Milano 2015, Milan is reconfirming its role as an international city, which has been celebrated since the universal Exhibition held there in 1906.

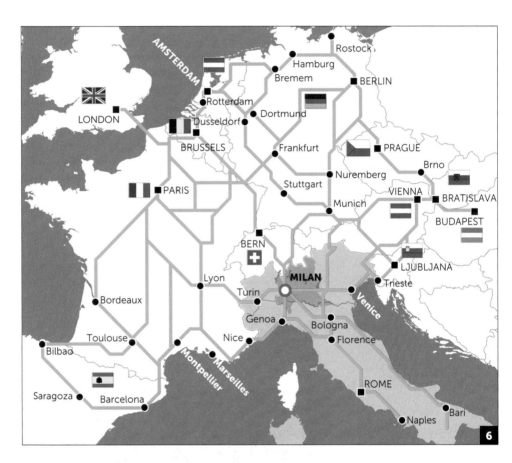

A choice for development

The Expo is giving the host city and its surrounding area the chance to not only make the most of its own characteristics and refurbish its urban landscape, but also to modernize its communications network.Structures that have been purposefully built for the occasion, very often the creative fruits of top-class ar-chitects and engineers, will be dismantled at the end of the event, but some of the more important installations will be left standing, to become symbols of the organizing city. This is how it's always been right from the first universal exhibition, held in London in 1851, when the Crystal Palace was designed and built by Joseph Paxton for the occasion. That structure was destroyed by fire in 1936 but lives on in the collective memory, as well as in books on architecture and history, as one of the symbols of universal exhibitions. The Eiffel Tower is an even more famous example, inherited from the Paris universal exhibition of 1889, in the century of the revolution, while the most evident symbol in Brussels is the Atomium, created for the Expo held in the Belgian capital in 1958.

Since ancient times, Milan has played a crucial role in exchanges between northern and southern Europe.

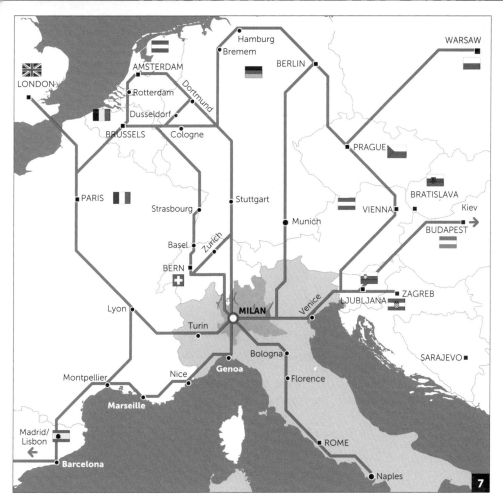

Hamburg
Bremem
BERLIN
WARSAW
AMSTERDAM
Dortmund
LONDON
Rotterdam
Dusseldorf
BRUSSELS
Cologne
PRAGUE
PARIS
Stuttgart
BRATISLAVA
Strasbourg
VIENNA
Kiev
Munich
BUDAPEST
Basel
Zurich
BERN
LJUBLJANA
ZAGREB
Lyon
MILAN
Venice
Turin
Bologna
SARAJEVO
Montpellier
Nice
Genoa
Florence
Marseille
Madrid/
Lisbon
ROME
Barcelona
Naples

7

Milan 1906

The 2015 edition will not be the first expo held in Milan; the Lombardy capital already held one in 1906. The idea then was to organize a major international exhibition on transport, to coincide with the opening of the Sempione Tunnel through the Alps, a 20-km rail tunnel connecting the Italian Val d'Ossola with Switzerland and thereby linking Italy to central Europe. The universal exhibition was officially inaugurated by the Italian royal family on April 28, 1906, on a site that was divided between Sempione Park and the area that was later to become the site of the trade fair. The numbers were impressive for the period: 40 participating nations, 205 pavilions, and 10 million visitors. The City Aquarium remains as testimony to the event.

6. The major communication routes in Europe

7. Milan in the European railroad network

WITHIN REACH

Long-distance travelers to Milan have a choice of three airports: Malpensa, the main hub; Linate, closest to the city center; Orio al Serio, for low-cost flights.

Choice of the site

The area to the northwest of the metropolitan boundary is the best developed of the regional-metropolitan area of Milan, from a transport point of view. There are fast and frequent connections to the city center, using the subway, the three highway routes, and the various railroad lines, including high-speed trains.

The underlying concept of the development of the exhibition site, set by the designers of the Expo, including leading architects such as Stefano Boeri, Ricky Burdett, and Jacques Herzog, is the idea of sustainability and harmony with the environment, which is in tune with the theme of the event. The organizers chose to go against the tendency of previous exhibitions and decided to discard the idea of a strikingly monumental archi-

The regional-metropolitan area of Milan is well served by an efficient airport system, planned for every kind of traveler.

tectural ideal in favor of giving form to a more agile, and therefore more sustainable master plan, which would be able to interact positively with its landscape and permit the use of biodegradable materials, eco-compatible transport systems, and the exploitation of solar energy.

A few numbers

Occupying a total area of **1.7 million sq.m**, there will be places for **132** participants (countries and international organizations) and **60** private companies. Over the **6** months that the event will be open (May–October 2015) **20 million** visitors are expected, an average of over **100,000** a day. Around **32,000** volunteers will be working to make the exhibition a success. Around **7,000** cultural and music events will take place during the Expo.

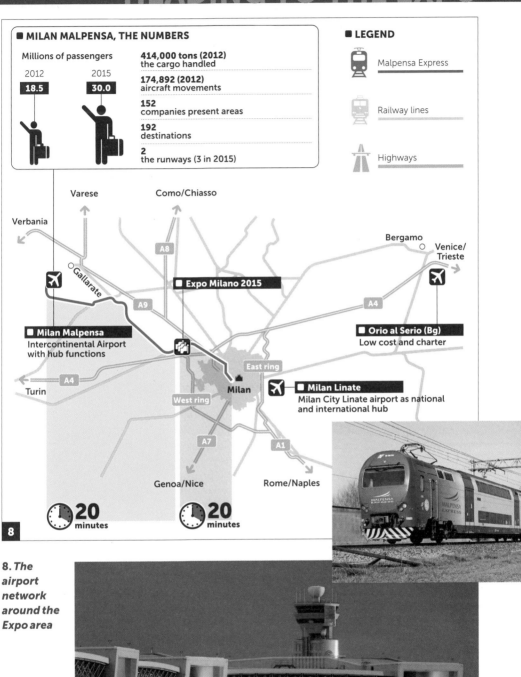

■ MILAN MALPENSA, THE NUMBERS

Millions of passengers

2012 **18.5**

2015 **30.0**

414,000 tons (2012)
the cargo handled

174,892 (2012)
aircraft movements

152
companies present areas

192
destinations

2
the runways (3 in 2015)

■ LEGEND

Malpensa Express

Railway lines

Highways

Varese

Como/Chiasso

Verbania

Bergamo

Venice/Trieste

A8

Gallarate

■ Expo Milano 2015

A9

A4

■ Milan Malpensa
Intercontinental Airport
with hub functions

■ Orio al Serio (Bg)
Low cost and charter

A4

East ring

Turin

Milan

West ring

■ Milan Linate
Milan City Linate airport as national
and international hub

A7

A1

Genoa/Nice

Rome/Naples

20 minutes

20 minutes

8

8. *The airport network around the Expo area*

21

DINNER IS SERVED

During this event it will be possible to taste an enormous range of food and wine specialties, out of a selection of offerings from all over the world.

Feed the Planet, Energy for Life. The theme of Expo Milan 2015

The theme of Expo 2015 is a universal one that affects the fundamental dimensions of nature and society: no life-form on Earth, starting with humans, can opt out of his or her nutritional process. At the same time the planet itself needs energy to guarantee sustainable development to be handed down to future generations. So there is a double challenge: reflect and find feasible routes for the nutrition of Man and the Earth at the same time. There is no alternative to facing these two problems jointly, since our future depends precisely on a balanced relationship between natural resources and food and energy production. In light of this, it is easy to understand the importance of the subthemes listed by the Expo Scientific Committee, which the various countries (public institutions, but also private companies, humanitarian associations, consumer representatives, and producers) will have to take into consideration, questioning themselves and attempting to make a constructive contribution.

The Expo is close to the trade fairground Nuova Fiera and is easy to get to from Milan center.

Food production: the memory of ancient techniques, and new technologies

The event will provide a chance to undertake a long journey, which will take us from the most ancient traditions of hunting, fishing, cultivation, and animal rearing of populations with thousands of years of experience, up to the confines of the "as yet unknown."

The history of Man really is identifiable in his capacity to produce food, a capability that has evolved over time, resulting in modern technologies for producing and conserving foodstuffs. It will be possible to analyze entire agro-alimentary production chains, to make comparisons, to find out where technological evolution has worked to the detriment of a healthy relationship with the ecosystem and where, on the other hand, beneficial strategies have been adopted, whether in the transformation of products or the distribution or consumption of food.

The memory of the ancient techniques and the awareness of the present situation will prove to be decisive presuppositions in evaluating and working out innovative solutions and future projects for the investment of human capital and economic resources.

Railways lines	—
Metro M1	—
Highway	—
Parking	
Expo Milano 2015	
New Milan Expo Center	
New civil works	- - -

Con
Vare

Milan

Va
Sem

Italia
Railway

SS

HS/HV li

A4

Turin

Novara

The food and drink on offer: excellence and traditions

Expo 2015, with a theme that is so focused on nutrition, offers a chance to translate the arguments into pleasant occasions for sampling, as well as getting to know the eating, cultural, and ethnic traditions of various countries.

The idea has been put to the participants to organize two dining areas inside their pavilions, both in tune with the architecture and the concept of their pavilion, where

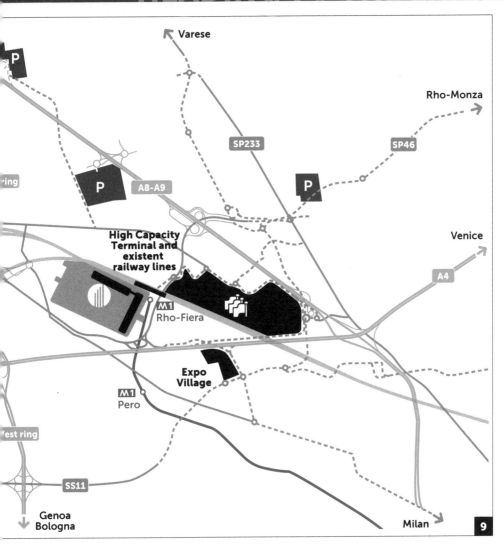

P

Varese

Rho-Monza

SP233

SP46

P

A8-A9

ing

Venice

High Capacity
Terminal and
existent
railway lines

A4

M1
Rho-Fiera

M1
Pero

Expo
Village

est ring

SS11

Genoa
Bologna

Milan

9

they can present their products in an original, decorative manner.

The food and drink on offer, which may not go outside the parameters of excellence and sustainability, something of a recurring slogan for the whole event, will be of two kinds: one destined for the

9. The transport links from Milan to the event site

general public—more dynamic and practical and aimed at the thousands of visitors looking around the exhibition areas; the other, though, destined for a more select public, one that is seeking a refined, meditative gastronomic experience, generally reserved for the evenings. It is certain the people from Milan and their guests will have every chance to satisfy all their eno-gastronomic whims.

THE LEGACY OF EXPO 2015

The Expo is an opportunity not only for the modernization of the transport network in the region of Milan, but also for the creation of a permanent center for research on nutrition.

Milan, city of waterways

It is amazing to think that a city without any major river that passes through it, far from the sea and lakes, has been the center of a dense network of commercial navigation for most of its history. The articulated network of canals built and enlarged several times over the centuries, and now almost completely buried, in the first decades after the unification of Italy, are the cause of this legacy.

The Expo 2015 led Milan to rediscover, albeit partially, its ancient "aquatic" soul, with restoration of the dock area and the construction of a waterway that cuts from the city center to the Expo area.

10. Waterways and bike paths around Milan

11. Works for the Expo at the Darsena (Harbour Area) of Milan

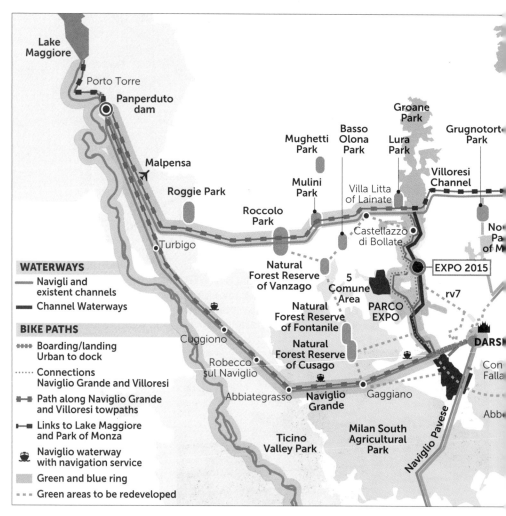

WATERWAYS
— Navigli and existent channels
— Channel Waterways

BIKE PATHS
••••• Boarding/landing Urban to dock
•••••• Connections Naviglio Grande and Villoresi
■-■ Path along Naviglio Grande and Villoresi towpaths
I-■ Links to Lake Maggiore and Park of Monza
⚓ Naviglio waterway with navigation service
▢ Green and blue ring
- - - Green areas to be redeveloped

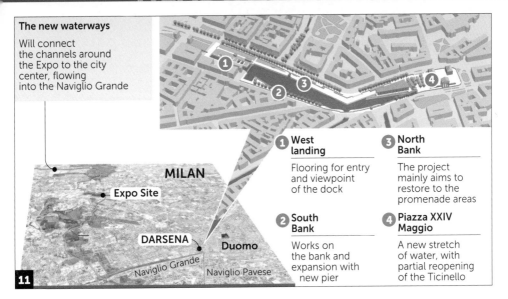

The new waterways

Will connect the channels around the Expo to the city center, flowing into the Naviglio Grande

MILAN

Expo Site

DARSENA

Duomo

Naviglio Grande

Naviglio Pavese

11

1 West landing

Flooring for entry and viewpoint of the dock

2 South Bank

Works on the bank and expansion with new pier

3 North Bank

The project mainly aims to restore to the promenade areas

4 Piazza XXIV Maggio

A new stretch of water, with partial reopening of the Ticinello

Lambro Park

Monza Park and Villa Reale

Adda Valley

Crespi D'Adda

Naviglio Martesana

Idroscalo

Linate

10

The lasting heredity of Expo 2015

The world and international expositions as well as other world events, such as the Olympics, always offer unique opportunities for the host cities, in terms of city layout and infrastructures.

Milan is preparing for the big event with important architectural works that will change the very perception of broad areas of the city. But the goal of Expo 2015 goes beyond the mere desire to leave a material legacy, and it aims to deliver a decisive contribution for, primarily, sustainable ideas and solutions, as well as greater and more diffused awareness on the issues addressed. With this in mind, the organizers gave life to the project Feeding Knowledge, with the aim of "promoting a network of knowledge, training, and cooperation initiatives for all countries on the issue of sustainable development, in order to establish a permanent legacy of the 2015 World Expo." Substantial resources have been allocated to this project, which has already led to the establishment—thanks to an agreement between the Expo Organizational Committee and the Ministry for the Environment—of a permanent international research center—the International Center Food and Environment Security—based in Milan. The center, the only one of its kind, aims to become a point of reference for scholars and experts in the field, with regard to research and dissemination in nutrition and food security, as well as issues linked to the environment and energy imbalance and food resources between north and south of the world. The center will also sponsor training projects involving international agencies and organizations.

7,000
performances

MILAN

MILAN

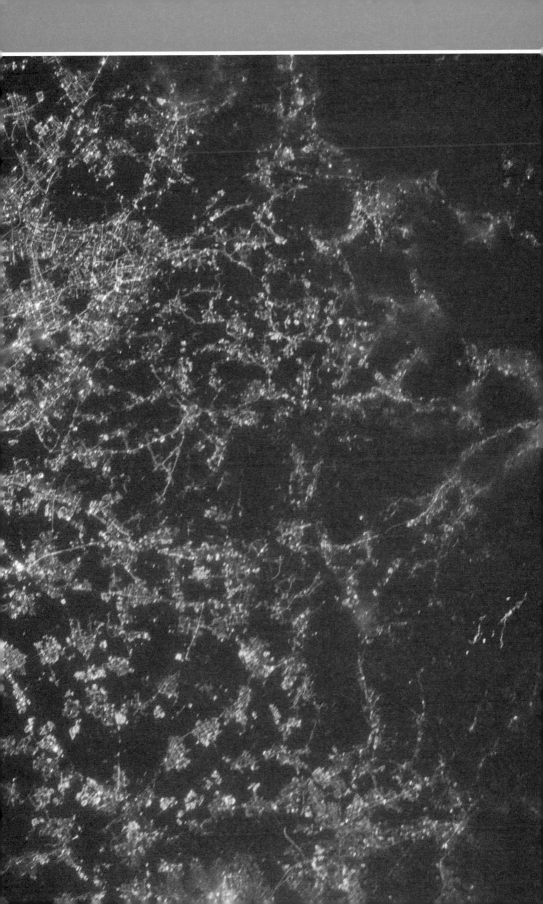

MILAN

VENUES AND MONUMENTS

The best the city has to offer in twenty stops, combining cultural tourism, relaxation, and entertainment.

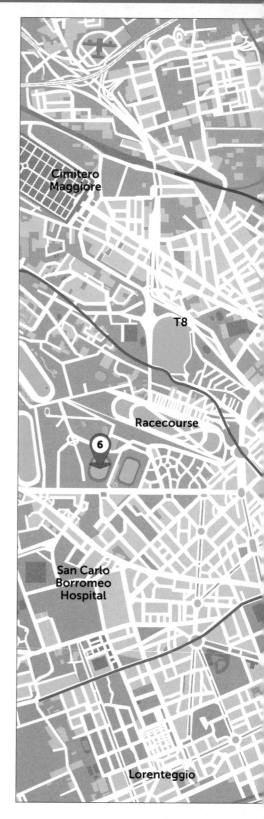

visa
.M.

Ca' Granda
Niguarda
Hospital

Greco

Dock area
Farini

Central
Railway Station

Cimitero
Monumentale

Garibaldi
Railway Station

Expo
Milan City

Parco
Solari

Polyclinic
Maggiore
Milan

Porta
Vittoria

Naviglio
Grande

Naviglio
Pavese

Dock area
Lodi T.I.B.B.

LONGING FOR EUROPE

**A monument symbolizing the city, Milan Cathedral—the Duomo—
is the only large, medieval, Italian church built
in the same style as the Gothic cathedrals on the continent.**

A gilded **Madonnina** sits 108 meters from the ground, on top of the best-known monument in Milan, as proof of its ancient international standing. Outside, the cathedral swarms with rampant arches, spires, and pinnacles stretching into the sky, and windows, and the interior is divided into five aisles with dizzying columns.

The decision to build it, on the site of a previous cathedral, was made in **1386**. It was financed by all the social classes, well-off and not, and especially by the lord of the city **Gian Galeazzo Visconti**, who wanted to make it a symbol of prestige for his ancient bloodline, who reigned over substantial lands in northern Italy at that time. He had marble shipped from the quarries at Candoglia, near Lake Maggiore, as he wanted the building completed entirely with this material. He also called in and paid experts from over the Alps, who worked closely with local architects, engineers, and craftsmen in a fruitful exchange of ideas and techniques.

The decidedly Gothic style of the building and its **exceptional size** (it remains the fourth largest in Europe, after St. Peter's in Rome, St. Paul's in London, and Seville Cathedral) made it a symbol of the city's political rise on the international scene.

The cathedral is dedicated to the Virgin Mary, as highlighted by the reliefs on the façade, which was

not finished until the 1800s. But the part that is older and more Gothic in style is the **apse**. This is perfectly aligned toward the east and enriched by the scene of the Annunciation standing out in the central window: the figures of the angel and the Virgin Mary are flanked by St. Ambrose, patron of Milan, and St. Galdino, the archbishop who encouraged the rebuilding of the city after its destruction by the emperor Barbarossa in the mid-12th century; God and the Holy Spirit are shown above the sun's rays, the heraldic symbol of the Visconti, as well as the emblem of Jesus Christ, the sun of justice.

The oldest spire is the one over the apse. This was completed in 1404 and dedicated to Marco Carelli, a rich merchant who donated all of his wealth, more than 35,000 ducats, to the cathedral at the end of the 1300s.

A magnificent place

A sense of magnificence strikes when you enter the cathedral. The **52 pillars**, which separate the five aisles (the central one twice the size of the others), are each topped by enormous capitals, with full-size statues of martyrs and angels standing on them. The chancel, erected in the 1570s by the bishop of Milan **Carlo Borromeo** soon catches the eye. Here, there is the altar and the tabernacle, the niche where the consecrated Host is kept. The heavy

emphasis put on this part of the cathedral is due to the fact that St. Charles, at that time, was a leading light in the Catholic Counter-Reformation after the Council of Trent, when the Church of Rome responded to the Protestant movement's refusal of some sacraments, including the Holy Communion.

This saint was a member of one of the most influential aristocratic families in the city, and his life is depicted in the so-called *Quadroni*, 44 large paintings from the early 1600s, commissioned for his beatification and canonization. They are on display from November 4, St. Charles' name day, until January 6, Epiphany.

The cathedral tour illuminated by its 164 windows, with nearly 3,000 square meters of glass, has a lot to offer; starting near the entrance with

the meridian line, a brass strip with the signs of the zodiac marked along it, designed in 1786 by the astronomers of Brera. As you enter the cathedral there is a small hole 24 meters up on the right-hand wall; a ray of sunlight shines through this hole at solar noon and casts a small circle of light on the floor on the zodiac sign of the moment (this phenomenon can no longer be seen, because of modern electric lighting).

Farther on, in the aisle furthest to the right, there is the sarcophagus of Ariberto d'Intimiano, a powerful archbishop in the first half of the 11th century; above it there is a copy (the original is in the cathedral's museum) of the crucifix in gilded copper laminae he commissioned. In this part of the building are the oldest windows, dating back to the 1400s. Particularly worth not-

The Piazza del Duomo was opened in the second half of the 1800's. In the center there is the monument to Vittorio Emanuele II.

ing are those with the stories of the Old and New Testaments, made in around 1470 from a drawing by Vincenzo Foppa, leading figure in renaissance painting in Lombardy.

In the right wing of the three-aisled transept, there is

the marble and bronze burial monument, sculpted in the style of Michelangelo by Leone Leoni (1560–68) for Gian Giacomo de' Medici, known as Medeghino, who was a warlord and mercenary, as well as being Pope Pius IV's brother and Carlo Borromeo's uncle. There is also a grisly statue of St. Bartholomew Flayed, carrying his skin over his shoulder like a stole. This work demonstrates Marco d'Agate's sculpting ability and knowledge of anatomy.

Relics and treasures

The holiest relics can be seen in the area around the altar. In the dome above the apse, a small red lightbulb marks the spot where a **Holy Nail** from Christ's True Cross is kept. According to tradition, Helena found the nails from the crucifix and gifted one to the son of Emperor Constantine, which later passed from Theodosius to Bishop Ambrose. This relic is shown to the faithful every year on September 13, the day of the invention of the crucifix. To do this the archbishop, accompanied by five canons, has to use the *nivola*, a sort of lift to reach the niche where the nail is kept. This lift, which resembles a cloud, was possibly the brainchild of da Vinci and was once raised by hand, but nowadays by electric winches.

The remains of Carlo Borromeo are below the presbytery, in the **crypt**, kept in a crystal coffin donated by the king of Spain, Philip IV. The burial chamber, dating from 1606, is decorated with silver bas-reliefs depicting scenes from the life of the saint.

Continuing in the ambulatory, there are some examples

The best view of the cathedral is from Piazzetta di Palazzo Reale (on the right of the building) and from Corso Vittorio Emanuele II.

of refined late-Gothic sculptures to admire, some of the most ancient in the cathedral: the two sacristy portals from the 1300s and Jacopino da Tradate's statue of Martin V, the pope who consecrated the cathedral in 1418. In the left wing of the transept there is the altar of the Madonna of the Tree, from 1614. Opposite that, there is the seven-arm **Trivulzio Candelabrum**, donated to the cathedral toward

The building of the cathedral of Milan, started in 1386, was only completed in the 1900's. As was customary with large medieval churches, work started on the apse, so that the altar could be added as soon as possible and make it possible to consecrate the church, which was done as early as 1418. For centuries the building remained an enormous building site: the transept was only closed in the 1500's to stop the traffic of ox-drawn carts, which passed through with indifference to the building.

the mid-1500s by the high priest Giovan Battista Trivulzio. This is a mysterious object: it is the largest medieval candelabrum in existence, and is of unknown origin. It was quite possibly forged around 1200, in France or England, and features figures of monsters sprouting from the branches and leaves of a plant. Continuing around the perimeter, you come to another important object of worship; the wooden cross carried by St. Charles in processions during the 1576 plague.

Before leaving the interior, you can go downstairs into the archaeological area (the start is near the main entrance) to see the remains of sacred buildings, such as the Basilica of Santa Tecla and the Baptistery of St. John at the Springs, one of Christianity's oldest octagonal-shaped baptisteries and the site where St. Ambrose baptized St. Augustine in the Easter vigil of 387 AD.

The forest of spires

On a clear day it's almost obligatory to go up to the **terraces** on the outside of the transept. You can walk along the whole of this cathedral roof, and it offers a unique view across the rooftops of Milan and into the distance, as far as the alpine peaks of Resegone and Monte Rosa. At the same time you get a close-up view of the jungle of statues and decorations that adorn the flying buttresses and abundant spires, as many as 135. This is an almost infinite collection of sculptures (around 3,400 statues and more than 700 figures in bas-relief), all in marble and produced continuously over the centuries: from the statue on the Carelli spire of St. George,

recognizable as a portrait of Gian Galeazzo Visconti, to the figures of modern-day saints. Among the bas-reliefs there is room for curious objects, too, such as a Roman helmet, tennis rackets and balls, mountaineering equipment, and even two pairs of boxers, in honor of Primo Carnera, the first Italian to win, in 1933, the world heavyweight title.

Anyone who wants to take a closer look at some of the more antique statues from the building, or examples of windows, tapestries, and sacred furnishings, should visit the museum, recently reopened on the ground floor of the Palazzo Reale, on the right of the cathedral. It's a wonderful chance to better appreciate the long process of building the cathedral and of preserving it.

MILAN'S PARLOR

The shopping passageway Galleria Vittorio Emanuele II is an elegant shopping intersection that emerged as an icon in Milan in the 1800s. Still loved by the residents of the city, it's an absolute must for visitors.

The idea of building an ultramodern "open air shopping passageway" in the heart of Milan goes back to the 1800s and major projects of urban replanning. The process of accepting bids for the projects was initiated internationally by the municipality in 1861, just after the proclamation of national unification, which explains why the passageway was named after the first king of Italy. **Giuseppe Mengoni**, architect and engineer, submitted the winning bid out of 176 applicants, and on March 7, 1865, in a snow-storm, Vittorio Emanuele II laid the first stone.

Mengoni's bid probably won because it was bold enough to put technological advances to architectural use. The passageway was given the form of imposing cross-vaulting,  with an iron frame covered with glass, reaching a height of 47 meters at the center of the vaulting. The two arms, 196 and 105 meters long, respectively, open up from two triumphal arches, forming a spacious octagonal hall in the center, covered by vaulting.

Mengoni did not survive to see the **inauguration**, as he died tragically a few days previously, after falling from the scaffolding during an inspection. Vittorio Emanuele could not make it either, as he was suffering from a bout of pneumonia, which was to kill him too. Despite these inauspicious events, the galleria aroused great pride and admiration among the citizens of Milan. In particular, the structure, with its exposed iron work and glass, brought to mind the marvelous Crystal Palace, built in London in 1851 for the first World Exhibition. The **lighting** also caused astonishment, as it was far ahead of its time; the first in Italy and state of the art in Europe. It was

In 1967, the 100th anniversary of the inauguration of the galleria, the Rizzoli bookstore opened while the publishing group's founder was still alive. Angelo Rizzoli (1889–1970) was one of the most extraordinary personalities of Italy in the 1900s. He was the son of a shoemaker who had died by the time he was born, and he started his brilliant career in publishing as a typographer, a profession he learned in the Martinitt institution, which educated orphans in Milan for centuries.

In the center of the galleria, you may witness a curious superstitious ritual: people performing a triple pirouette, turning clockwise with the right heel firmly planted on the "equipment" of the bull (in a mosaic on the ground, the emblem of the city of Turin). The original purpose of this ritual was to break any curses associated with Mengoni's unfortunate demise, but nowadays people do it just for good luck.

the first time a public area was illuminated by arc lamps, at first in 1881 and permanently after 1885.

From the very start this pedestrian passageway became a meeting place for the Milanese, thanks to its elegant cafès, restaurants, and stores. Some of the original businesses are still operating and have become famous in the history of the Milanese lifestyle. The venues that are most steeped in history have to include the cafè, Biffi, opened in 1867 by Paolo Biffi, royal confectioner. This cafè immediately became

a classic appointment for the Milanese bourgeoisie. Then, on the corner of the cathedral square, there is the bar, **Campari**, still bearing the name of the company that is symbolic of the Italian aperitif. Another venue with a history is **Savini**, a top-notch restaurant, in the shorter arm of the galleria going toward Via Ugo Foscolo. At the turn of the century, between the 1800s and 1900s, many famous figures from the cultural and entertainment world dined here, including Giuseppe Verdi and Giacomo Puccini, Gabriele D'Annunzio and Giuseppe Verga.

Publishers also voted for the galleria as a shop window for their profession. The newspaper *Corriere della Sera* had its head office here and

the names of two other major Italian family-owned publishing groups stand out among the advertising signs. **Rizzoli** have a large bookstore at the entrance to Piazza Scala and Ricordi, the music specialists, have a basement multimedia store, which also sells books in conjunction with Feltrinelli publishers.

One other top store is the **Prada** boutique, a business that opened in 1915 as a luxury leather laboratory and remains high on the list of shopping destinations. Above the shop there is the only seven star hotel in Italy, the Seven Stars Galleria (www.sevenstarsgalleria. com), an exclusive VIP hotel born to respect its décor, stuccoes, frescoes, and its original architecture.

THE TEMPLE OF OPERA

La Scala theater is the icon of Milan for anyone in the world who loves classical art and music. Its stage has confirmed the glory of exceptional performers and seen a procession of the world's greatest orchestra conductors.

On the night of February 25, 1776, carnival Saturday, the Regio Ducale theater, in a wing of the Royal Palace, burned down. This happened not long after an acclaimed appearance by Mozart. Work started immediately on a new theater, no longer within the palace premises, but in the same place as a crumbling 1300s church, the Santa Maria alla Scala. The church was demolished to make way for the new building, but the name remained.

The building's history

The project was entrusted to **Giuseppe Piermarini**, undisputed expert in neoclassical building in Milan. Despite several renovations and modernizations, the theater basically remains unchanged. The exterior still has its accommodating gallery, and the in-

The elegant square, Piazza della Scala, was not opened until the 1800s, long after the theater was built.

terior maintains its horseshoe layout, with four tiers of boxes and the original galleries. The cost of building La Scala was partly financed by selling the boxes in the new theater to the owners of boxes in the burned down one. The opening took place with great pomp on August 3, 1778, with a performance of Antonio Salieri's opera *Europa Riconosciuta* (Europa Recognized), composed for the occasion.

Major modernization work was carried out in the early 1800s. In 1814 the stage was made deeper, and in 1821 the candle lighting was replaced by a large central light with safety lamps, substituted in 1860 with a gas-burning system, which was only used until 1883, when the hall and stage were fitted with electric lighting.

Looking at the theater from the square, two new parts are clearly visible over the rooftops, one oval shaped and the other rectangular—the work of the architect Mario Botta and built between 2002 and 2004. They contain, respectively, rehearsal rooms and the scenery tower.

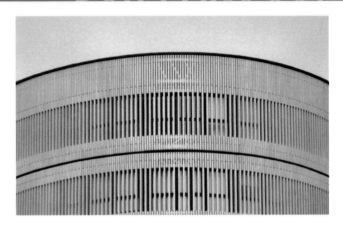

More than just a theater

From the moment it was opened, La Scala was the most prestigious **venue for high-society**. The various owners of the private boxes decorated them in splendor, as they liked. They dined in them, received guests, used them for courting purposes or for business meetings. The theater was available for dancing, fancy dress balls, and even for gambling (something that was completely prohibited in the rest of Milan). At the same time, the stage was becoming ever more famous internationally, so much so that Stendhal wrote this in 1816: "For me this is the first theater in the world, because it is the one that brings the greatest pleasure out of music . . . As for the architecture, it is impossible to imagine anything grander, more majestic and new."

In 1951 the traditional opening of the opera season was moved from September to **December 7**, the patron Saint's day of St. Ambrose, a public holiday in Milan. This has given the "premiere" more importance, and not just culturally. With the mayor and important officials presiding over it, it has now become a high-profile event for Italian high society.

The splendor of the 1800s

In terms of performances, while Neapolitan opera and its top performers (Giovanni Paisiello and Domenico Cimarosa) were originally given the most space, the artistic scene started to broaden at the end of the 1700s, toward a French flavor and the romantic opera

Of all the composers whose names are associated with the theater, Giuseppe Verdi has always been the favorite of La Scala audiences.

of Gioacchino Rossini, who made his debut in 1812 with *La Pietra del paragone* (The Touchstone) and then turned La Scala into the **temple of Italian melodrama**. The 1800s were a succession of historic premieres: Vincenzo Bellini's *Norma*, Gaetano Donizetti's *Maria Stuarda* (Mary Stuart), and Giuseppe Verdi's *Nabucco*.

Arturo Toscanini

At the start of the 1900s, Arturo Toscanini was, without doubt, a leading figure, after conducting his first concert at La Scala in 1896 and then becoming a highly demanded artistic director. He was forced to flee from Milan and then Italy because of his conflict with the fascist government (he was famously slapped by a fascist paramilitary Blackshirt in Bologna, because he refused to play the fascist anthem before a performance), but it was Toscanini who conducted the theater's memorable reopening concert, May 11, 1946, after the damage that had been done by the Second World War bombings. A large crowd of Milanese listened to the event on speakers in the squares.

A bust of Toscanini, with his usual worried expression, is displayed in the theater lobby.

out, the hall still maintains its neoclassical look, with its splendid stuccoes and gilded friezes, elegantly dominated by its crimson damask wall covering.

The specialist library is also part of the tour. This is used for short-term exhibitions, often showingcasing period costumes to illustrate the excellent standard of work the theater's tailors are historically renowned for.

The Theater Museum

Looking at the exhibition inside the theater is a great way to review the most important events in its history and get to know the major figures.

The museum opened in 1913, when the invaluable collection of theater memorabilia was bought at auction in Paris, from the antique dealer Jules Sambon. The core of the collection has been added to over the years by purchases and donations of costumes, scenery sketches, letters from composers, musical autographs, and antique musical instruments. The silk paneled rooms, recently set up with paintings and memorabilia, by scenographer Pier Luigi Pizzi bring back to life the famous figures

of Toscanini, di Donizetti, Puccini, and the prima donnas of opera, Maria Callas, Giuditta Pasta, and Eleonora Duse. The leading figure of the tour is Giuseppe Verdi: portraits from various moments of his long life are on display. The paintings show him with the people closest to him, such as his first wife, Margherita; his father-in-law Barezzi, who helped him so much early in his career; and his beloved Giuseppina Strepponi, his companion for much of his life.

The museum visit includes a look at the theater hall. Although the boxes have been completely reconstructed after their destruction in the 1943 bombings, and other recent work has been carried

Teatro alla Scala
Via Filodrammatici 2,
For a schedule of events
and to buy tickets:
Phone: 0288791
www.teatroallascala.org

Museo Teatrale
Largo Ghiringhelli 1,
Piazza della Scala
Hours: Weekdays:
9:00 a.m.–12:30 p.m.
1:30 p.m. –5:30 p.m.
Phone: 028879.2473/7473

Tickets to shows can be purchased with a credit card on the theater's official website or at the underground ticket counter in Piazza Duomo (open weekdays, 12:00 p.m.– 6:00 p.m.) or for tickets to shows scheduled on the date of purchase, in the evening at the ticket counter on Via Filodrammatici (open from 6:00 p.m.).

Ticino.
Where Swiss quality meets Italian lifestyle.

ticino.ch
Your gateway to Swiss mountains and lakes – in a blink of an eye!

Ascona, Lake Maggiore and Valleys

INSIDE THE DUKES' CASTLE

In the second half of the 1400s Castle Sforza was one of the most important and well-known buildings in Europe. It is where the Sforza family ruled the richest country in Renaissance Italy. Today it's one of the most extensive museum complexes in Italy.

Although they were formally subject to the emperor, the dukes of Milan behaved just like kings. They handed down power by dynasty and reigned absolutely over their lands, which included most of Lombardy, the Canton of Ticino, and large areas south of the River Po. Under their control, Milan grew to a population of almost one hundred thousand and acquired great wealth, thanks to the prosperous surrounding countryside, commerce, and manufacturing, especially of luxury goods, including top quality armor. Some of the brightest geniuses of the period worked for the ducal court, including Leonardo da Vinci, who moved to Milan in 1482 and stayed there until the fall of the Sforza family, but also Donato Bramante.

Milan in the 1400s

The dynasty was founded by **Francesco Sforza**, established leader of a mercenary army. Shortly after coming to power, in the mid 1400s, he ordered reconstruction work to start on a partly destroyed castle that had been erected in the previous century by the visconti, the first dukes of Milan. The son of Francesco, Galeazzo Maria, who ruled from 1466, settled in the new building and, over the years, developed it more and more into a multifunctional complex: it was not only the duke's residence, but also a representative seat, main garrison, and headquarters for the state administration. The prestige of the Sforza family and their residence was such that the fame of Milan spread all over Europe. Even in far-off Russia, Tsar Ivan III, who wanted to freshen up the image of his power and his premises, called in architects from Milan to give a new look to the Moscow Kremlin, which nowadays, with its walls and turrets, still reminds us of the Sforza Castle.

After the French invasion in 1499, followed by the Spanish and Austrian occupations, which did not effectively end until 1859, Milan and a large part of Lombardy became provinces under foreign rulers. The Spanish turned the castle into a **barracks and fortress**, encircled it with a solid brick protective wall known as the garland (remaining ruins may be seen on the side facing the park), and put it at the center of the city fortifications system, the southern point of the new city walls built in the 1500s. From then on, for centuries, what had been the symbol of the city's ancient glory became, for the people of Milan, the place they hated most, filled with nasty soldiers who were oppressing their city. The castle then suffered changes and damage: it lost its imposing entrance tower, the work of the architect Filarete. That

was only rebuilt after the unifi-cation of Italy, when the com-plex became the headquarters of the city museums and other important cultural institutions.

A stroll around the Castle

Entrance to the castle is through Filarete's Tower, re-erected in 1905, which carries a statue of St. Ambrose, the city's patron saint, and a bas-relief of King Umberto I on horseback. This overlooks the castle square on the outside, with a sparkling ornamental fountain from the 1930s.

Passing through the tower, you step out onto the wider castle courtyard, called Pi-azza d'Armi, venue for sum-mer shows and fashion shows. On the right-hand side of this courtyard there are displays of Roman remains and archi-tectural remains of buildings from the 1400s and 1500s. On the long side, opposite the entrance, there are two arch-ways. The left one leads to the fortress, the Rocchetta, which was built as a last refuge if the castle was besieged. The one on the right comes out onto the ducal courtyard, where the more graceful-looking archi-

tecture shows what this wing of the complex was built for; the duke's apartments were here on the first floor, while the court chapel and the offi-cial reception rooms were on the ground floor.

Leonardo, Michelangelo, and other treasures

The most important items in these extensive **castle mu-seums** are displayed in the rooms of the ducal court. The Museum of Antique Art takes up the ground floor, laid out

in chronological order. Any tour of the city has to visit here. The masterpiece of the first room is a 16th-century Byzantine female head, prob-ably Empress Theodora. In the next room, pride of place goes to the burial monument of Bernabò Visconti, lord of Milan in the latter half of the 1300s. It's remarkable how this monument highlights Vis-conti's talents as a defender of peace and order. It's the work of Bonino da Campione, who belonged to a major medieval school of sculpture, the Cam-pionese Masters, which was active over most of northern Italy from the 12th- to 14th-centuries. A few rooms on, the original reliefs that decorated the Roman gate are worth admiring. These were made after 1172 and show the de-feated population of Milan be-ing expelled from their city by the emperor Barbarossa, and their return to Milan in 1167, events which led up to the victory of the League of Lom-bardy over the imperial army at Legnano in 1176. At the far end of this room there is

The statue of St. Giovanni Nepomuceno, patron saint of Bohemia, commemorates the time when Milan was part of the Austrian empire.

another relief from that period, with an obscure meaning: it shows a woman shaving her pubic hairs with a large razor. This might be just making fun of the defeated empress or, more likely, it's just a good luck image (its original position was on one of the city gates called the Porta Tosa probably because of the presence of this relief).

The next room displays the city banner from 1566, picturing St. Ambrose chasing away Aryan heretics. The biblical tapestries from Brussels hanging on the walls also date from the 1500s.

Next we come to the famous **Sala delle Asse**, still decorated with the wall paintings of Leonardo. At the time of the Sforza family court, the room was used as the state room, thus explaining the

The city museums of the Castello Sforzesco (www.milanocastello.it) are open daily, except Mondays, 9:00 a.m.–5:30 p.m, (last admittance 5:00 p.m.). Closed on December 25, January 1, and May 1. The most visited section is the Museum of Antique Art, which can be reached by passing between the Piazza d'Armi and the Ducal Court.

complex symbolism of the structure. There is a plausible but unproven theory that the twine that covers the ceiling and part of the walls is made up of mulberry shoots, a plant whose Latin name is *morus*. "Moro" (Moor) was the nickname of Ludovic, duke of Milan. The protection and harmony that allow the *morus* plant to thrive are in contrast

with the opposite wall, showing a barren landscape, which the branches of the plant don't reach.

The room after is the beautiful ducal chapel, finely decorated with frescos, is dedicated to the armorers of Milan. Armor made in Milan in the 1500s was so good that it was considered a status symbol all over Europe.

The dramatic events that shook northern Italy in the first half of the 1500s, as France and Spain used it as a battleground to determine who ruled Europe, left an extraordinary funerary monument, on display at the end of the Sala degli Scarlioni, a room decorated with red and white zigzag stripes. This is a reclining statue of Gaston de Foix, the king of France's handsome young lieutenant, killed in battle by the Spanish at Ravenna in 1512. This statue, with its surrounding reliefs, should have been part of a great

The entrance archway to the Piazza d'Armi, left of Filarete's Tower, frames the modern sculpture Needle and Thread, the work of Claes Oldenburg, and stands on the nearby Piazza Cadorna.

tomb created by the sculptor Agostino Busti, also known as Bambaja, but it remained unfinished.

The Rondanini Pietà was also on display on the ground floor of the ducal court until 2013, when it was moved to other premises. This was Michelangelo's last work, and he worked on it for more than a decade, up until his death. He never finished it, and he changed his mind while he was working on it (the signs of the previous version are clearly visible). This work gave a completely new image to the theme of compassion, one of the Madonna holding a dead Christ, with Maria and Jesus both standing. A Roman funeral altar from the first century AD was used as a base for this statue from the 1700s on.

Among tapestries and violins

On the upper floor of the ducal court there is a rich collection of furniture on display.

Some are very antique and belonged to the Visconti and Sforza families, but a section is also dedicated to the design of the 1900s. Then there is the art gallery, which includes major works by Italian Renaissance artists, such as Antonello da Messina and Mantegna. But even that is outshined by the collection of **antique musical instruments**. This is one of the best in Italy, with a total of over 900 items and around 500 on display, including a rare inlaid lute from the early 1500s, a flute from the mid 1600s, and a violin made in 1761 with Antonio Stradivari's scroll. Immediately after this display you come to the Sala della Balla (named after a Renaissance period game, similar to tennis), where the **Mesi tapestries** (dedicated to the months of the year), made in Vigevano in 1503 from drawings by Bramantino, are on display.

The other museums in the castle are more of educational interest, featuring archaeological and coin collections. The Sala del Tesoro, with its entrance on the courtyard of the Rocchetta, is used for temporary exhibitions. It is decorated with a fresco from the late 1400s (probably by Bramante) showing Argo the dog, watching over the duke's valuables, which were kept here.

THE GENIUS OF LEONARDO, BETWEEN FAITH AND MYSTERY

The Last Supper has been copied thousands of times, and it is one of the world's most famous paintings. It was painted on the refectory wall of the former Dominican convent of Santa Maria delle Grazie.

To Milan from Florence in 1482, da Vinci presented himself to Ludovic the Moor as an accomplished player of the lyre. In his famous "application letter" addressed to the duke, the painter states that he is an expert in matters of military art and in the construction of machines of war, while only at the end does he mention his aptitudes in "times of peace;" that is, architecture, painting, sculpture. **The artistic genius, during his first stay in Milan lasting 18 months, completed several masterpieces, such as the two versions of the *Virgin of the Rocks* and *Lady with an Ermine*, a sophisticated portrait of Cecilia Gallerani, a favorite of Duke Ludovic the Moor.**

The duke of Milan, Ludovic the Moor, commissioned **Leonardo da Vinci** to carry out the work, which took him from 1494 until 1498. It can be viewed inside the large rectangular hall, used as a dining room by the monks. There is a more modest fresco on the opposite wall, *Crucifixion* (1495) by Donato Montorfano.

The magnificent mural painting (460 x 880 cm) immortalizes the moment when Jesus, during a meal with the apostles, reveals, "Truly, I say to you that one of you will betray me." The choice of this dramatic moment allows Leonardo to create a sort of scene from a play, where the imposing figures of the apostles show how upset they are with their expressions and gestures. **Flows of mood** was a favorite area of interest for Leonardo. Each flow starts from the figure of Jesus, alone at the center, and spreads in a tight rhythmic chain around the apostles, gathered in groups of three, like musical triplets.

The portraits of the apostles

On the left there are John, the youngest apostle, painted with his traditional long hair and soft features; Peter, holding the knife he will use to cut off Malchuss' ear; and Judas. Farther left is the group of Andrew, James the Lesser, and Bartholomew.

To the right, there are Thomas; James the Greater, jumping up with outstretched arms; and Philip, with his hands on his chest as if to say: "Could it be me, my Lord?"; then, at the end of the table, Matthew, Jude Thaddeus, and Simon.

Judas, holding the little bag of money, is not on his own on the other side of the table as in other pictures of this scene. Nor is he the only one with no halo, because nobody has one here, but he is left in shadow. Thanks to Leonardo's expert command of perspective, with the vanishing point on Jesus' face, the painted room seems like an open stage, enlarging the space and giving the impression that the meal is actually taking place in the refectory. This trompe l'oeil effect is magnified by the

details of the laid table: food, plates, transparent glasses, and the embroidered tablecloth. The painting we see today is the result of **major restoration** (1977–1999), which tried to restore as much as possible of the original, which had been devastated by misguided conservation procedures (also by the opening of a door in the center and the bombing in 1943, which hit the refectory, leaving the masterpiece miraculously intact). The original work began to deteriorate very

The Last Supper is included on the Unesco World Heritage List, as is the church of Santa Maria delle Grazie.

quickly, and this was partly due to the technique used by Leonardo himself. He didn't like the idea of a traditional fresco, because it meant having to work quickly and with no changes of mind, so he chose to work with tempera on a plaster base surface. This was like painting on canvas and allowed him to make extraordinary effects with light, but caused continuous flaking of paint from the wall, since the room was very damp.

Several restoration attempts were made over the centuries, but they often made things worse by heavy repainting, which obscured the scene and altered the figures.

Santa Maria delle Grazie

This brick church was built in a Gothic style and decorated inside with fresco figures of Dominican saints. Before it was built, on the site there was an ancient chapel named after Our Lady of Grace. In 1492,

only two years after the building was completed, Ludovic the Moor decided to make it a mausoleum for himself and the Sforza family. He called on Bramante, one of the top Renaissance architects, to rebuild the presbytery area and erect a stately **tribune** on it. A space built on the model of a circle inscribed within a square and loaded with symbolism is something out of the ordinary. Its nature sets it apart from the Gothic style of the nave. The fourth chapel to the right, decorated with Gaudenzio Ferrari's *Passion* (1542), featured Titian's famous *Crown of Thorns* as an altar piece, until it was requisitioned by the French in 1797 and taken to the Louvre.

The Last Supper is open Tue. to Sun., 8:15 a.m.–7:00 p.m. (last admittance 7:45 p.m.). Visits are limited to 25 people at a time for 15 minutes. No admission without a ticket booked in advance (+39.0292800360; www.cenacolovinciano.org). The church is open Mondays to Saturdays, 7:00 a.m.–12:00 p.m. and 3:00 p.m.–7:00 p.m. and Sundays and public holidays 7:30 a.m.–12:15 p.m. and 3:30 p.m.–9:00 p.m.

THE FANS' TEMPLE

The San Siro stadium, Giuseppe Meazza, has won the most titles in Europe, seeing that its two teams have ten times been winners of the top continental trophy—once called the European Cup, now known as the Champions League: 7 to Milan, 3 to Inter.

Italian soccer, except in Turin, is different from the rest of Europe in that two teams from the same city share a stadium, which is not their own property but belongs to the municipality. To make it feel like their own, the fans call it by different names. For the fans of Milan it is San Siro, the district where it stands, while fans of Inter call it Meazza, using the name of the great soccer hero of the 1930s and '40s, and one of the very few Italian soccer players ever to win two World Cups—in 1934 and 1938. Giuseppe Meazza was born in Milan and spent almost all his glorious career playing for Inter, playing just two seasons for Milan. When he died, the stadium was named after him, but the decision left a lot of Milanese fans disgruntled, especially the older ones who remembered that San Siro had once been just "their" stadium.

A. C. Milan (Associazione Calcio Milan) was founded in 1899 by a group of British people living in Milan. In 1908, after an internal split in the company, Football Club Internazionale was formed. Inter (the club has always been called by this name) had to use the name Ambrosiana during the fascist period.

The structure

The stadium is made up of three tiers, called rings, which have each been added on to the others. The bottom tier was built in the mid 1920s, holding 35,000 spectators, just for the Milan games (at the time Inter still played in the Arena stadium). The second tier was added in 1955, by which time Inter was also playing in the same stadium as their "cousins," and the capacity increased to 85,000 spectators. There was only a small area with a roof, the majority of the seats were not numbered, and there was also standing space. Two years later floodlights were installed, so it became the first stadium In Italy to play night games. The third tier was added on when the 1990 World Cup was held in Italy. That was when the stadium first looked the way it does today, with numbered seats for all **81,389 spectators**.

The stadium tour

The stadium is open for daily tours, except when a game is coming up (www. sansiro.net). The tour includes a visit to a large area on the ground level dedicated to a museum, as well as a visit to the spectators' areas and the

locker rooms. In the center of the museum, some of the trophies won by the two teams from Milan are on display. From there, you can follow two separate exhibition trails recreating the history of Milan (left trail) and Inter (right trail) through old photographs, newspaper cuttings, and the shirts of the all-time greats. The earliest items on display are curious, for the cleats and balls that were used in the early days of soccer, when the players went onto the field after a heavy lunch dressed up in

clothes more suited to a stroll in the country than playing a game of sport. Farther on, the exhibits start to show the favorite stars of the two teams in the past, or particular periods of their histories that stick in the minds of the fans. They are not necessarily always the winning times. The last showcases on the right display the shirts of star players who have played in the stadium as opponents of the Milanese.

In the heart of the stadium

Every 15 minutes there is a guided tour of the spectators' areas, including the more expensive seating areas and the VIP boxes used as hospitality areas made available by the club to sponsors during games. The big moment on this tour is the visit to the locker rooms, where fans never miss the chance to have their picture taken sitting at the place usually used by their personal favorite player. The locker rooms used by opposing teams and the game referees are not included in this visit.

The tour guides speak several languages and give explanations about the stadium. They also show the players' benches at the side of the field (the Milan bench is actually a set of armchairs) where the players sit during games.

Despite its age, the stadium offers an excellent view from all areas. There is also no athletics track or anything else separating the playing field from the spectators.

The south of the stadium, with the blue seats, is used by the Milan fans; the north, with green seats, is for the fans of Inter.

THE HISTORY OF MILAN IN A BASILICA

Related to the origins of the Church in Milan and the eminent figure of the city's patron saint, who it was named after, St. Ambrose is one of Italy's most important Romanesque-style churches and much more.

Ambrose was born in the German town of Treviri; became an official in the Roman Empire; and, on the death of Bishop Aussenzius (374), was given the task of smoothing over the conflicts among different Christian groups troubling Milan. Then the population wanted him as bishop. But Ambrose, who at the time was not even baptized, did not want to accept. He was convinced by the emperor himself. His consecration took place in 374, on December 7, today the Patron Saint's Day, and is the principal celebration in the city. Ambrose is the saint and doctor of the church.

It was founded in 386 by **Ambrose**, bishop of Milan, in an area where Christian victims of persecution had been buried. He dedicated it to the martyrs, and to Gervase and Protase, twins murdered under Nero, and chose it as his own burial place. The church underwent major work in the Carolingian period, and, between 1088 and 1099, became the building we see today. Since then, restoration has been carried out a number of times, especially after the bombings in 1943, which badly damaged the apse.

The arched **portico**, used in the first centuries of Christianity to receive pilgrims and catechumens (people not yet baptized who could not join in the full mass),

separates the church from the city and acts as an introduction into the sacred area. The plain architecture of the area, rebuilt in the Romanesque period, is enhanced by the color contrast of the bricks, typical of Lombard building, with the stone used in the supporting structures and decorative sculptures. The façade has an unusual hutlike shape and is flanked by two bell towers that express the divided use of the basilica by two separate religious communities down the centuries. The tower on the right, lower and simpler, belonged to the monks from the neighboring Benedictine monastery, founded in 784, while the one on the left, known as the "Canonici," belonged to the canons,

or lay priests, who built it in the 12th century.

The **interior** is surprisingly solemn, with its rigid mathematical proportions, underlined by the two colors of the cotto tiles and stonework.

Antique treasures

The church is a treasure trove of precious works, starting with the **Romanesque capitals**, decorated with animal and plant motifs. Many were retouched in the 1800s, but some are originals, especially in the atrium and on the first pilaster on the left of the nave, where there are also frescoes, signs of more painted decoration in the 1200s.

In the second span, on the left, there is a single column topped by a bronze serpent, reportedly the one made by Moses, brought from Constantinople as a gift to the Bishop around the year 1000. A little farther on there is the **sarcophagus of Stilicone** (fourth century), resting place of the famous general and his wife, Serena, daughter of Emperor Honorius. The sarcophagus is richly decorated with sacred and symbolic themes, including one of the first images of the Nativity, and stands beneath a pulpit from the Romanesque period.

The jewel of the basilica is the golden altar: completely plated with chased gold and silver and decorated with gemstones and colored enamel. The altar bears the signature of Volvinio, and was commissioned by Bishop Angilbert II (824–860). It was his idea to create the apse mosaic, with Christ on a throne between the two martyrs, Gervase and Protase, and scenes from the life of St. Ambrose at

the sides. This was heavily restored in the 1800s and after the bombings in the Second World War. Above the altar is a ciborium on Roman columns made of porphyry stone, decorated with colored stuccos from the mid-tenth century. Proceed through the nave and take the stairs beside the presbytery to go down to the crypt, where the remains of St. Ambrose lie, flanked by Gervase and Protase.

The seventh chapel on the left leads to the chapel of **San Vittore in Ciel d'Oro**, a small

On the interior of the church, above the side aisles, there is a gallery called the matroneo, which is reserved for women only.

separate building built in the fourth century to hold the remains of the martyr St. Victor and much liked by Ambrose, who had his brother Satyrus buried there. The mosaics (fifth century), which completely cover the room, provide us with one of the oldest and most realistic portraits of St. Ambrose. From the sides of the chapel you come to Museo del Tesoro, set out in an area once used as a passage between the basilica and the Benedictine monastery, which is now the lecture halls of the Catholic University.

La Basilica of St. Ambrose is open daily for worshippers and visitors. Visitors are admitted Mondays to Saturdays, 10:00 a.m.–12:00 p.m. and 2:30 p.m.–6:00 p.m., Sundays, 3:00 p.m.–5:00 p.m. There is a charge for admission to the Chapel of San Vittore in Ciel d'Oro and to Museo del Tesoro. www.basilicasantambrogio.it

ROYAL ART

The Brera Art Gallery is the oldest public museum in Italy and displays wonderful Renaissance paintings. It was inaugurated in 1809, when Milan was the capital of the kingdom of Italy.

The same building that houses the gallery is also home to the Fine Arts Academy, the Braidense National Library, an observatory and a botanical garden. In the courtyard, there is a bronze statue, a copy of a statue by Antonio Canova, of **Napoleon** as Mars the Peacemaker (*Napoleone come Marte pacificatore*). The museum was created thanks to the French emperor. On August 15, 1809, Bonaparte's 40th birthday, the Viceroy of Italy, Eugenio di Beauharnais, invited the people of Milan to visit the Royal National Gallery, and around one year later the gallery was opened to the public.

There was already a collection of artworks in the building, which had been a Jesuit monastery in the 1500s. This collection had been used as models by the students of the art academy, but Napoleon had a much more ambitious project in mind and planned to "build a collection with a number of works and a range of interests worthy of the capital of the Italic [sic] Kingdom."

The museum of Milan, the capital

The French troops entered Milan in 1796, which coincided with the start of an important period for the city, which became the capital, first of the Cisalpine Republic and then of the Italic Kingdom, until 1814.

The first Italian "public museum" did not result from a private collection, but from a political project, which meant it could display works of greater importance, requisitioned by the French army. This is why the rooms of the Brera Gallery contain shining examples of altar pieces from the churches and monasteries of Lombardy, Veneto, Emilia Romagna, and the Marche (all the areas conquered by Bonaparte).

The gallery tries to show the evolution of European

In room 18, there is an interesting restoration workshop on view, where gallery visitors can observe how the experts work on antique paintings.

painting between the 15th and 18th centuries, so the originals were enriched by the addition of important works from other Italian regions and from foreign schools, such as the paintings of Rembrandt, Rubens, and Van Dyck, which arrived here after exchanges with the Louvre in 1913.

The works not to miss

There are a lot of masterpieces not to be missed,

starting with the *Valle Romita Polyptych, Polittico di Valle Romita* by Gentile da Fabriano (ca. 1410, in room 4). This is an enchanting work with figures of sophisticated elegance and graffiti created with gold leaf, making it almost a goldsmith's art. The nucleus of Renaissance works is impressive and includes **Dead Christ** by Andrea Mantegna (ca. 1480, in room 6), an intensely dramatic painting, recognized for its view of the body of Christ supine on a marble slab; *Pietà* (1465–1470, in room 6) by the Venetian master Giovanni Bellini; and the large-scale scenic painting, which Bellini worked on with his brother,

Sermon of St. Mark in Alexandria (1504– 1507, in room 8), showing a magnificent basilica, inspired by St. Mark's in Venice, as backdrop to the evangelist's sermon to a group of people in Asian costumes.

In room 9, there are several large paintings, including *The Finding of the Body of St. Mark* (1562–1566) by Tintoretto, with its dramatic perspective effects. These paintings demonstrate the spectacular evolution of Venetian painting in the 1500s, dominated by Titian and Paolo Veronese.

After that, there are the renaissance masterpieces from other regions of the Italic Kingdom. Room 24 is maybe the

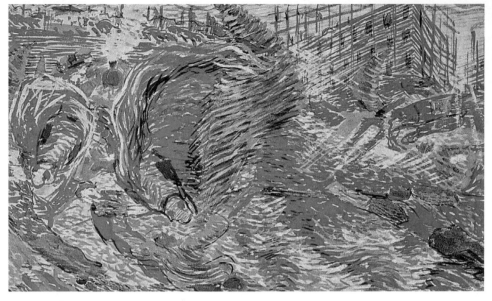

most prestigious of the whole museum, displaying paintings from Urbino: *Brera Madonna*, by Piero della Francesca (ca. 1472), which is enchanting with its clever use of light and perspective; Raphael's *The Marriage of the Virgin* (1504), donated by the Città di Castello to a Napoleonic officer for sparing the town; Bramante's *Christ at the Column* (1490), which makes a strong emo-

Among the masterpieces, in sequence according to period, the gallery displays works by Mantegna, Raffaello, Caravaggio and Boccioni.

tional impact with its bold spatial slant. In the top ten of the not to be missed: Caravaggio's *Supper at Emmaus* (room 29), painted by the artist in Rome in 1606 with passionate realism and dramatic use of light and shade, and two well-known paintings from the 1800s, *The Kiss* by Hayez (1859, room 37), completed at the peak of the Risorgimento and a symbolic message of love and *Fiumana* (1895–1896, room 38) by Pelizza da Volpedo, a manifesto of social emancipation. Lovers of modern art should also not miss the rooms with the works of the leading Italian artists of the early 1900s, such as Boccioni, Carrà, De Pisis, Marino Marini, Modigliani, and Morandi, all of which were acquired by the gallery in the 1970s as part of the Jesi donation.

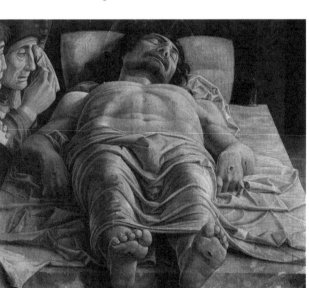

The Art Gallery
Hours: 8:30 a.m.–7:15 p.m.
Closed Monday
For info and bookings:
Phone: 0272263264-229
www.brera.beniculturali.it

BETWEEN ART AND FAITH

Long established institutions of Milan, the Ambrosian Library and Picture Gallery are a treasure trove of masterpieces that go back to the beginning of the 1600s and are due to the patronage of a great cardinal.

The library and picture gallery were both founded by **Federico Borromeo** (archbishop of Milan from 1595 - 1631), a cousin of the Carlo Borromeo, who had so much to do with the Catholic reforms after the spread of Protestantism. Federico was a man of rigid doctrine, and he was aware of the importance of cultural instruments in teaching the clergy and in the struggle the Roman Church was facing then. In 1609 he opened his grand **library** for public reading (in the building in Piazza Pio XI, where the two institutions are still housed today, after several extensions and refurbishing), and he called it the Ambrosiana, after the city's patron saint. Because of the initiative of its patron, the library's reading room made books more accessible to the public. Here the books were set on shelves along the

walls instead of being chained to benches, as they were in other libraries at that time.

Federico sent learned experts around Italy and Europe and built a large collection of important manuscripts and incunables, such as the *Ilia Picta* (Ambrosian Iliad), a fifthcentury manuscript showing scenes

from the Iliad; the *Virgil*, a collection of texts by the Latin poet, annotated by Francesco Petrarca, with a frontispiece by the 1300s painter Simone Martini; authentic codices, such as *De prospectiva pingendi* (On Perspective in Painting) by Piero della Francesca. Federico's considerable core collection, boasting 30,000 books and 15,000 manuscripts, has grown continuously over the centuries. One of the library's treasures, which arrived just after Federico's death, is the highly acclaimed *Codice Atlantico* (Atlantic Codex), the world's most comprehensive collection of drawings by Leonardo da Vinci.

In 1618, Federico donated his personal collection to the Ambrosian, founding the picture gallery. This substantial collection of about 250 works was intended for public pleasure and to stimulate creativity

The Ambrosian also includes the Settala Museum, created from the eccentric collecting of Manfredo Settala, a canon and friend of Borromeo. This sort of "cabinet of wonders" displays peculiarities from the world of nature, scientific instruments, drawings, and also automated robots.

in the students of the annexed academy (inaugurated by the cardinal in 1621 but then transferred to Brera in the 1700s, on the wishes of the empress Maria Theresa of Austria).

The fascinating tour, covering two floors, initially follows the original layout, described by Federico Borromeo himself in *Musaeum* (Museum), based on previous descriptions of museums, printed in 1625. The large staircase leading from the main lobby to the rooms is decorated with plaster copies of important statues, like Michelangelo's *Pietà* in the Vatican, which the academy students used as models, while the library's imposing reading room is visible from the first rooms, a reminder of how the cardinal's two institutions were designed to complement each other.

The first rooms show paintings such as *Adoration of the Magi* by Titian and *Madonna del padiglione* (The Virgin and Child with Three Angels) by Botticelli (ca. 1493). The tour continues with the enormous cartoon (8.04 x 2.85 m) of Raphael's *Scuola di Atene* (School of Athens), which was the last model in the preparation of the famous fresco completed in the Stanza della Segnatura in the Vatican. This cartoon, brought from Rome

on the back of a donkey, must have cost the cardinal a lot of money, while one of the museum's jewels, Caravaggio's *Canestra di Frutta* (Basket of Fruit) (1599), was donated to his collection, probably during a visit to Rome, by Cardinal Del Monte, an important protector of the painter.

For six years, since the exhibition of Expo 2009, the pages of Leonardo's *Atlantic Codex* have been on show in the room Sala Federiciana of the Ambrosian Gallery and in the sacristy of the church of Santa Maria delle Grazie. www.leonardo-ambrosiana.it

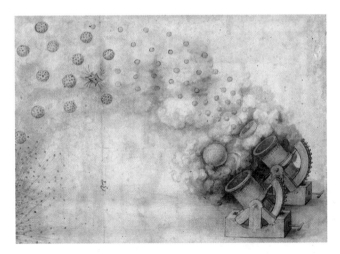

Federico Borromeo is one of the background figures in events of the *Promessi Sposi* (The Betrothed), the Italian historical novel, where he is an example of Christian virtue for "his habit of kind and noble thoughts, the inner peace of a long life, love of mankind, the lasting joy of ineffable hope," so much so that he managed to convert the Unnamed, a well-known powerful evildoer.

The penultimate room contains an interesting set of paintings done between the 1400s and 1500s in Lombardy by pupils of Leonardo, the so-called "Leonardeschi," as well as *Ritratto di Musico* (Portrait of a Musician)(1485–90), painted by Leonardo himself during his period in Milan and

is considered a masterpiece of Renaissance portrait painting. The last room shows series of Leonardo's drawings.

La Pinacoteca (Picture Gallery)
**Hours: Tuesday–Sunday
10:00 a.m.–6:00 p.m.
www.ambrosiana.it**

ART, LEISURE, AND NATURE BACK OF THE CASTLE

Milan boasts a large green estate of 47 hectares, loved by its residents because of its location and various attractions, including a stadium, Museum of Design, Acquarium, and meeting places.

The park extends from the rear of Castle Sforza, in the woods the Visconti and the Sforza families called the Barcho, which they used as their breeding and hunting grounds. The architect Emilio d'Alemagna designed it in 1894 as an English-style park, creating the picturesque scenic effect that was the fashion at the time. It features high ground, pathways among the bushes, waterways and groups of trees and shrubs.

At the foot of the arch

The park was conceived as a telescopic perspective between the castle and the **Arch of Peace**, a magnificent triumphal arch designed in 1807, in Milan's Napoleonic period, by Luigi Cagnola, as a grand entrance into the city along

The park claims 50 tree species, including elms, which the park rangers point out along two separate educational trails.

the main route called Corso Sempione. It was completed in 1833 under the Austrians, who crowned it with its 4 meter high chariot drawn by six horses, the *Dea Minerva in Pace* (Goddess Minerva at Peace).

The park gets its name from the roadway laid as a monument in the Napoleonic period, which goes from the road toward the Sempione pass, and connects the city to Switzerland and then France.

Leisure park

The area has something to offer everyone. There are those who walk, ride bikes, jog, follow a training trail, play sports, or go skating. There are also those who prefer an aperitif at **Bar Bianco**, a busy venue that becomes an absolute must in the summer evenings. The kids have their playgrounds, a mini-train, and go-

Sport and concerts

For some rather more serious sport, there is the monumental **Civic Arena**. Today it's named for the top Italian sports reporter Gianni Brera, but it was designed by the neoclassical architect Luigi Canonica, inspired by Roman amphitheaters, especially the Circo Massenzio in Rome. It is monumental (238 x 116 meters), as well as elegant in the interior (it has been used for weddings in recent years), and when it was opened, in 1807, it could hold 30,000 people (a quarter of the population of Milan at that time). It was used for a long time as a soccer stadium by Inter Milan, before the

The park reflects the multiethnic nature of the city, as several different nationalities stand side by side: Chinese get together to hold a session of Tai Chi, while Americans play basketball, and women of Eastern Europe have organized a quiet picnic.

kart circuit, while lovers will not miss out on the romantic bridge of sirens, **Ponte delle Sirene**. This little 19th-century bridge was constructed for the Martesana canal, but moved to the park when that canal was filled in. The Milanese fondly call it *"delle sorelle Ghisini"* (the cast-iron sisters), after the four cast-iron sirens, each with an oar in one hand, who stand in pairs at each end of the bridge to greet passing couples.

team moved to the San Siro, where A. C. Milan played. Now it's a multisports center and also used for rugby games and summertime concerts.

"Secret" places

Up toward the highest point in the park and near to a city library, which has a well-lit reading room where it's pleasant to sit for a while. There is the *Statue of Napoleon III on Horseback*, greeting the crowd and waving his

beret. This statue was commissioned after the emperor's triumphant arrival in Milan in 1859.

Lovers of modern art should not miss two works that were featured in a 1973 exhibition: *Accumulazione Musicale* (Musical Accumulation) by the French artist Arman, who re-created a miniature amphitheater with a stepped structure in cement, and *Bagni Misteriosi* (Mysterious Baths) by De Chirico.

The Branca Tower stands next to the Triennale, and offers the highest rooftop view open to the people of Milan. It was designed by Giò Ponti in 1933 and built from steel in just four and a half months. It is 108.60 meters high, taller than the cathedral's Madonnina.

Designer mecca

The De Chirico sculptures are in the grounds of the Palazzo dell'Arte, an art gallery better known as the **Triennale**, the name of the applied art exhibition held there for decades. The clinke-and-marble building was constructed in 1932–33 by Giovanni Muzio and renovated in 1994 by Gae Aulenti. It's a high-profile exhibition center for architecture, design, fashion, and modern art. Since 2007 it has also held the Triennale Design Museum,

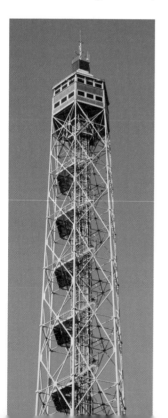

the first Italian museum dedicated to design, which has a dynamic, constantly self-renewing layout. In the Triennale's basement, there is the art theater, Teatro dell'Arte, set up by Muzio and reconnected, in 2011, to the exhibition stands. This is a landmark in Milan for the performing arts.

Fish in the splendor of Modern style

A walk round the park should also include a visit to the **city aquarium**. It's housed in an elegant Modern-style building, embellished by friezes and majolica, built in 1906 for the Milan International Exhibition, of which it is the only reminder left standing. The aquarium, third oldest in Europe, vamped all its tanks in a recent major renovation, to give a much better view of the various displays of Italian freshwater and saltwater life.

The Park
Hours: October–April:
6:30 a.m.–9:00 p.m.
May: 6:30 a.m.–10:00 p.m.
June–September:
6:30 a.m–11:30 p.m.
To book a guided botanical tour organized by the volunteer park rangers:
Phone: 02.88464456

Triennale of Milan—Triennale Design Museum
Viale Alemagna 6
Hours: Tuesday–Sunday:
10:30 a.m.–8:30 p.m.;
Thu.: 10:30 a.m.–11:00 p.m.
Closed Monday
Phone: 02.72434208
www.triennale.it

City Aquarium
Viale Gadio 2
Hours: Tuesday–Sunday:
9:30 a.m.–1:00 p.m.
and 2:00 p.m.– 5:30 p.m.
www.acquariocivicomilano.eu

A TECHNOLOGICAL JOURNEY BETWEEN LEONARDO AND THE FUTURE

A museum dedicated to Leonardo da Vinci, who spent quite a large and prolific part of his life in Milan; the world's largest collection of machines made from his designs are on display.

The main body of the museum is formed around two wide cloisters of an ancient monastery, built at the beginning of the 1500s as an annex to the lovely church, San Vittore al Corpo, which stands on the right of the museum entrance. The monastery was turned into a military hospital during the Napoleonic wars, then became barracks for the Italian army, and, finally, was badly damaged during the

Second World War bombings. Shortly after the wartime destruction, on April 27, 1947, a sign was put up outside San Vittore to announce the start of the rebuilding as a museum. It was designed by Piero Portaluppi and Ferdinando Reggiori and opened in 1953.

The original collection in the museum included a large number of scientific instruments, models, and machines, but also works of art. Over the years, more and more exhibits have been added that illustrated scientific and technological advances, as well as helping to understand the great strides in human knowledge.

Coming into the museum, you immediately get the feeling that you are in a living, multiformed space, where everyone can invent their own tour and visit the categories that interest them most. There are seven categories: Materials,

The workshops are the museum's pride and joy. They develop the themes of the various categories and are intended especially for children, but can be for older age groups, who can take part in different learning experiences.

Transport, Energy, Communications, the Art and Science of Leonardo, New Frontiers, and Junior Science. In each category, the exhibits are dynamically linked to interactive workshops, following an "informal education" approach.

When visiting the museum for the first time, there are some things that should not be missed, things that stand out among the 15,000 exhibits as special inventions or important discoveries.

The very first exhibit that greets you, for instance, is the

The collections in the museum have been built up since the 1930s, and this is thanks to the contribution made by leading Italian scientists, such as Guglielmo Marconi.

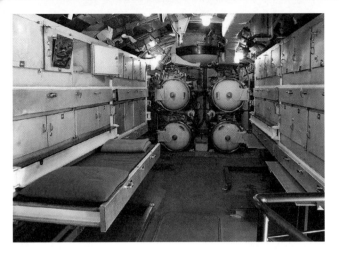

One of the major attractions in the museum is the *Toti*. She was the first submarine built in Italy after the Second World War. It was launched in 1967 and patrolled the Mediterranean to identify Soviet submarines. Hours: Tues.– Fri.: 10:00 a.m.– 5:00 p.m. Sat. and public holidays: 10:00 a.m.– 6:30 p.m. Visits have to be booked and a supplementary ticket is payable.

Regina Margherita, an impressive turbine from a thermoelectric generator that drove 1,800 looms in a silk factory in Brianza, inaugurated in 1895 by the royal family. Near that is a display of the particle detector from CERN in Geneva, which enabled Carlo Rubbia and Simon van der Meer to prove the existence of the W and Z particles in 1983 and win the Nobel Prize for Physics.

The second floor of this historic building contains a collection of models by Leonardo da Vinci. This collection was assembled in 1953 by military architects and modelmakers from the Italian army, to celebrate the 500th anniversary of the birth of the artist-cum-scientist.

On the same floor there are the Vetturetta Bianchi 8, one of the first Italian automobiles, first presented in 1903 by Bianchi, the famous cycling manufacturers from Milan; Giovanni Dondi's Astrario, a medieval world clock, reconstructed according to the original designs of its inventor; the telescope used by Schiapparelli in the Brera Observatory in 1861, when he discovered the asteroid Esperia and studied the phenomenon of falling stars; an example of an early PC, the Programma 101, a desktop calculator made by Olivetti between 1962 and 1964; and the magnetic detector used by Guglielmo Marconi in 1902, for his experiments on electronic waves, which led to his development of the first working telecommunications system (the basis for radio and television) and made him a Nobel Prize winner.

Downstairs in the basement, there are three more important exhibitions: a historic dynamo, taken from the first European thermoelectric power plant, inaugurated here in Milan in 1883, based on the model of the one put into operation in New York the year before by Edison; the Stassano furnace, the first electric arc furnace used for steel production in 1898; and the workbench on which Giulio Natta invented isotactic propylene, the molecules of plastic, which meant that he too would win a Nobel Prize, in 1963.

In the Transport category, which extends into two separate buildings (the rail and naval air pavilions), there are full-scale exhibits to wonder over. Sixteen locomotives retrace the history of transport on rail tracks, as well as the training vessel *Ebe*, launched in 1921, one of the largest ships in a museum. It had to be cut into sections and reassembled inside the pavilion. Aviation enthusiasts should not miss the deltaplane *Stratos*, in which Italian Angelo d'Arrigo made the first flight over Everest in 2005, nor the Macchi MC. 205V, one of the most flyable fighter planes in the Second World War, nor Enrico Forlanini's experimental helicopter, the first motorized object to take in flight in 1877.

Participation in program activities in the workshops or exhibition areas must be booked at the information desk near the entrance. Via San Vittore 21 Hours: Tues.–Fri.: 9:30 a.m.–5:00 p.m. Sat. and public holidays: 9:30 a.m.–6:30 p.m. Phone: 02485551 www.museoscienza.org

THE HOUSES OF ART

Four historic homes converted into museums provide a view of almost two centuries of urban history through the lives of prominent families.

The oldest museums, the Poldi Pezzoli and the Bagatti Valsecchi, show the passion for collecting that was common among the aristocracy in the latter half of the 1800s, when the city was under rapid expansion and establishing itself among the economic and cultural forefront of the newborn nation. Villa Necchi Campiglio and the Boschi di Stefano Museum House elegantly paint a picture of the first half of the 1900s, when Milan was the leading Italian city for contemporary art: this was where futurism was born in 1909, the Italian 1900s in 1922, and Lucio Fontana's spatialism in the 1940s.

For information about the tour, visit the website: www.casemuseomilano.it

The **Poldi Pezzoli Museum** reveals the lifestyle of a great 19th-century gentleman: the wealthy Gian Giacomo Poldi Pezzoli, a friend of art connoisseurs and renowned artists. In 1849, this enlightened collector returned from exile, forced upon him by Austrian repression, and began to set up his "special apartment" in a part of the family palace. He later decided to donate the area for the "use and benefit of the public" and it opened as a museum in 1881.

The entrance to this aristocratic home is on Via Manzoni, in the city center. Passing through an elegant courtyard, you come to a scenographic oval staircase that lead up to the main floor. Even though the 1943 bombings caused damage to the palace (the Gothic armory was destroyed and rebuilt in 2000 by Arnaldo Pomodoro), the palace tour winds through sumptuously decorated rooms inspired by various periods of history. The rooms are furnished in period style and embellished by important paintings, sculptures and valuable objects of decorative art, including weapons, glass, clocks, porcelain, rugs and tapestries, furniture, and jewelry. The Poldi Pezzoli jewels include Renaissance masterpieces, such as Pollaiolo's *Dama*, the museum's icon, and works of Piero della Francesca, Botticelli, and Giovanni Bellini.

The Poldi Pezzoli Museum
Via Manzoni 12,
Hours: 10:00 a.m.–6:00 p.m.
Closed Tuesday
www.museopoldipezzoli.it

Fausto and Giuseppe **Bagatti Valsecchi** also dedicated themselves to the care of their family residence and collected works of art to embellish it. The two brothers shared a dream to build their palace in the heart of Milan in the 1800s, but in a neo-Renaissance style, turning it into a sort of "time machine," truly Renaissance in every detail. In their palace, which was opened to the public at the end of the 1800s, you can visit sumptuous rooms where works of art, furnishings, weapons, and original household appliances stand alongside period reproductions, while technological innovations are cleverly disguised; a bathtub with a shower, for example. The most important original pieces include paintings by Giovanni Bellini, such as the *Santa Giustina*, and a bed from the 1500s in the bedroom, which belonged to Fausto.

A totally different cultural ambience emanates from **Villa Necchi Campiglio**, designed in the 1930s by Piero Portaluppi. This mansion, built on one of the most elegant streets in the city and adorned by a spacious garden with swimming pool and tennis court, reflects the taste of the upper bourgeois class, to which the two sisters Gigina and Nedda Necchi, as well as Gigina's husband, Angelo Campiglio, belonged. It was a meeting place for intellectuals and artists, and guests included such important figures as the Savoy and Spanish royal families as well as Prince Henry of Hesse-Kassel, the scenery designer for La Scala, who slept in the so-called "Prince's bedroom." Over the years, the palace has acquired paintings and sculptures from the Italian 1900s, along with works from the 1700s.

Villa Necchi Campiglio
Via Mozart 14
Hours: 10:00 a.m.–6:00 a.m.
Closed on Mon. and Tues.
www.fondoambiente.it

The **Boschi di Stefano Museum House**, in a smaller building, which was also designed by Portaluppi, is worth a visit for its collection of contemporary art, with paintings,

sculptures, and drawings from the first decade of the 1900s up to the end of the 1960s. On show are around 300 works by painters associated with futurism, such as Soffici and Boccioni, di Morandi, de' Pisis, and other artists who were part of their circle; one example is Mario Sironi, who has a room dedicated exclusively to him, while another is Lucio Fontana.

Bagatti Valsecchi Museum
Via Santo Spirito 10/
Via Gesù 5
Hours: 1:00 p.m.– 5:45 p.m.
Closed Monday
www.bagattivalsecchi.
house.museum

Boschi di Stefano
Museum House
Via G. Jan 15
Hours: 10:00 a.m.–6:00 p.m.
Closed Monday
www.fondazione
boschidistefano.it

THE MANSION THAT WAS NAPOLEON'S

In the most aristocratic area of Milan stands a neoclassical mansion, home of the Gallery of Modern Art, with masterpieces from the 1800s. In front, there is the elegant greenery of the public gardens, with the Planetarium and the Natural History Museum.

This illustrious residence was built in the 1790s, when Milan was ruled by the Austrians, for Count Ludovic Barbiano di Belgiojoso, a diplomat who had carried out important missions in Europe for the Viennese court. The site chosen for the **luxury neoclassical residence** was strategically placed between the center of the city and Corso di Porta Orientale, now Corso Venezia, the symbolic entrance for anyone coming to the city from the empire. The project was entrusted to the Austrian Leopoldo Pollack, one of the top architects of that time and favorite pupil of Piermarini, the architect of La Scala opera house who had originally been chosen also for this project. Pollack conceived the house as an elegant construction of three floors, balanced out by two lower wings jutting forward, framing a courtyard of honor. The building was completed in 1793 and then enriched with sculptures, such as the statues of classical deities on top of the balustrade above the attic, and the bas-reliefs of mythological figures adorning the windows of the first two floors, the ideas of the poet, Giuseppe Parini, who was a leading intellectual of the period.

The count left half of the property to the French, when they entered the city in 1796, and the whole mansion was given to Napoleon at the start of the 1800s and then chosen as the official residence of **Eugène Beauharnais**, adopted son of the emperor, and of his wife, Amalia.

The most spectacular façade of the great neoclassical mansion is to the back, facing the splendid garden.

In later times the house continued to play a historically important role, being visited by major figures of the city's political scene, such as **Marshal Radetzky**, who signed the Peace Treaty of Milan there in 1849 and who also died there in 1858; and Napoleon III, who chose it as his residence. The more composed rear façade of the building faces the garden, opened to the public in the 1930s. The garden was also designed by Pollack, assisted by Count Hercules Silva, one of the leading botanists of the period, and they followed the fashionable landscaping style to bring the garden

> The public gardens enjoyed one of their most glorious moments in May 1881, when the grand national exhibition was held there, inaugurated in the presence of the sovereigns Umberto I and Margherita.

alive, with a pond, a stream, grottoes, and little bridges. A notice on the entrance gate reminds adults that they may not enter the garden unless they are accompanying children. However, this is not so much a categorical ban as a way of conserving this little corner of peace and quiet in the heart of Milan.

A rich but little known museum

After a spell of relative abandon in the wake of the unification of Italy, the municipal administration renovated the interior of Villa Belgiojoso Bonaparte and in 1921 opened the **Gallery of Modern Art** there. This museum stands out for the perfect match be-

tween the exhibition premises and works on display, which are largely in the neoclassical. The collections were built up thanks to private donations (first and foremost by the sculptor Pompeo Marchesi, who donated a large part of his creations), as well as those of public bodies and academies, specially the Brera Academy. The exhibits span two floors in chronological order, with some rooms often half empty. Nevertheless, the collection is quite rich and displayed in ornate rooms with valuable period furnishings. The displays include sculptures by Canova, undisputed leading figure in neoclassical art; and from the 1700s, the paintings and preparatory cartoons of Andrea Appiani. This Milanese neoclassical artist was described by Napoleon as "our first painter in Italy," and Eugène Beauharnais commissioned him for the frescoe Parnassus with *Apollo among the Muses* for the dining room of the villa. On the upper floor, the 1800s are introduced by the paintings of Francesco Hayez, including the *Ritratto di*

Alessandro Manzoni. After the ballroom, one of the most important examples of neoclassical interior design in Milan, and the sumptuous dining room, you come to the paintings by other locally known painters from the 1800s, including exponents of the Scapigliatura movement (a wholly Lombard romanticism), such as Daniele Ranzoni, Tranquillo Cremona, and Mosè Bianchi. The 1800s category finishes with the works of two figures from Ital-

ian Divisionism: Giovanni Segantini and Gaetano Previati. The gallery is also enriched by two important collections: the Grassi collection, on the third floor, with masterpieces from the 13th through the 20th century, and the Visnara collection, on the first floor, with major examples of Italian and foreign works from the 1900s, including Picasso, Matisse, and Renoir. To the right of Villa Belgiojoso Bonaparte, there is the Contemporary Art Pavilion (**Padiglione d'Arte Contemporanea, PAC**), built in 1951. Designed by Ignazio Gardella, the agile structure of the PAC, illuminated by large windows and skylights, is a top-notch exhibition area, dedicated to 20th-century art and new experimental art.

The oldest park in Milan

In front of villa, there are the Public Gardens, named in

Among the numerous events that take place in the public gardens, special mention goes to Orticola, a floral/nursery fair, held every May and always well supported by the Milanese.

2002 after the reporter Indro Montanelli. They were created in the 1780s, when Ferdinand of Hapsburg-d'Este, viceroy of Milan, commissioned Giuseppe Piermarini, the most prestigious neoclassical architect in Lombardy at the time, to design them. They were considered as a park open to the public, the first in the city, and laid out French style, which can still be seen today in the geometric layout of the flower beds and the perspective framing of the tree-lined paths, surviving partial changes made in the 1800s. At that time a scenic garden was pre-

pared on the west side, with artificial rocks, water features, and an eclectic building, the so-called Coffee Pavilion, a favorite meeting place for artists of the period.

The gardens contain a number of tree species, including Magnolias, Cedars from Lebanon and the Himalayas and a monumental Metasequoia. There are various play areas for children, and the younger ones also have the obligatory attractions of the mini train, running between the statues of the Seven Dwarfs, ponies that will take them for a ride around the park and the Butterfly Oasis.

Inside the gardens, there is a historic institution, founded in 1838—the **Natural History Museum**, made up of five subjects: mineralogy, paleontology, natural history of man, invertebrate zoology, and vertebrate zoology. The

whole exhibition is spread over 23 rooms, where numerous examples of existing plants and animals are displayed together with minerals and fossils. The strong point of the museum are the nearly 100 stands recreating natural environments that faithfully illustrate the biodiversity of our planet. This is one of the favorite attractions for Milanese children, especially the rooms dedicated to **dinosaurs**. Giant casts of skeletons win the day here, including the skeleton of a pliosaurus, a marine reptile from the upper Jurassic period, hanging from the ceiling in room 6; Tyrannosaurus rex, one of the largest carnivores ever to have walked Earth; and the triceratops, whose spectacular reconstruction has become a mascot of the museum. The museum is open to

a dynamic learning approach, and in recent years, has improved the original exhibition area with the addition of learning workshops, a perfect complement to the exhibition tour. The Paleolab is dedicated to paleontology and mineralogy, and offers the chance, for example, to simulate excavations in a fossil layer. This has now been joined by Biolab, for life sciences and meteorology, in the greenhouses of Palazzo Dugnani (a 1600s building to the west of the park, boasting a wonderful Tiepolo fresco) and the Verdelab (Greenlab), handling the botanical subjects.

Under the starry dome

Next to the Natural History Museum, there is the **Planetarium**, a building shaped like a small, domed classical temple, designed in the 1930s by Piero Portaluppi. The famous publisher Ulrich Hoepli had it built and donated it to the people of Milan, being convinced that "understanding astronomy, through contemplation of the infinite order of all Creation, could constitute the most relaxing spiritual evolution." The largest in Italy in terms of the size of its pro-

jection room, the Planetarium has been using, since 1968, a powerful instrument for these purposes, a Zeiss model IV. During the week it is used for school groups, while at weekends it offers guided stargazing for people of all ages who are interested in identifying the constellations and learning the basics of astronomy.

Gallery of Modern Art
Via Palestro 16
Hours: Tuesday–Sunday:
9:00 a.m.–1:00 p.m.
and 2:00 p.m.–5:30 p.m.
Phone: 028844594.7/4
www.gam-milano.com

Royal Villa Gardens
Hours: May–October:
9:00 a.m.–7:00 p.m.
November - April:
9:00 a.m.–4:00 p.m.

Contemporary Art Pavilion
Via Palestro 14
Phone: 0288446.359/360
www.comune.milano.it

Public Gardens
Indro Montanelli
Hours:
November–February:
6:30 a.m.–8:00 p.m.
March and April:
6:30 a.m.–9:00 p.m.
May: 6:30 a.m.–10:00 p.m.
June–September:
6:30 a.m.–11:30 p.m.

Natural History Museum
Corso Venezia 55
Hours: Tuesday–Sunday:
9:00 a.m.–5:30 p.m.
Bookings for Paleolab,
Biolab, and Verdelab
Phone: 0288463337
www.comune.milano.it

Planetarium
Corso Venezia 57
Phone: 0288463340
www.comune.milano.it

> **In the 1800s the Public Gardens were a meeting place for Milanese bohemian artists, especially the Scapigliatura painters.**

MUSEUMS AND GALLERIES

During the 20th century, Milan saw the birth of many artistic styles and movements, which are detailed in the testimonials of museums. It is also rich in galleries, documenting the vitality of the collector market.

Museo del Novecento

In the heart of Milan, in Piazza del Duomo, stands an important museum, which opened to the public in 2010 to permanently accommodate the public collections of contemporary art, with works ranging from the beginning of the century to the 1970s. The venue chosen is itself a historical monument: the left wing of the Arengario is a marble-clad building consisting of two specular, massive pavilions designed in the 1930s by a team of four architects, among the most prestigious of the time, and decorated with reliefs with historical scenes by sculptor Arturo Martini. With its conversion into museum, the building's interior underwent a complete change in order to adapt the historic space for the exposition of

about 400 works: a selection of the many that form the civic collection, while the others, many of high quality, are put on rotating exposition in temporary exhibitions.

The tour starts with a spectacular spiral staircase—left exposed to create continuity between the space of the mu-

seum and that of the front located piazza—which vertically connects the stories of the metro. In a niche of the grand staircase, the exhibition of works opens with a large painting from 1902 of the *Quarto Stato* by Pelizza Volpedo. It is a well-known work still tied by social subject to the 1800s but which in modern times heralds the future as per technique of execution. The route unfolds in chronological order through the main artistic movements of the 20th century and closes significantly with 1968, the year that marked the history of Europe, while awaiting its continuation in the MAC, the Museum of Contemporary Art (Museo di Arte Contemporanea), designed by Daniel Libeskind that should be built in the near future within CityLife, the former Expo area.

On the first floor, after a taste of the international avant-garde of the early 20th century, documented by a number of paintings of the Jucker collection—including masterpieces by Braque, Klee, Kandinsky, Matisse, Modigliani—we find a large section dedicated to futurism, the revolutionary movement of European birth, born in 1909, in Milan. The first room, called "delle Colonne," is dominated by Umberto Boccioni, father of the movement, of whom the museum has the largest collection of works in the world, including some masterpieces

The neon tube structure by Lucio Fontana, made for the Triennial of 1951, illuminates the large room on the second floor of the Museo del Novecento and has quickly become a "night" icon of the Piazza del Duomo.

such as *Stati d'animo* of 1911 and *Elettricità* of 1913. There are paintings by other futurist painters, such as Balla, Carrà, Soffici. Three smaller rooms are in monographic tone dedicated to outstanding personalities in Milan between the two wars: Giorgio Morandi's *Still Life* with its shards and bottles; De Chirico, with his metaphysical mannequins; and Arturo Martini. The works of this sculptor, one of the greatest of the 20th century, also made of clay, bronze, and stone hearth, to accentuate the expressive effects, are also exhibits such as *La Sete* (1934), in which a woman is on all fours, in search of water, with her child clinging to the neck.

The long trail of works that leads to the second floor documents Italian art from 1920 to 1940. The artists of the so-called 20th-century Italian movement—such as Mario Sironi, Carlo Carra, Felice Casorati—are united by the desire for a "return to order" after the excesses of the vanguard, followed by a section devoted to abstraction. The top floor of the Arengario is entirely devoted to a great protagonist of the 20th century: Lucio Fontana. The large dining room, which offers a unique view from the Duomo, features the ceiling that the artist created in 1956 for a hotel on Elba and also shows an impressive selection of *Tagli*, the great Neon of the

Triennale from 1951. The next rooms are where to meet the masters of the informal world, with famous works by Alberto Burri and Piero Manzoni. In the part of the museum that occupies the adjacent royal palace, we proceed into spaces dedicated to kinetic art along with analytical paintings and new figurations.

Gallerie d'Italia

Recently inaugurated in historic buildings of Milan to expose the enormous artistic

heritage of two major banking groups were Intesa San Paolo and Fondazione Cariplo.

With their 8,300 square meters, these areas offer an immense showcasing space. The first section, opened in 2011 in the 18th- and 19th-century buildings Anguissola and Brentani, that faces Via Manzoni, displays about 200 works of the **19th century**, grouped into a thematic exhibition entitled *Da Canova a Boccioni* (*From Canova to Boccioni*). The 23 rooms you can admire plaster bas-reliefs by Antonio Canova, the best-known neoclassical sculptor, works by Francesco Hayez and other protagonists of the Lombard Romance, canvases of renown Macchiaioli and Divisionisti, such as Frederick Zandomeneghi, Giovanni Boldini, Telemaco Signorini, Giovanni Segantini, and Gaetano Previati. The itinerary of the 1800s ends with an important group of symbolist painting, and ushers in the next century with the works of Umberto Boccioni. Some sections of the exhibit restore life to the 19th-century Milan, with urban views of the Duomo and of the Navigli, which have disappeared, representations of bourgeois salons, and battles and scenes of the period.

A second section is devoted to the **20th century** and was inaugurated in 2012 in the 19th-century Palazzo Beltrami, overlooking the Piazza della Scala. It is the historic seat of the Italian Commercial Bank, filled with lavish structures and timeless furnishings that include a number of bank desks of the period. The exhibition, entitled *Cantiere del 900*, seeks to represent

Contemporary Art Galleries

Galleria Blanchaert

Founded in 1957 by Silvia Blanchaert, who still works with his son, Jean, the venue stood out in its early years by proposing to see out alternatives to traditional antiques and for a strong gravitation toward the decorative arts, ancient but mostly contemporary. Without giving up the exhibition of paintings, photographs, and videos, the research and exhibition activities of the gallery focus primarily on works in ceramics, enamel, wood, glass, and marble and have become a point of reference for artists and collectors in the enhancement of arts and crafts in Europe.

Piazza Sant'Ambrogio 4
www.galleriablanchaert.it

Antonio Colombo Contemporary Art

Ushering in this space in 1998, in the heart of Brera, Antonio Colombo undertook the task of promoting young Italian art, for which the gallery soon became a point of reference on a national level. Even through major exhibitions, the business has expanded to foreign artists, effectively putting young Italian talents into contact with the international art community, in search for new paths not only in painting but also in photography, sculpture, installations, and videos.

Via Solferino 44
www.colomboarte.com

Fondazione Forma per la Fotografia

Within the exhibition rooms of the foundation, built inside a historic tram depot in the Navigli area, visitors can find alternative exhibitions dedicated to the protagonists of Italian and international photography. The friendly multipurpose area also includes sections dedicated to educational workshops and screenings; a restaurant ; and Forms Galleria, the specialized bookshop, with collector photographic prints on sale.

Piazza Tito Lucrezio Caro 1
www.formagalleria.com

Studio Guenzani

Opened in 1987 by Claudio Guenzani, this gallery debuted on the Milanese art scene with a strong focus on photography, from the first exhibitions of Americans Louise Lawler and Cindy Sherman, to personal showings of photographers, such as Hiroshi Sugimoto, Nobuyoshi Araki and Gabriele Basilico. The studio's activity goes down the road of multidisciplinary contemporary art, with a special predilection for artists of the West Coast and Japan (such as the personal exhibitions of Yayoi Kusama), but with a strong interest in the most recent generation of Italian artists, such as Stefano Arienti, Margherita Manzelli Pessoli, and Alessandro Pessoli, all of whom are figures on the international stage.

Via Bartolomeo Eustachi 10
www.studioguenzani.it

Galleria Antonia Jannone

Since its inception in 1979, it has distinguished itself by having a keen interest in architecture, soon becoming an authoritative point of reference in Italy and in Europe, producing monographs devoted to notable players, such as Leon Krier, Aldo Rossi, and Giovanni Muzio. The research was then extended, in the 1980s, to scenery and design, with exhibitions by Luigi Serafini, Borek Sipek, Ettore Sottsass, and Daniel Weil. Recent exhibitions have been devoted to historical names along with important protagonists of contemporary architecture: Aldo Rossi, Vittorio Gregotti, Michele De Lucchi, Alessandro Busci, Alvaro Siza Vieira, Velasco Vitali, and Mario Botta.

Corso Garibaldi 125
www.antoniajannone.it

Galleria Giò Marconi

Designed as an exhibition center (it hosted exhibitions of artists the likes of Marc Chagall, Man Ray, Joan Miro, Pablo Picasso, and Mario Schifano), it was inaugurated in 1990 by Giò Marconi, who, at the onset, managed the gallery in partnership with his father Giorgio, founder of the Studio Marconi, a sort of laboratory for emerging artists, critics, and cultural players. Gallery programs, which continue to promote the artists of the Studio, are open to the experiences of young talent and players in the international scene.

Via Alessandro Tadino 15
www.giomarconi.com

Galleria Robilant + Voena

The gallery of Edmondo di Robilant and Marco Voena, in addition to the headquarters in Via Fontana, boasts another seat in London. The two art dealers, specialized in antique and 19th-century paintings, have launched major exhibitions that often include first showings of works that range from the 17th-century to present day (from Caravaggio to David LaChapelle and Julian Schnabel). Their customers include leading institutions on an international level, such as the Tate Britain in London, the National Gallery of Scotland in Edinburgh, and the Museo di Capodimonte in Naples. The Galleria Robilant + Voena is distinguished by its significant presence in major exhibition markets, such as Tefaf di Maastricht, the Biennale of Paris, and Milan MiArt.

Via Fontana 16
www.robilantvoena.com

Galleria Suzy Shammah

Inaugurated in 2004 in the heart of Brera, the gallery has focused on contemporary art since its opening, often exclusively selecting and promoting the activity of Italian artists, without leaving out the British, American, German, and Iranian scene— this last still new to Italy though well-established internationally. The gallery promotes the realization of ad hoc works through important exhibitions and strives to foster collaboration between artists and collectors.

Via Moscova 25
www.suzyshammah.com

Salamon&C

This gallery is in its fourth generation, established in 1956 and now run by the Salamon brothers, and focuses on graphic and antique pictorial art. In 1992 thanks to the contribution of Lorenza Salamon, the field of contemporary figurative art entered the reality of the gallery, with the aim of promoting Italian talents, whether engravers, sculptors, or painters. These are all emerging international artists, such as Marzio Tamer, Ugo Riva, Safet Zec, and Ivan and Luciano Zanoni.

Via San Damiano 2
www.salamon.it

Galleria Lia Rumma

After decades of activity in Naples, where the gallery of Lia Rumma has established itself as a point of reference on the international art scene, in 1999, the Neapolitan art gallery (though Lombard in birth) opened a space in Milan, on Via Solferino, followed by another gallery in 2000 on Via Stilicone: a white essentialist cube, which replaces the old disused transistor factory with an exhibition space on four floors, illuminated by large windows. The Galleria Lia Rumma has hosted major contemporary artists such as Marina Abramovic, Andreas Gursky, and Gino de Dominicis, and has, in a few short years, taken on the role of contemporary art temple and point of encounter for artists, curators, collectors, and art buffs.

Via Stilicone, 19
www.liarumma.it

the dynamic, artistic reality of the century, a continuous laboratory for new languages. The 12 sections of the layout documents the most important artistic currents that have occurred after the Second World War—such as informale, the concrete art movement, arte povera and conceptual art, and pop art—and provides an in-depth thematic voyage dedicated to *colore in forma plastica* (color in motion). Among the 189 works put on display, you can admire many a masterpiece by the elite of the Italian and international scenes, such as Alberto Burri, Lucio Fontana, Mario Schifano, and Alighiero Boetti.

Hangar Bicocca

It was conceived as a center for promoting research and training in the field of contemporary art, and is located in a northern district of the city. The spaces created inside the factory belonged to Breda, a company established in the late 19th century, which was among the most important in Italy and produced passenger cars, steam engines, and even aircraft during the First World War. With the decommissioning of plants, the vast district of Breda was reclaimed. Hangar Bicocca was created, along with the implementation of the Arcimboldi Theater, a large and modern structure designed by Vittorio Gregotti, which, during the last decade hosted shows by La Scala Opera House during the theater's restoration, which called for temporary closure.

Hangar Bicocca is home to two major permanent works. One of the three *Navate* (Aisles) created in the monumental building, which once housed transformers, hosts *I Sette Palazzi Celesti* by the German artist Anselm Kiefer. The evocative site-specific installation, created in 2004, consists of seven towers, varying in height—between 14 and 18 meters—and is built from reinforced concrete and containers that were once used to transport goods. The work, including the latest and most celebrated artist, is full of symbolic meanings and is inspired by an ancient Hebrew text that tells of a spiritual person who wants to reach the sight of God. In the garden, Hangar Bicocca visitors are greeted by *La Sequenza* by Fausto Melotti, a great installation where several scenes open at depth.

Exhibitions

There are many **exhibition spaces** in the city dedicated to international exhibitions on

Modern and Contemporary Art, which takes place every year in Fiera Milano City. MiArt is a must for all art lovers and for those who work in the sector, and is not only a showcase of prestigious Italian and European galleries, with spaces dedicated to specialized publications, but also an event animated by conferences and meetings.

contemporary art and to the 20th century. Among the most important, the Museo della Permanente, which inherited the spaces of the ancient "Società delle belle arti ed esposizione permanente" (Society of Fine Arts and permanent exhibition); the *Fondazione Stelline*, housed in an historic building in front of Santa Maria delle Grazie, the multipurpose center Spazio Oberdan, and the Fabbrica del Vapore, a creativity workshop born in an abandoned locomotives and tram factory.

The city also boasts a large number of **tunnels**, which often promotes festivals and cultural events, where collectors can learn about the latest news related to the art market, get professional advice, and make significant investments.

The art market finds its utmost expression at **MiArt**, at the International Exhibition of

Museo del Novecento (Via Marconi 1, phone: 0243353522)
Hours: Mon. : 2:30 p.m.–7:30 p.m.; Tues., Wed., Fri., and Sun.:
9:30 a.m–7:30 p.m.; Thurs. and Sat.: 9:30 a.m.–10:30 p.m.;
www.museodelnovecento.org

Gallerie d'Italia (Piazza della Scala 6, phone: 800 167619)
Hours: Sunday–Tuesday: 9:30 a.m.–7:30 p.m.
Thursday: 9:30 a.m.–10:30 p.m.; www.gallerieditalia.com

Hangar Bicocca (Via Chiese 2, phone: 026611573)
Hours: Thursday–Sunday: 11:00 a.m.–11:00 p.m.
Free admission; www.hangarbicocca.org

THE EMPEROR'S BASILICA

The Basilica of St. Lawrence, San Lorenzo Maggiore, probably was once a chapel of the nearby imperial palace, between the fourth and fifth century, at the time when the city was the capital of the Western Roman Empire.

If you come from Corso di Porta Ticinese, a row of 16 Roman columns, eight and a half meters high, taken from a second-century building, give a clear indication that you are approaching one of the oldest monuments in Milan. The people of Milan, down the centuries, have always loved this building as a symbol of their glorious past and have tried to protect it. So the ancient architectural structure has been preserved, even though it was renovated after fires in 1070, 1075, and 1124 and after the dome collapsed in 1573. The dome was immediately rebuilt on the orders of St. Carlo Borromeo, who was bishop of the city at the time.

A portico from the 1800s gives access to the interior, which is particularly majestic. Walking to the right, along the corridor created by the colonnade, known as an ambula-

tory, you come to the Chapel of St. Aquilino, which is the part that is closer to its original state than any other in the whole complex. Traditionally known as the "Queen's Chapel," it contains an ancient Roman sarcophagus, said to be the tomb of Galla Placidia (388/392–450), daughter of the emperor Theodosius. The empress actually died and was buried in Rome, but this little octagonal-shaped building was originally intended to be an imperial mausoleum, completely covered with precious decorations: marble inlays at the base of the walls, mosaics, and frescoes. All that is left of

these rich fifth century decorations are traces of paintings on the gallery in the upper part of the chapel, and, most of all, the mosaics. Of these, a few fragments, but extremely beautiful ones, can be seen above the atrium and on the sides of the altar. On the right, there is *Christ the Lawgiver among the Apostles* (*Cristo maestro tra gli Apostoli*) with Christ shown beardless, recognizable by the halo and his gesture of blessing. He is holding a book of the apocalypse, and there is a basket at his feet, containing scrolls of the Old and the New Testaments. Below him, and to the sides, the apostles are sitting behind two pools of water, representing the rivers of paradise. In the left mosaic, the one that is more badly damaged, a pastoral scene can be made out, with shepherds and sheep, while high up, in the center, a chariot rising into the sky can just be made out, partly from the preparatory drawing, where the tiles have come away. This scene has been interpreted as a representation of Christ as

The impressive effect of the dome, still the biggest in Milan, must have been even more marked when it was covered by its original gilded mosaic. A eighth-century description stated that St. Lawrence's Church was "magnificent, with its colored cladding and golden dome."

the Unconquered Sun, *Cristo come Sol Invictus*, meaning a permanent sun reawakening the world. This interpretation is supported by the fact that on December 25 (Christmas Day), the rising sun shines through the window right above this mosaic.

An urn from the 1500s on the altar holds the remains of St. Aquilino. The frescoes on the vault show how he was killed, in 1015, by the heretics, who cut his throat. History says his body was carried to the basilica by porters, of whom he is the protector.

A stairway at ack of the altar leads down into an underground mausoleum, recovered during excavations in the early 1900s. Here, there are carved blocks of various materials, some of them held together by cement. According to archaeologists, these blocks, including capitals and pieces of columns, which were used for the foundations, had been recycled from a previous Roman building, probably a nearby amphitheater.

The Piazza della Vetra, which opens from the back of the basilica, gives a wonderful view of the main body of the basilica, with its dome surrounded by four towers (making the edifice look like a turreted fortress), together with its three satellite chapels. Beside the Chapel of St. Aquilino, there are two other paleochristian octagonal chapels, erected as if on the spokes of a wheel. South of the basilica there is the Chapel of St. Hippolytus and to the north, that of St. Sistus.

During the Middle Ages, houses were put up, between the façade of the church and the columns. They were knocked down in the early 1900s, when it was decided to visually rejoin the two ancient structures once again. The statue in the middle of the square represents Constantine, the emperor who, right here in Milan in 313 AD, issued the famous edict of tolerance, a bronze copy of which is kept in Rome, in the Lateran Basilica.

The Basilica
Hours: Mon., Fri. and Sat.: 7:30 a.m.–6:30 p.m. Tues., Wed., and Thurs.: 7:30 a.m.–12:30 p.m. and 2:30 p.m.–6:30 p.m. Sun.: 9:00 a.m.–7:00 p.m. A fee is payable for admission to the Chapel of St. Aquilino www.sanlorenzo maggiore.com

MILAN

ZONES
AND DISTRICTS

Strolling through the different souls of the city, take our advice on the restaurants and venues to visit while experiencing world-class shopping.

1. Piazza del Duomo
2. Around Monte Napoleone
3. Brera - St. Mark
4. Navigli
5. Centrale - Repubblica - Buenos Aires
6. Ticinese
7. Corso Como - Isola
8. Arch of Peace - Sempione - Sarpi
9. Garibaldi - Solferino
10. Porta Romana

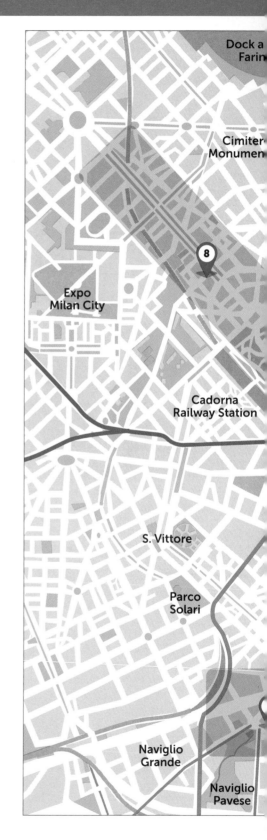

Central
Railway station

Piazzale
Loreto

Città
Studi

Public
Garden Indro
Montanelli

Piazza
5 Giornate

Porta
Vittoria

Dock area
Lodi T.I.B.B.

THE FASHION QUAD

Its cathedral, its castle, its art galleries, and its ancient churches all help make Milan famous with tourists, but not as much as this little network of streets, which, in recent years, have become symbolic of elegance, made in Italy.

At the ends of Via Manzoni, Via Monte Napoleone, Corso Venezia, and Via della Spiga, there seems to be nothing but an uninterrupted parade of high-fashion shop windows, often displaying such refined originality that they really seem to be artistic creations. In particular, you will notice that, unlike in other cities renowned for shopping, here there are no shops offering discount products or kiosks selling souvenirs between one fashion boutique and the next.

The importance of the Quad (quadrilatero) as a calling card for products made in Italy becomes much more obvious during the fashion

Strolling past windows that look like artworks, street level of illustrious buildings.

weeks, which attract professionals from all over the world, and during special fashion events. One of these events is always at the beginning of September, Fashion's Night Out, a long evening with the boutiques staying open to all, and VIPs and designers vying for attention at parties and shows. Another special is the so-called Vendemmia in Boutique (in October), when some of the most prestigious national wine producers present in fashion boutiques their latest vintage to the public.

All the major international labels are present in the Quad, but most of the space is taken up by national designers.

Some of these, such as Franco Moschino and Domenico Dolce, did their professional training in the Marangoni Institute, which is based at Via Pietro Verri 4, inside this quarter of Milan. This is a world-famous fashion school, founded in 1935, with locations also in Paris and London.

On the corner of Via Verri and Via Monte Napoleone, there are the windows of one of the city's most original shops, Lorenzi's cutlery shop (via Monte Napoleone 9, www.lorenzi.it). The interior is wonderful, with valuable articles for sale and excellently trained sales staff. They sell scissors, razors, and knives of all shapes and forms and for all purposes, as well as articles for smokers and other truly original objects, like chain-mail gloves for opening oysters or telescopic walking sticks.

The aristocratic homes

The impression of measured elegance that comes from the shop windows in the Quad finds an echo in the residential buildings in the area, many of which date back to the 1700s and early 1800s, when ideals of harmony and moderation were predominant in architectural taste. Some of these buildings accommodate museums, like at Via Gesù 5 (the Bagatti Valsecchi Museum, see page 65) and Via Sant'Andrea 6. The latter address is the Morando building, a splendid patrician residence, still furnished in part with furniture from the 1700s and 1800s, which is open for visits to collections of period costumes and paintings, showing Milan as it once was (www.costumemodaimmagine.mi.it, closed Monday). The

The house, now a museum, of the great poet and novelist Alessandro Manzoni is adorned by friezes in cotto, created in the 1860s.

Morando building is also the location for short-term exhibitions on original or curious aspects of Milan in the past. It is also worthwhile just taking a glance at the courtyard here, to understand the relationship, totally Milanese, between the almost austere simplicity of the façades and the richness of the courtyards, hidden from the gaze of passerbys. This confirms a principle, which was once quite commonly shared, that opulence should certainly be enjoyed but never shown off. From a historical and documentary point of view, the museum at Via Morone 1 is even more interesting. It is set up on the premises where the most important Italian novelist of the 1800s, Alessandro Manzoni, lived for almost 60 years, until his death (May 22, 1873) and displays his documents and memorabilia.

The home of Manzoni (www. casadelmanzoni.mi.it, closed Saturday and Monday) opens onto a cozy courtyard, which is overlooked by the neoclassical palazzo Belgioioso, designed by Giuseppe Piermarini and completed between 1772 and 1781. The first floor of this building houses a renowned restaurant with traditional cooking, Boeucc (Piazza Belgioioso 2, www.boeucc.it).

Along Via Manzoni

Via Morone leads off from the square, and here, at number 3, there's a shop that is almost an institution for Milan: Colla, the barbershop, (www. anticabarbieriacolla.it), open 1904 and still furnished as it once was. Portraits of the shop's customers line the walls and form an almost complete collage of Milanese life from the last century.

The buildings that overlook nearby Via Manzoni are just as illustrious. The street itself starts from Piazza della Scala and finishes at the remains of a gate in the 12th century wall. This is the Archi di Porta Nuova (Porta Nuova Arch), where copies of Roman tombstones have been placed,

and there is, on the façade, a 1300s tabernacle with statues of saints in it. Among the many buildings worth noting, there are two that house museums: the Galleries of Italy complex (see page 71) and the Poldi Pezzoli (see page 64).

The big hotels

Via Manzoni is also known for its two luxury hotels. The **Grand Hotel et de Milan** (Via Manzoni 29, www.grandhoteletdemilan.it) was the residence of great cultural figures, including Giuseppe Verdi, who stayed here and, in fact, died in

one of the rooms on January 27, 1901. The Milanese felt so much affection for the maestro, that, while he was on his deathbed, people had straw put on the paving of Via Manzoni so that the noise of the passing carriages would not disturb him. To the right, at number 31 on Via Manzoni, there is the **Armani Hotel** (milan.armanihotels.com), part of a building long occupied by the famous fashion house, with shops selling flowers, housewares, perfumes, and other items. (High-end clothes and accessories are sold in the boutiques in nearby Via Monte Napoleone and Via della Spiga). Inside the building, now renamed **Armani Concept Store**, there are also the famous Japanese restaurant Nobu; the Armani Club, which is one of Milan's most exclusive nightspots; and the Armani cafè, where you can enjoy light bites in an elegant but informal environment. At the opposite end of the Quad, at Via del Gesù 6-8, there is the **Four Seasons** (www.1.fourseasons.com), a five-star luxury hotel, housed

in what was the 1400s convent of Gesù. A good view of the large cloister can be enjoyed from the tables of the restaurant Teatro, which is on the basement floor. Opposite the Four Seasons, in the same building that houses the Bagatti Valsecchi Museum (see page 65), there is the chic deli **Salumaio of Via Monte Napoleone** (Via Gesù 5/Via Santo Spirito 10, www.ilsalumaiodi-

Italian restaurant of old. Another for the list is **Bagutta** (Via Bagutta 14, www.bagutta.it), no less typical, with a simple, family restaurant look, crowded and lively. Since the 1920s, this place was a meeting place for artists and intellectuals, so

cake, the panettone (see page 120). Almost as famous, especially since they have branches in Manhattan, is **Sant'Ambreus** (Via Matteotti 7; www.santambroeusmilano.it), a sort of flag bearer with the name of the city's patron saint in the local

montenapoleone.it), which sells classic Italian dishe, in premises adorned by antique columns and paneled ceilings. The outside tables are no less fascinating since they take up part of the courtyard of the Bagatti Valsecchi building.

The **Carlton Baglioni** hotel (*www.baglionihotels. com*), another great classic of Milanese luxury accommodation is not far away. It has two entrances, at Via Senato 5 and on Via della Spiga, the loveliest street of the Quad. Il Baretto is the hotel's renowned restaurant, offering traditional Milanese dishes.

To take a break

Any list of top eating places in the Quad has to include Bice (Via Borgospesso 12, www.bicemilano.it), a restaurant that is very much in vogue for the city's international clients, yet has kept its atmosphere as an

much so that by 1927, a literary prize was established there. To find another famous spot with a different atmosphere, you just have to go to Paper Moon (Via Bagutta 1, www.papermoonmilano.com), a very chic pizzeria/restaurant.

Near Via Bagutta is the legendary confectioner's **Cova** (Via Monte Napoleone 8, www. pasticceriacova.it), an elegant tearoom, which also serves light meals. In business since 1950, on the first floor of the building on the corner of Via Monte Napoleone and Via Sant'Andrea, it descends directly from the confectioner's shop, opened in 1817 by Antonio Cova. The shop had much to do with establishing the typical Milanese Christmas

dialect. On very elegant premises and with attentive service, it has been open since 1936, specializing in confectionery and aperitifs served with their own savory finger snacks. They also serve restaurant lunches.

Via Matteotti starts from Piazza Meda, in the middle of which there is a bronze statue of the **Sun**, created in 1972 by Arnaldo Pomodoro, who has work on display around the world, from the Vatican to the United Nations building in New York City.

THE HEART OF THE CITY

The cathedral square is surrounded by big stores and renowned restaurants, but also some quaint little side streets hidden away from the nonstop downtown hustle.

For one of the best views over the city's central square book a table at the restaurant Giacomo all'Arengario (Via Guglielmo Marconi 1, www.giacomoarengario.com). It's on the second floor of the building to the right of the cathedral, home of the Museum of the 1900s (see page 70) and its windows overlook the cathedral façade (see page 32), the entrance to the Galleria shopping mall (see page 36), and the monument to Italy's first king, Victor Emanuel II, on horseback. The restaurant is done out in Art Deco style with an open kitchen, and specializes in fish dishes and traditional Milanese recipes.

On ground level, in the courtyard of the **Palazzo Reale** (Royal Palace) built in the 1700s and now used for exhibitions and civil weddings, have coffee in the elegant cafè, with its mezzanine reading room. This cafè is almost never overcrowded because it's out of sight of most passersby, and it's a great place to take a good look at the building it is in. The palace was built in 1778 for the Austrian governor of the city and then became the seat for the court of the kingdom of Italy. This kingdom was founded by Napoleon and en-trusted to his viceroy, Eugène de Beauharnais, the son of his companion, Josephine. During that decade (1805–1814), Milan was the capital of a modern state covering about one-third of the Italian peninsula and underwent major development, economically and artistically.

The street of big stores

The colonnades along the opposite side of the square lead to the opening of the Galleria shopping mall and, beyond that, to the start of **Corso Vittorio Emanuele II**, a pedestrians-only street entirely under porticoes and lined with stores and malls along its whole length. The biggest name is the first store on the left, **Rinascente** (Via Santa Radegonda 3,

> As the evening draws in, the frenetic activity in and around the square calms. There are other areas that attract the night owls. The restaurants and cafès in the Galleria are an exception, though, since they are favored by foreign tourists.

www.rinascente.it), a department store selling upscale goods. The seven-floor 1950s building (there was a shopping mall here for 100 years before) offers clothing, accessories, homewares, cosmetics, and a tax-back office for non-EU citizens. The top floor is mostly given over to the food market and eating places, including a Japanese restaurant and a diner with a superb view over the cathedral terraces. But there is also room on this floor for a top hairdresser. Milanese hair stylist, Aldo Coppola, who is an established international name, has one of his salons here. Another Rinascente claim to fame is that Giorgio Armani once worked here. Before he started his brilliant career in the world of fashion, he was a buyer for Rinascente, Milan.

The big stores of **Excelsior** (www.excelsiormilano.com) may not have the same history, but they are also here, at the end of the Galleria del Corso mall, a short, covered gallery that opens up from around halfway down Corso Vittorio Emanuele II, on the right. They offer a very wide range of wares, but all in the spirit of an unconventional, sometimes quirky, luxury image. They try to get away from the look of the label, following the trend of the more modern concept stores. Some of the leading lights of Milan fashion, such as the chief buyers for the renowned boutique Antonia, help to choose the articles on sale. The talented chef Davide Oldani is head of the culinary section, which is a sort of flagship of the mall; his supermarket Eat's, full of culinary delights and imaginative deli dishes, has become a standard for many Milanese, rivaling the excellent bistro on the first floor.

On the other side of Corso Vittorio Emanuele II, a short walk along Via San Paolo leads to the square, Piazzetta del Liberty. This is dominated by the shop windows of **Ferrari** (www.store.Ferrari.com), where you can buy clothing and gadgets bearing the logo of the most famous Italian car makers and actually get a close-up look at some of the Formula One race cars produced by the Maranello team. Next door to this shop is one of the most chic pizza restaurants in town, the Charleston (www.ristorantecharleston.it); well-lit premises for dining on tasty Tuscan dishes,

For almost a century, Rinascente is the symbol of high-end shopping. The building was reconstructed after a 1917 fire. Its name, conceived by the great poet Gabriele D'Annunzio, means "the resurgent." Nowadays, it boasts branches in 11 major cities.

open till late and ideal for after-theater meals.

Corso Vittorio Emanuele II finishes in **Piazza San Babila**, a modern-looking square. Across this square, to the right of a short gallery, there is one of Milan's favorite cocktail bars, the **Ginrosa** (Galleria San Babila 4B; www.gin-rosa.it), a venue that first opened 150 years ago. Their specialty is the cocktail the bar is named after, but which does not actually contain any gin. It is a mixture containing "only" 25 percent alcohol and based on more than 30 different herbs, and shaken. It can be drunk like that or used as a base to mix with various different spirits. Opposite the bar, there is the entrance to one of the Mazzolari (Corso Monforte 2) stores, a large cosmetics shop, selling all the top brands and rarest of perfumes and essences for personal use and use in the home. They also sell candles, incense, and personal care products.

The average person's alternative to the elegant shop-

ping of Corso Vittorio Emanuele II can be found on Via Torino, starting from the southwest corner of the cathedral square. This is where you find the shopping malls with affordable prices and a number of clothing stores where you can buy quality clothes at a reasonable cost.

This old street is not just for shopping, though. There are also some ancient churches here, and one of the most beautiful is right at the start, on the left, number 17. It's called **Santa Maria at San Satiro**, and

it was embellished by Donato Bramante. The great Renaissance architect worked on it starting in 1482 and managed to overcome the lack of space for a new apse by creating an amazing effect of illusion. He used a trick of perspective with a bas-relief of gilded and decorated clay. As you enter the church, it seems to have a deep recess behind the altar, but as you get closer, it turns out to be just one meter deep.

Between cooks and merchants

On the other side of **Via Torino**, the first street leading off it to the right is the narrow Via Spadari, much loved by those who like their food. This is where to find the best-known deli in town, one of the best stocked and lavish in Europe: **Peck** (Via Spadari 11, www.peck.it) opened in 1883 by a deli owner who came to Milan from Prague. His shelves and counters are loaded with every imaginable delicacy, with special attention paid to the maturity of the foods. At the back of the store, you can take a peek at the cooks while they prepare dishes, and downstairs in the base-

ment there is an excellently stocked wine store, selling top-notch wines and spirits. There is a tearoom upstairs on the second floor. Right across the narrow street, there are the windows of a food market that is no less a part of local history: the fish shop Pescheria Spadari (www.pescheriaspadari.it). It sells marinated fish and shell-fish snacks to eat on the premises any time of day.

A few paces further along Via Spadari, you come to **Via Hugo**, where at number 4 there is the restaurant Cracco (see page 126) and opposite that, at number 6, the Peck Italian Bar, offering excellent snacks or cocktails made as they should be.

Crossing over Via Orefici, which is not pedestrianized, you come back to the cathedral square by way of an attractive merchants' square **Piazza dei Mercanti**. At one end, there is the palace, Palazzo della Ragione, built at the start of the 1200s as the seat of government. At that time, Milan was like other free mu-

nicipalities in Italy, which had a system of democratic participation, where the citizens were called upon to decide for themselves the principal matters of state. Political work was done in the rooms upstairs, which are now used for short-term exhibitions, while the downstairs area under the porticoes was

The Piazza dei Mercanti is a charming part of medieval renaissance Milan.

used for business. In this area, there is an acoustic effect that makes it possible to hear what people are saying from one side of an arch to the other, even if they lower their voices. Legend has it that the merchants particularly liked this because it helped them with their bargaining over prices.

IN THE ALLEYS OF OLD MILAN

The Brera Art Gallery is not just the richest art museum in the city, it is also the epicenter of a charming quarter, with good shops, restaurants, and trendy places to hang out. Brera is the best-known image of Old Milan.

For decades, it was the quarter of the artists, the brothels, and cheap restaurants. Today it's one of the most expensive areas of the city. The main axis of the district is **Via Fiori Chiari**, and a number of restaurants are lined up along here, all of which offer a decent service to international customers without being "touristy." The is that they are always used by the Milanese themselves. The restaurant with the longest history on the street is the Torre di Pisa (Via Fiori Chiari 21, www. trattoriatorredipisa.it), with a menu of Tuscan cuisine and meat dishes. The premises are very cheerful, with the tables

Behind the church of Santa Maria del Carmine, a web of really enchanting little alleys teems with life until the wee hours.

close together and something going on all the time. Nearby, just as popular and busy, is Nabucco (Via Fiori Chiari 10, www. nabucco.it). They have a few tables outside, too, and offer plenty of fish dishes.

Around Carmine Square

About halfway along Via Fiori Chiari, you turn onto Via Madonnina, one of the most interesting streets in the quarter. It leads into Piazza del Carmine (**Carmine Square**), dominated by a large church, Santa Maria del Carmine, which was built in the 1400s, even though its façade has an end-of-the-1800s look. In the middle of the square, there is *Frammento di Torso* (*Fragment of a Torso*) by contemporary sculptor Igor Mitoraj, while on the south side, there is Trattoria del Carmine (Piazza del Carmine 1, www.trattoriadelcarmine. com), a restaurant appreciated in fair weather, when the tables outside allow you to admire the pretty, pedestrians-only square.

If you want to pay a little

less, go to **Pizzeria Sibilla** (Via Mercato 14), just a few yards away from the square, where customers sit around long, shared tables to eat either the tasty thin-crust pizzas or a typical simple trattoria dish.

Stop to eat

Stepping just outside the borders of Brera, you come to Da Claudio (Via Cusani 1, www. pescheriadaclaudio.it), which has been the best-known fish shop in Milan for decades. The classic "Meneghino" (a nickname for the typical Milanese man) would eat a small plate of fresh fish standing at the long counter in the shop, maybe washed down with a glass of spumante. Now, though, it's also possible to have lunch sitting comfortably in the elegant upstairs restaurant that opened a few years ago.

If you go along Via dell'Orso, you get to another of this quarter's renowned restaurants, Coriandolo (Via dell'Orso 1, www.ilcoriandolo.com). It's more formal, but not too much so, and they serve classic Italian dishes accompanied by wine from a well-stocked cellar. Nearby, but a little hidden away, is the restaurant in the **Hotel Bulgari** (Via Privata Fratelli

The street-cum-square in front of the church of St. Mark holds a street market twice a week, and other district events.

Gabba 7b, www.bulgarihotels. com), considered by many to be Milan's most sophisticated five-star hotel. The dining room is minimalist but luxurious, and they serve quality dishes prepared by Andrea Ferrero, who specializes in fish. The inner garden, which is next to a vegetable garden, can be admired from large windows.

Among artists and market stalls

This district is not only famous for its restaurants but also for bars, the haunts for bohemians and intellectuals, especially in the 1950s and '60s. The most famous is **Jamaica** (Via Brera 32, www.jamaicabar.it), on the corner of Via Brera with an alley named after Piero Manzoni, a postwar Milanese artist who spent a lot of time here with friends and colleagues.

At the end of this alley, beyond Via Fatebenefratelli, is the ancient **church of St. Mark**. This church was once used for a concert by Mozart, when he was still young, and also for a requiem mass for Alessandro Manzoni, with music by Giuseppe Verdi. Inside there is a burial monument from the mid-1300s, sculpted by the great artist from Pisa Giovanni di Balduccio. Twice every year, at the start of spring and in the fall, they hold one of the city's most colorful charity markets, **Floralia**, in the church sacristy. Milanese women often go there to buy plants for their balconies.

Speaking of **markets**, one is held biweekly on Via San Marco, near the church. It's held every Monday and Thursday and reconciles the casual tone of the marketplace with the elegant surroundings of the quarter. It's not unusual to find something valuable among the stalls, even if the price is not always right.

Via San Marco is also known for its venues. Some are steeped in tradition, such as the restaurant **Stendhal** (Via Ancona 1, www.osteriastendhal.it), an elegant os-

teria serving traditional Lombardian food, and **Tombon de San Marc** (Via San Marco 20), an English-style pub that has been here for decades and is named after the Darsena ("Tombon" in Milanese), a port that used to stand here on the canal, until it was filled.

Just a few yards farther on, you move into the district of Solferino-Garibaldi, which mostly has the same atmosphere as Brera.

IN THE CANAL QUARTER

Because they did not have a river to facilitate trade, for centuries the Milanese dug artificial canals, called navigli. As modern Milan grew, between the 1800s and the 1900s, they had to start filling them in to make way for roads, leaving just stretches of the navigli.

Along the main canals, Naviglio Grande and the Naviglio Pavese, there are glimpses of fairly typical corners of Old Milan. The easiest to reach, if you are coming from the city center, is the first stretch of the Naviglio Grande, on the right-hand bank, between the Darsena (an ex-port) and the first iron footbridge.

The Naviglio Grande

After just a few yards, you come to a typical "**casa di ringhiera**" (Alzaia Naviglio Grande 4), a type of lower-class housing construction, common in the 1900s, where there was a continuous, shared balcony running along the length of each floor of the building, giving access to the apartments from the courtyard. There are

When the weather is good, you can take a trip on the tourist boats leaving from the Naviglio Grande (near the Darsena) and returning about an hour later, viewing the main points of interest on the urban stretch of the two navigli, such as historic churches and ancient lochs.

still many of these houses in the city, but this is one of the most beautiful because it has had a lot of excellent improvement work done on it, and it is now used to house artists' studios and craft workshops.

In front of the building, there is a landing dock for small boats for tourist trips on the Naviglio Grande and the Naviglio Pavese. These trips last about an hour, without any stops, following what is called the **Itinerario delle Conche**, a tour of the canal basins (www.naviglilive.it; round trips start and finish at the same point).

Another typical sight is the porticoed area where the washerwomen worked in times past. This place is called **Brellin**, a term in the local dialect for the footboard the

women stood on while working. The same name is also used for the restaurant that has always stood behind the structure. The restaurant serves typical Milanese food (Alzaia Naviglio Grande 14, www.brellin.it). The Brellin has helped to bring culinary fame to this first stretch of the Naviglio Grande, and so has the Pont de Ferr (www.pontdeferr.it). This "starred" osteria can be found on the other bank of the canal at 5 della Ripa di Porta Ticinese (the roads on each side of the canal have separate names).

Nightspots and market stalls

The banks of the Naviglio Grande are known for their big-name restaurants, but more so for the number of osterias, pizzerias, and pubs, suitable for all pockets and all ages and which make this quarter the most overcrowded place in the entire city on summer evenings.

The boutiques here are just as well-known, especially those selling vintage clothes. The area is also a favorite for those interested in period clothes and objects. The last Sunday of every month, except July, from 9.00 am to 6:00 p.m., the banks are crammed with 380 stands, selling antiques, modern art, and vintage articles at the **antiques flea market**. One of the well-known shops from this stretch of the canal is a specialized second-hand bookshop (this is the original store of the Libraccio, nowadays a chain of bookstores in several Italian cities), on the corner of Alzaia Naviglio Grande and Via Corsico (www.libraccio.it). Last but not least, there is a well-stocked supplier of vinyl records, Discomane, at Alzaia Naviglio Grande 38.

The Naviglio Pavese

This stretch of canal has a similar air as Naviglio Grande,

One
of the Expo
projects involving
the Navigli
is a plan to bring
real gondolas
from Venice
and use them
on the canals
during the
exhibition period.

but is less crowded and it has two venues with quite different atmospheres and prices. **Le Scimmie** (Via Ascanio Sforza 49; www.scimmie.it), is a lively pub/restaurant with live jazz and a history of shows by top performers. **Sadler** (www.sadler.it) is a restaurant at Via Ascanio Sforza 77, run by one of Milan's top chefs.

Not far from Le Scimmie is the **Conchetta del Naviglio Pavese** (Little Basin). This is the smallest of the 14 *conche*, or basins, built at intervals along the canal from Milan to Pavia and it has recently been re-

> **On summer evenings, the Navigli quarter is the liveliest in the whole of Milan, with a thousand packed venues and shops open late.**

stored. These ingenious structures, which were probably perfected by **Leonardo da Vinci** (some of his drawings would suggest this) served as lochs on

the canal, to resolve the problem of differences in height at different points along the waterway. Once out of its urban stretch, the naviglio reaches Pavia, after skirting past the Certosa monastery. Before crossing the city boundary, the waterway passes a rural area, which has in recent years undergone reclaiming work. The area comprises of a beautiful medieval church called **Chiesa Rossa** (Red Church); a nearby farmhouse with a portico enclosing it; and an unfinished canal loch called Conca Fallata (Faulty Basin).

CARTA DEI VINI DI LOMBARDIA

Come and find out Wines of Lombardy.

50 Restaurants are waiting for you.

Download the list from

www.ascovilo.it

LOMBARDIA

RegioneLombardia
Agricoltura

Vini di Lombardia

ASCOVILO
Associazione Consorzi Vini Lombardi

RegioneLombardia

Fondo Europeo Agricolo per lo Sviluppo Rurale: l'Europa investe nelle zone rurali
PSR 2007-2013 Direzione Generale Agricoltura

THE COSMOPOLITAN QUARTER

Around the considerable mass of the main train station, there are a series of five-star hotels and corners of a multiethnic Milan, with shopping opportunities to suit every pocket and a large numbers of restaurants with all kinds of different cuisine.

Central Station

The station was built between 1927 and 1931, in a historical style and is the best-known edifice in the quarter that stands northeast of Milan's center. It has always had a lot of admirers who appreciate its grandiose appearance, but there are a fair number of critics too, who do not appreciate all the fascist symbols peeping out of statues and friezes or the bizarre, excessive style, jokingly described as "Assyrian-Milanese."

From when it was opened until the rise of mass air transport, Central Station was the door to Milan. In 1944, the Jewish victims left the city fon their journey to the concentration camps. The trains left from track 21, where today there is the *Monument to the Shoah*. Central Station was also the first glimpse of a metropolis for the large number of citizens from the southern Italy who came to work in the north in the 1950s and 1960s, and became a symbol of the wealth and potential offered by Milan.

Following recent changes to its layout, the large areas between the ticket desks, on the ground floor, and the tracks, on a raised level, have been transformed into a large shopping mall, selling a little of everything.

To the left of the station, in the square, Piazza Duca d'Aosta, one of the most famous works of 1900s Italian architecture stands out. The **Pirelli skyscraper** is a little over 127 meters high, with a total of 31 floors, and is set up on an irregular hexagonal base, which gives it its characteristic shape. It was designed by Gio Ponti, working with Arturo Danusso and Pier Luigi Nervi, and was built between 1955 and 1960 for the giant Milanese tire manufacturer.

Hotels, restaurants, and high society

On the wide, modern street that stops opposite

Central Station, **Via Vittor Pisani**, there is a restaurant that is better known for its glamorous clients than its culinary delights. It's called Giannino (Via Vittor Pisani 6, www.giannino.it), and the Milanese soccer stars go there to eat in their time off, as well as showbiz stars of all ages. If it's full or if you don't care to spend hand over fist to sit next to some personality from the tabloids not far away, right at the center of the three-four-star hotel area surrounding the station, there is another restaurant, the **Osteria del Treno** (Via San Gregorio 46, www.osteriadeltreno.it). It is just as well-established, but far easier on the pocket, with a family atmosphere and simple, good, quality food accompanied by good wine, all at the right price.

Via Vittor Pisani leads into the square, Piazza della Repubblica, where there are two large five-star hotels. One

Between Central Station and Piazza della Repubblica, there is the biggest concentration of hotels in the city. For this reason, the area is one of the busiest for tourists, Italians, and foreigners.

is the **Westin Palace** (Piazza della Repubblica 20, www.westinpalacemilan.com), and the other is the legendary **Principe di Savoia** (Piazza della Repubblica 17, www.hotelprincipedisavoia.com), which has scenic halls that are often used for events and presentations and which boasts the most prestigious suite in the whole of Milan (three bed-

rooms, sitting room, pantry, kitchen, and swimming pool). Next door, at number 13, there is the restaurant Dal Bolognese, perhaps the classic restaurant for business breakfasts in the city. The cuisine, typical of the region of Emilia, is excellent, and the service is impeccable. Most of the patrons, especially at lunchtime, have in mind successful deals with their fellow diners rather than the quality of the meal.

Another Milan

In the network of streets that spread out behind the Westin Palace, there is a completely different atmosphere. This is one of Milan's most interesting quarters, with all the **multiethnic flavors** of the world's populations. For the most part, these are immigrants who have lived in Italy a long time and are well integrated. So there's no worry about not finding a Russian-Ukraine food store, an African

restaurant, or an authentic kebab. If you are also looking for color and liveliness, go to Via Benedetto Marcello on Tuesday or Saturday morning for the market, where you can find real bargains.

The ethnic group most in evidence, and who have been in Italy for the longest time, are West Africans (who, for the most part, come from the pre–Second World War Italian colonies). A popular meeting point for the Eritrean community is Martha's Bar (Via Panfilo Castaldi 19), where the traditional dish called 'ngera reigns. It consists of soft, spiced bread with cubes of stewed meat and vegetables on top, all to be only eaten with your hands.

A restaurant run by a Senegalese man, Rougui, is just as well-known. It is called Baobab (Via Tadino 48, www.ristorantebaobab.com) and serves food mostly from the owner's country, but with some recipes from other ar-

> **The famous American architect Frank Lloyd Wright defined Central Station as the "world's most beautiful station."**

eas of Africa. The restaurant's name is also one of their specialties, since their customers can always ask for baobab juice, which is very rich in iron. If you want an Indian restaurant, you can get quality food at Just India (via Benedetto Marcello 34, www.ristoranteindianojustindia.com), spe-

cializing in dishes from northern India, where the owner comes from.

Another possibility for those who like Indian cuisine is the excellent nearby takeaway at Via Spallanzani 6, the Kashmir (www.kashmirindia-no.it), which uses an original tandoori oven brought from India by the owner. If you want to stay exotic, but closer to Europe, drop in to Magazin Kalin-ka (Via Boscovich 40), where the owners, from Ukraine, sell products from their native land, as well as from Russia. The food is always fresh,

because the store is regularly supplied by a shuttle bus service that arrives daily in Milan from Eastern Europe.

Shopping in Buenos Aires

The boundary of the quarter is drawn on one side by Via Vittor Pisani and on the other by a long commercial artery, lined by a succession of shop windows of all kinds and for all pockets. On this street, there is also a theater, which has a long history and has recently been refurbished, Elfo Puccini (Puccini the Elf; Corso Buenos Aires 33, www.elfo.org), with a billboard for contemporary drama. It now has three rooms for shows, a library, a media shop, and refreshments. The crowds of people going in and out of the stores, bars, and

hotels on Corso Buenos Aires never stops, especially on Saturdays, the holy day for shopping in Milan. If it's aperitif time, have one in the bar of **Hotel Diana Majestic** (Viale Piave 42, www.sheratondianamajes-tic.it) and enjoy a moment of peace and quiet in its luxurious Belle Epoque atmosphere. The hotel has been here since 1912, but the building itself was built in 1842, when it contained baths, a public swimming pool (the oldest in Italy), a ballroom, a shooting gallery, and various tearooms.

WHERE THE PARTY IS IN THE STREET

The venues in this district have the youngest customers in the city, but it is the most ancient urban area. It is here that you find the clearest traces of Mediolanum (Roman Milan).

The Basilica di San Lorenzo Maggiore (Basilica of St. Lawrence; see page 76–77), with an "urban sitting room" in front of it, a stage set created by sixteen Roman columns, is the classic meeting place for twenty-year old Milanese. The expression *"vedersi in colonne"* ("See you in the columns") is now a city buzzword. The area is **littered with bars**, where you can get a quick drink, because, weather permitting, not many people can resist the temptation to spend time outside. A different, older, set of customers crowd the shop windows and sidewalk cafès lining the nearby block, including the

streets Via Celestino V, Via Gregorio XIV, and Via San Vito, behind the basilica on the left. This is a cafè area, particularly full at aperitif time.

The snapshot of the apse of the Basilica di San Lorenzo

Maggiore is one of the city's best-known images. This can be seen from the gardens in the square, **Piazza della Vetra**, named after a river that used to flow there. Despite its beauty, this square is considered to be "cursed." This is because it is the place where witches were burned and other executions carried out, like the 1630 execution by torture of Gian Giacomo Mora, accused of being a propagator who spread the infection of the plague by selling evil remedies. The tragic end of this most unfortunate citizen is recalled in Alessandro Manzoni's story *Storia della colonna infame* (History

venues on the main street. A bit farther on, you can get an ice cream from Grom (Corso di Porta Ticinese 51, www.grom.it), a nationwide ice cream chain (also available outside Italy now) selling semi-homemade ice creams and gelato. The ice cream shop is under **the medieval gate, Porta Ticinese**. Despite its mistreatment in the 1300s and again in the 1800s, it is one of the most important remains of the city

The Porta Ticinese is really two: the medieval gate, in bricks, and outside it, the early 1800s gate, built in neoclassical style.

of the Infamous Column). As a reminder of this barbaric act, a piece of twisted iron has been placed in the square, on the side closest to Via Molino delle Armi, with the Latin word "Pax" (Peace) written over it.

wall that was built in the 12th century. It is decorated on the façade by a recess, with a Virgin Mary on a throne, baby Jesus on her knee, and two classic Milanese saints, Ambrose and Peter the Martyr, standing on each side of her.

Church, the largest orthodox Christian community in Milan. Behind the church is the archaeological site of the **Anfiteatro Romano** (Roman Amphitheater; Via De Amicis 17), a small, quiet open park among the ruins of the ancient structure. In the second and third centuries, this large amphitheater of Mediolanum (the Roman name for Milan) accommodated no less than 35,000 spectators.

Far from the madding crowd

Just a short way along **Via Molino delle Armi**, toward Corso di Porta Ticinese, you come across Dogana del Buongusto (Via Molino delle Armi 48, www.ladoganadelbuongusto.it), an osteria-cum-restaurant, with two lovely basement dining areas designed in a pleasantly vintage style. The wine cellar is well-stocked, and the cheeses and cured meats are top quality, so it may be ideal not just for lunch or evening meal, but also for a quick bite. It would be a good destination too, if you are looking for a moment of peace and quiet away from the crowded

After the intersection with Corso di Porta Ticinese, Via Molino delle Armi becomes Via De Amicis. Here, immediately to the left, is the beautiful 1600s façade of the church Santa Maria della Vittoria (St. Mary of the Victory), the official place of worship for the Romanian

The historic venues

The Cap Saint Martin (Via De Amicis 9), the café to the left of the façade of Santa Maria della Vittoria, is considered one of the historic businesses of the

In the Park of the Basilicas

This stretch of **Corso di Porta Ticinese** is crowded with people; even the tramcars (the only vehicles, apart from taxis, that can use the street) have difficulty passing through the clamor. To find some peace and quiet and to see attractive corners of ancient Milan, it is worth going to the nearby park, Parco delle Basiliche (Basilicas Park), which is closed at night but can be circumvented on Via Antonio Banfi. The park is actually a series of gardens that stretch from Piazza della Vetra to the apse of the Basilica di Sant'Eustorgio (Basilica of St. Eustorgius). This is one of Milan's most beautiful churches and dates back to the fourth century, despite its mainly Romanesque look and its façade, which was completed in the 1800s. According to legend, the basilica was erected at the spot where the wagon bringing the remains of the Three Kings from Constantinople to Milan was mysteriously stuck. Today the basilica has only some fragments of the precious remains, which were appropriated in the 12th century by the bishop of Cologne.

district, since it was one of the first to launch the idea of the happy hour in Milan.

The nearby restaurant **Trattoria Toscana** (corso di Porta Ticinese 58, www.trattoriatoscana.net) has made an even bigger contribution to local habits over recent decades. All the major changes in youth culture can be seen reflected in this restaurant, which started as a simple trattoria, and then became a meeting place for radical left-wing supporters in the 1970s, before turning into an icon for trendy Milanese in the 1990s. That is how it remains today, as can be seen just by taking a look at its clientele.

The Ark of St. Peter the Martyr was created in marble in 1339 by Giovanni di Balduccio and holds the remains of the revered Dominican preacher.

The Portinari Chapel, inside the basilica, is considered a true masterpiece. It was built in the 1460s and financed by Pigello Portinari, who was director of Florentine bank in Milan. He earned the gratitude of Bianca Maria Visconti—the wife of the lord of the city, Francesco Sforza—and then built this splendid chapel in the new Renaissance style of Tuscany, to hold the revered remains of St. Peter the Martyr, a Dominican preacher who was worshipped in Milan. The edifice is probably the work of the great Florentine architect Michelozzo, while the frescoes adorning the upper part of the walls (from 1468) are considered to be by Vincenzo Foppa. Anyone who happens to be in Milan on January 6, Epiphany, should go to the basilica in the morning to see the end of the colorful procession of the Three Magi in costume, which starts from Piazza del Duomo and finishes with the placing of gifts in front of a live nativity scene in the basilica's sacristy.

Near the basilica, you can go into the cloister of the convent of St. Eustorgius, where they hold various cultural events (conferences, lectures, and concerts) in the summer, or you can just take a drink at the open-air bar. The cloister also leads to the Museo Diocesano (Diocesan Museum; Corso di Porta Ticinese 95, www.museodiocesano.it), which has some interesting paleo-christian items.

Corso di Porta Ticinese finishes at Piazza XXIV Maggio, and is overlooked by the imposing neoclassical Porta Ticinese, with its two tollhouses. It was built in 1800 by the architect Luigi Cagnola, immediately after Napoleon's victory at Marengo, which chased the Austrians out of Lombardy. To the right of the gate, before crossing into the Navigli district, you can take a look around the covered market behind the old port area, the Darsena. Inherited from an old city market, identical to those that existed in every local district a few decades ago (today there are still 26 open), the Ticinese market has been "colonized" by Latin Americans, mostly Peruvian, who have transformed it into a lively, colorful area, with exotic fruit stalls, languages, and aromas you really wouldn't expect to find in the center of Milan.

BETWEEN MOVIDA AND SKYSCRAPERS

For a long time, it was the biggest unused area in the center of Milan. Today it is a conglomeration of brand-new buildings of dizzying heights. You get there along the short Corso Como, packed with in-places and trendy boutiques.

Why has this old street on the edges of the center become the place to be for the "trendies"? The main reason may be found in the local housing, with a large number of *ringhiere* (a type of lower-class housing construction, common in the 1900s). These houses were always ignored by the well-off in Milan until they became popular at the end of the last century. To parallel the increase in housing prices and the demographic changes in the local population, boutiques and services have opened up on the street.

To get onto Corso Como, you pass through Porta Garibaldi (Garibaldi's Gate), built

in 1826, with a tollhouse on either side. This stands at the center of Piazza XXV Aprile and has a larger building to the right of it, which contained one of the most famous concert stages in the city, Teatro Smeraldo (Emerald Theater) and is soon to become an outlet for the culinary chain Eataly.

Next to the former theater, at number 12 on the square (entrance on the courtyard), there is the well-known furniture and housewares store **High Tech** (www.cargomilano.it). It's not quite in vogue as it was a few years ago, but if you show off their dinnerware (especially a recent collection), you won't have to worry about raised eyebrows from the "smart set."

Before going onto Corso Como and the realm of all that is trendy, you could take a short stroll along Viale Pasubio, where they are currently building the new headquarters for the Giangiacomo Feltrinelli Foundation, designed by the Swiss architects Herzog & de Meuron. You can still see the original corners of Old Milan around it. One example is the historic restaurant Antica Trattoria della Pesa, with its typical interior and traditional cooking (Viale Pasubio 10, www.anticatrattoriadellapesa.com).

In the street's boutiques
The place that is most emblematic of the whole area,

At 232 meters high, the Unicredit tower is the highest building in Italy. It dominates most of the views of the area.

which has now acquired international status, is **10 Corso Como** (www.10corsocomo.com), an entire building that was re-invented in the early 1990s by Carla Sozzani, a leading name in Milan fashion. Stepping through a little door, you find yourself inside a real microcosm, including a cafè, a bookstore, an art gallery, a roof garden, and a clothing and accessories store, all blended together with an identical idea of the beautiful. It's hard to remain indifferent to a place like this, which can fascinate or, just as easily, repel, since it completely represents an entire world.

Some of the boutiques on this street are equally well-known: Boule de Neige, taking up three separate shops, is a landmark for wealthy eccentrics (in moderation) in their thirties and forties, while the same goes for the shops of the designer Massimo Rebecchi (www.massimorebecchi.it) and the high-end optician's store selling glasses with the French label Alain Mikli.

The nightlife

In the evening, the type of person you meet on Corso Como changes slightly. The nightspots here—some stay-ing open till late—are very popular with the younger set, especially the nightclubs: **Hollywood** (www.discotecahollywood.com), **Tocqueville 13** (www.tokvill.com), and **Loolapaloosa** (www.loolapaloosa.com). They have built their reputation over decades (Hollywood is the biggest name in the city), with the help of showbiz and sports celebrities who have spent hot nights there under the lenses of the paparazzi.

At the end of the street, on the left, there is a fitness center in tune with the spirit of the area. Virgin Active (www.virginactive.it) combines health and fitness with hi-tech, and makes use of Asian techniques.

Daring architecture

At this point, Corso Como meets the heavy traffic of the avenue that separates it from the railroad station Porta Garibaldi (second largest station in the city) and gives way to a brand-new district of sky-scrapers. The **Unicredit tower** stands tall, easily identified by its 232-meter-high pinnacle (twice as high as the Madonnina on top of the cathedral), candidate to become the new "Milan lighthouse." It is the tallest building in the whole of Italy and was designed by the Argentinian Cèsar Pelli. The structure is concave, and inside the curve, there is a raised circular plaza dedicated to Gae Aulenti, the top Italian architect who died recently. Pedestrian walkways and footbridges link the tower to the rest of the district. We are talking about a totally new corner for Milan, and the Milanese, who don't go there very much at the moment, but it is perfect for a bike ride or for anyone interested in skating.

To the "Island" of Milan

Walk past a loud splashing fountain and passageways in the middle of ingenious architectural views and you get to the so-called **Vertical Wood**,

The Palazzo Lombardia stands on the edge of a nice quarter of Old Milan, known as Isola (Island). This is one of the newly emerging areas of the city, thanks to the look of many of its buildings; a reminder of the Milan of the past and the fact that there are a lot of places to go here that are full of life in the evenings and at night. The heart of the local *movida* is Via Borsieri and the **Blue Note Jazz Club** (Via Borsieri 37, www.bluenotemilano. com), where top names on the Italian and international music scene play in a real jazz club atmosphere (the club is part of network founded by the famous Blue Note in New York), with tables for a drink or a full-blown meal. Sunday brunch at noon (October–March only; concert starts 1:00 p.m.) is a regular date for a lot of fans.

a pair of skyscrapers (one has 23 floors, the other 16) that got their name because they have so many terraces with plants, opening on to each floor of both buildings. These are the work of the architect Stefano Boeri, who saw this as an advanced technological answer to the problem of environmental sustainability in a high-impact structure, such as a skyscraper. A few hundred meters on, next to Via Melchi-orre Gioia, is Palazzo Lombardia, the **Lombardy Regional Government building**, which is a little more traditional but no less spectacular than the others. It is 161 meters high, designed by Pei Cobb Freed & Partners, and conceals, on the inside of the structure, a broad plaza called Piazza Città di Lombardia, where they screen shows and other events to the public and set up an ice rink in the winter.

THE EMERGING QUARTER

This pleasant area, almost completely pedestrianized, around the Arch of Peace is one of the hot spots of the Milan nightlife. Around here, there are a lot of very lively streets: Piero della Francesca (especially in the evenings) and Paolo Sarpi, the heart of Milan's Chinatown.

The bars and bistros on Piazza Sempione and at the start of Corso Sempione fill up with people, especially in the summer evenings. But the crowds are not there for the bars themselves, although some are nice, without being a "big name." The big attraction is the chance to be outside, in a space that is free of automobiles, in front of Milan's iconic monument and with a really spectacular view of Sempione Park and Sforza Castle. The people are mostly youngsters, twenty to thirty year olds, but not exclusively so. This is a place for everyone to be: pleasure seekers out for the night or families with kids who will play in the wide space under the arch while their parents enjoy a chat on the steps.

In the restaurants of the Milanese

The bars and restaurants at the "Arch" (using the regulars' catchphrase) are the starting or finishing point for a night out in this district, which has plenty of attractions. If you are not content with the finger foods that go with a drink at the bar and are looking for a full-blown meal, try Corso Sempione 12, Taverna dei Golosi (www.tavernadeigolosi.com), a good restaurant with standard Italian food and some tables outside on the street, or the well-known fish restaurant Montecristo (Corso Sempione 28, www.ristorantemontecristo.com), or again,

a bit arther on, at number 49, **L'Aquarius** (www.ristoranteaquarius.com), one of those hidden treasures of Milan that makes its visitors so happy when they are lucky enough to find it. In the daytime, it looks like an elegant bar in a rich area of Milan, but in the evening, it turns into a trendy restaurant and meeting place for showbiz folks and celebrities, attracted to a light, varied menu and a wine list with some top labels.

Temptations in the park

If you are looking for a place to spend a late night out, the best thing is to move from the Arch of Peace into the park.

Within a few yards you come to **Just Cavalli** (Via Camoens s/n, www.justcavallicafe.com), the club that belongs to the famous fashion house and operates as a restaurant, cocktail bar, and nightclub. It is right underneath the Branca Tower (see page 60), favorite lookout point over the city. Next door you'll find **Old Fashion** (Viale Emilio Alemagna 6, www.oldfashion.it), one of Milan's oldest nightclubs, occupying part of the Triennale building, which also houses the Museum of Design (see page 58). The **Design Cafè** (Viale Emilio Alemagna 6), on the first floor of this building (admission free, whether you visit the museum or not) provides good, simple, light meals on premises given an original look with distinctive décor, and nonmatching tables and chairs, albeit all rigorously designed furniture.

In the warmer seasons, don't miss a chance to try the bar that stands right inside the park, in a fenced-off area accessible only from inside the

Beside Corso Sempione, with its tall, RAI TV tower, the different souls of a many-sided, lively area go their separate ways.

Triennale building. It is adorned by a De Chirico scenic sculpture, *Bagni Misteriosi* (*Mysterious Baths*) and gazebos constructed in a distinctive shape, that of bottles of Campari soda.

Glamour and gourmands

Instead of going toward the park, a lot of nighthawks prefer to go the other way, toward **Via Piero della Francesca**, where there are some venues that are no less well-known. The one they all want to go to is **Gattopardo** (Via Piero della Francesca 47, www.ilgattopardo-cafe.it), a nightclub in a deconsecrated church, where they decide who to let in and guests have to sit at a table and pay for a drink. During fashion week or the furniture fair, when Milan's nightspots become catwalks for high society, it is impossible to get in without advanced booking. A little farther on is **Roialto** (Via Piero della Francesca 55), a venue that is also well-known but with reasonable prices. It made its name as an aperitif bar, but nonetheless is crowded until late at night. The furniture is special, the lights are low, the staff is impeccable, and it has a pretty roof terrace.

Apart from these two iconic venues of Milan nightlife and a large number of restaurants

of all kinds (including some pizzerias), all visited almost exclusively by true Milanese, Via Piero della Francesca also offers some interesting stores that may make it worthwhile to hang out there in the daytime, too. It's obligatory to take a coffee break at number 8, in **Hodeidah** coffee shop, part of history because it still does its own roasting. The owner himself has operated the old coalfired roasting machine since 1949, which gives the beans their delicious aroma. They don't just sell coffee of all possible qualities, though. Hodeidah is also recognized by the Milanese with a sweet tooth as the place to go for a great choice of teas and high-quality sweets and cakes, made on the premises.

The coffee shop is a few paces away from **Via Procaccini**, a long street with its own famous establishments (the best-known is **Milano**, at number 37, with a similar atmosphere to Roialto but better lit and more suited to conversation) and big name restaurants.

The art factory

At Via Procaccini 4, there is the steam factory **Fabbrica del Vapore** (www.fabbricadelvapore.org), 30,000 sq. m. of former industrial space converted and run by the municipality to hold short-term exhibitions and occasional shows and to provide a place for cultural associations involved in contemporary art. Its specialist library keeps almost 20,000 volumes and an archive of portfolios of around 3,500 Italian artists, while the video archive has film clips of around 4,000 artistic installations. On the third Saturday of every month, the large

109

courtyard of the steam factory holds the **Mercato della Terra** (Earth Market). This is run by the slow-food organization, and you can buy bread, wine, cheese, and cured meats directly from the producers. All the products are of high quality and healthy, many of them bio and zero food miles, which means they come from growers close to Milan.

Hints of the Orient

Via Procaccini borders on the legendary Milanese Chinatown, whose original core goes back as far as the first decades of the 1900s. The central street of the Chinese quarter is **Via Paolo Sarpi**, pedestrianized several years ago and full of stores, bars, and restaurants. It goes without saying that the street is dominated by those Chinese who have countless little stores selling inexpensive plastic products, which often cover for large wholesale warehouse suppliers. But there is also room for lots of little restaurants, where you can get an authentic Chinese meal, especially Shanghai style, where the majority of the local inhabitants come from. One of the most appreciated by the Chinese themselves is **Hua Cheng**, at Via Giordano Bruno 13, where really tasty meals (the soups are recommended) are served in a simple place and at a low price.

The quarter is multiethnic, though. The Chinese may predominate, but others are present, as proven by a pleasant Sri Lankan restaurant, Little Dream (Via Rosmini 3), where a few euros will buy you dishes prepared using true Sri Lankan recipes. However, the globalization of the area has not completely erased the traces of Old Milan from the street. We are reminded of old times by the structure of the houses, many of which have preserved their shared balcony so typical of the popular building style of the start at the last century, as well as one or two stores that survived the decades. A couple of examples are the Cantine Isola (Via Paolo Sarpi 30), a very popular, legendary wine bar; and the herbal store, Erboristeria Novetti (Via Paolo Sarpi 63), open since 1952, when herbal cures were not as trendy as they are today. The number of loyal customers demonstrates the ability of the owner, Francesco Novetti, to find the best remedies for every kind of problem.

On the edge of Chinatown, beside Sempione Park, there is **Via Cesariano**. On this street, every Monday and Thursday morning, they hold a street market selling food, clothes and accessories, which is appreciated and well supported by the local residents, both from the lower-class streets (Via Sarpi and others nearby) and from the elegant avenues flanking Sempione Park.

CONSORZIO VOLONTARIO VINO D.O.C.
S. COLOMBANO

lls of Milan "Isola di Terra" that are cultivated with vineyards in the "sea" of Lodigiana of plains to produce sophisticated that bear the label Designation of Origin: D.O.P.: San Colombano Red and White I.G.P.: Collina Milanese Verdea and rape varieties. For some years the hill has been safeguarded in cultivation by the birth of Hill Park covering its total surface the municipalities of Miradolo Terme, Inverno and Monteleone (PV), Sant'Angelo Lodigiano and Graffignana (LO).

SAN COLOMBANO WINE CONSORTIUM DOC
Via Ricetto - Castello Belgioioso - San Colombano al Lambro (MI)
Tel. 0371 898830 - Fax 0371 201161
info@sancolombanodoc.it - www.sancolombanodoc.it

emagna Canteen

Our company is located in an ancient rural courtyard just a few hundred meters from the Viscount castle. This courtyard, called old municipal barracks was bought by my mother's great-grandfather in 1878 as a result of regular public sale. The auction sale was held by the standard "virgin candle" method. First my great-grandparents, followed by my grandparents, then our mother and finally us, an infinite chain mitted art, made of smells, feelings and strong sensations. Ten years tured by those smells, feelings, and strong sensations, we decided, yful spirit, not to lose the ancient art of wine making, an art that soon mply repay us, so much so that the playful spirit has given way to a very ated production.

a Emilio Azzi, 94 - 20078 San Colombano al Lambro (MI)
Tel. 347 9668891 - www.casavaldemagna.it

Guglielmini Giuseppe Farm

The Guglielmini farm is now a wine reality in Miradolo Terme and in the territory of the San Colombano hills. It has produced wines for three generations, evolving both in care of the vineyards and canteen production. Over the past twenty years, in particular, the leadership of Giuseppe Guglielmini has combined technology and tradition, acquiring new vineyards and equipping the canteen with state of the art technology to increase production size and wine quality. Each label veils a year of intense work, hope and painstaking care for the raw materials, vineyards and end product of the canteen.

Via del Nerone, 9 - 27010 Miradolo Terme (PV)
Tel. e fax 0382 77183
www.viniguglielmini.com - info@viniguglielmini.com

tare dei Santi Farm

The Nettare dei Santi winemakers is located on the San Colombano Hills in a suggestive setting where vineyards, hills and wide horizons make up the countryside. The history of the canteen dates back to the 40s inside the courtyards of the San Rocco Oratory by the Riccardi family. The Nettare dei Santi brand was created by fencing Olympian from 1928, 1932 and 1936, who was internationaimed and deeply linked to these lands. His son, Enrico, spurred the s, focusing both on the vineyards and on the winemaking process. ico has been at the side of his father and manages sales with the assion. The canteen specializes in red, white and sparkling wines, ering certain aged and straw wines.

a della Capra, 17 - 20078 San Colombano al Lambro (MI)
Tel. 0371 200523 - Fax 0371 897381
www.viniriccardi.com - E-mail: info@viniriccardi.com

Antonio Panigada Farm

At San Colombano, a quaint hamlet between the lowlands of Pavia and the plains of Lodi, where the grasslands transform into suggestive hillsides, the Panigada family, aside from the famous deli, has been producing wines for over three generations. The label bears a curious name of Banino®. San Colombano owes its name to the Irish monk that Christianized it in the VI century, also importing his vineyards. The inhabitants of the town are known as banini, thus giving way to the exclusive name of the wine.

Via Vittoria, 13 - 20078 San Colombano al Lambro (MI)
Tel. 0371 89103
www.banino.it - vinobanino@hotmail.com

rasanta Canteen

Located in the heart of San Colombano al Lambro, the Pietrasanta Wines and Spirit Farms occupies the country estates on an ancient and lovely home that dates back to the mid-1700s, which is the residence of the Pietrasanta family. Carlo Giovanni Pietrasanta, is the owner, and is devout to his work, following every phase that goes with wine-making and canteen procedures in order to achieve the quality that distinguishes the company, assisted by the wine-maker Professor Leonardo Valenti.

Via P. Sforza, 57
20078 San Colombano al Lambro (MI)
Tel 348 7122717 - Tel 346 7219996
www.cantinepietrasanta.it

Poderi di San Pietro

The San Pietro Estates has been producing DOC and IGT wines since 1998 on the San Colombano hills. On the 75 acres of its own grounds planted with vines with an annual output of 4,500 hectoliters of wine. It is the Company Representative of wine excellence for the entire district of Milan and its province. The 6,000 square meter canteen, of which 2,000 m dedicated to barrels, already employs intelligent technology and stainless steel tanks that are thermo-conditioned and saturated

with nitrogen. Only the best selections continue aging in oak barrels until their complete maturation giving rise to the precious reserves that have obtained significant international awards including the Starwine of Philadelphia.

Via Steffenini 2/6 - 20078 San Colombano al Lambro
Tel. 0371 208054 - Fax 0371 208781
info@poderidisanpietro.it - www.poderidisanpietro.it

AT THE HEART OF SHOW BUSINESS

The incomparable theater district, lively 24 hours a day, is particularly animated in the evenings, when its many venues, ranging from old-style trattorias to cafès fill up with customers from all walks of life.

Corso Garibaldi starts on the boundary with the Brera district and is similar to it in atmosphere. This district is different, though, because it has kept some of its old, working-class feel. The typical Old Milan houses, just as overcrowded as in the neighboring district in the past, are now occupied by professionals from the fashion business, who have moved in over the last few decades to live next to the working-class families who have always been there.

You can get to know the soul of Garibaldi in the community center opened by the city authority in a former church (Corso Garibaldi 27). It's a bit of a surprise; a place where kids' activities and art exhibitions alternate with afternoons of ballroom dancing for pensioners. After dancing, they sit and chat on the benches in the yard, closed off by a portico.

A great Little Theater

Walking along Via Giorgio Strehler from Corso Garibaldi, you get to the heart of the Milanese theater life (apart from La Scala, obviously). The Piccolo Teatro (Little Theater) is a repertory group with three separate premises: two of them, the Strehler and the Studio, stand close to each other, while the third, the original theater, is on nearby Via Rovello. The Piccolo was formed in 1947 by two giants on the Italian cultural scene, director Giorgio Strehler and the impresario Paolo Grassi, and became internationally famous over the decades. It has kept up its reputation thanks to the wise guidance of its current director Sergio Escobar, who manages to organize a playbill full of quality and variety every year, relying on the artistic direction of Luca Ronconi.

The **Studio** (Via Rivoli 6) is used for more innovative works. It was designed by the architect Marco Zanuso as a re-creation of a typical Old Milan house, with the audience looking down from the balcony railings onto the stage in the

courtyard. The **Strehler** (Largo Greppi 1), also by Zanuso and again very much Milanese, has a more traditional design (the use of bricks is a clear tribute to traditional Lombardy architecture). It is the largest of the three theaters, with the largest audience capacity. It's used for the Piccolo Teatro's principal plays, as well as operas, concerts, and other cultural events, such as film showings during the Milano Film Festival, an internationally famous festival for short films.

Wineglasses and shop windows

The mixed nature of Corso Garibaldi is reflected in its shops, where you can find temples of secondhand items, such as Surplus (at number 5), specializing in vintage fashion long before it reached its peak; a favorite address for freaks of all generations, Don Quijote (at number 53, www.donquijote.it), specializing in cowboy boots and accessories; and a high-design furniture showroom, Il Piccolo (Via Delio Tessa 1, www.ilpiccolo.com).

The food and drinks panorama is no less varied, with

> **The presence in the district of two Piccolo Teatro venues and the cinema Anteo make it the most popular with the intellectuals.**

some pizza chains and aperitif bars with no particular character but it also has some really historic venues. Among these is the wine shop Moscatelli (at number 93), where, for

decades, the Milanese drank glasses of casked wine at low prices in a cheerfully noisy atmosphere. There is also Matarel (Via Mantegazza 2), a real temple of Milanese cooking that is known for its loyalty to the local cuisine, as well as for having several generations of Milan's VIPs, especially politicians, sitting at its tables. At lunchtimes, it is not unusual to find newspaper reporters from the *Corriere della Sera* and *Gazzetta dello Sport* eating here, not far from their head offices on **Via Solferino**, a street that is also known for its elegant fashion and accessories boutiques, especially along its first part.

Around the ancient basilica

Between Corso Garibaldi and Via Solferino, there is one of the most historical churches in Milan, dedicated to **St. Simplician** (Basilica di San Simpliciano, Piazza San Simpliciano 7). The basilica was founded in the fourth century by Bishop Ambrose and still has an essentially Romanesque look, even though the façade is almost totally 1800s. On the interior, in the

The Anteo area

The second part of Corso Garibaldi, from the intersection with Via della Moscova onward, is pedestrianized for a short distance and lined by an almost uninterrupted series of bars, which makes it one of the hot spots of Milan nightlife. The most famous bar is Radetzky, a regular for wealthy forty-year-olds and carefully avoided by anyone who knows the history of Milan (Radetzky was head of the Austrian occupation army in the mid-1800s).

apse vault, there is *Incoronazione della Vergine* (*Coronation of Mary*), a fresco from around 1515, a masterpiece accredited to Bergognone, and a carved wooden choir, also from the 1500s. There are also two beautiful cloisters (one from the 1400s, the other from the 1500s) on the interior

cating the atelier of BBPR, the most important architectural firm in Milan since the 1900s. At the end of the street, a small door leads into the oratory of St. Simplician, where there are play areas for kids, and park benches, but also a view of the apse of the basilica that is not to be missed.

Going right to the end of Corso Garibaldi brings you into Piazza XXV Aprile, the gateway into the neighboring and no less trendy district of Corso Como.

There is a different atmosphere, though, if you turn right, onto Via Marsala, at the 1400s church of **Santa Maria**

of the former convent's annex. Today, these are part of the Theology Faculty of Northern Italy and are open to the public only on special occasions or events (entrance from Via Cavalieri del Santo Sepolcro). The street that runs from behind the basilica, Via dei Chiostri, is one of the most romantic features of Old Milan, with an ancient silence hanging over it. There is a plaque indi-

Incoronata (Coronation of St. Mary). This building has a curious split façade, which corresponds with the interior division into twin naves. Legend has it that this structure was the wish of the financers of the work, Francesco Sforza and his wife, Bianca Maria, who wanted to underline the happiness of their relationship. The first intersection on the left on Via Marsala is the street where the Milanese cinema enthusiasts go for their favorite movies, the **Anteo** (Via Milazzo 9, www.spaziocinema.info). Its success is due to its ability to choose quality films that are not too intellectual nor too dependent on the box office. This recipe has enabled them to thrive during a period of crisis for traditional cinemas, without betraying their faithful audiences, who can watch films without background chatter and popcorn. They can concentrate and enjoy a film here in a way that is hard to find in other cinemas. Apart from the three screens, there are also a bookstore and a restaurant in the building, the Osteria del Cinema, offering a few select dishes, good quality wine, and a wall completely covered with pictures of films or actors off set, eating or cooking.

Almost opposite the Anteo is the Giallo (Via Milazzo 6), a restaurant serving a traditional menu, and stays open late, making it ideal for a meal after the film.

The last part of Via Solferino runs parallel to Via Milazzo, and Andrea Berton, the chef who built up the reputation of the restaurant Trussardi in Piazza della Scala, has recently opened a new restaurant here, **Pisacco** (Via Solferino 48, www.pisacco. it). The new establishment is well decorated in a modern style and customers can also drop in just for a glass of wine. Food and wine are upscale, but prices are affordable, especially if you don't have a full meal. A few yards on, there is a wine shop, **Cotti** (Via Solferino 42, www.enotecacotti. it), which is one of the best stocked (and historic) in Milan. They sell all the top Italian labels and a good selection of foreign ones.

> **Corso Garibaldi retraces the route of the Roman road that led to Como. On this street there are still many houses from the 1800s, which make it one of the most historic areas of Old Milan.**

THE ANCIENT SOUL OF THE CITY

This is the central district least visited by tourists, but it is not lacking in appeal, especially in one or two hidden corners where the heart of Old Milan is still beating.

The avenue that is now **Corso di Porta Romana** was the finest street in the city in ancient Mediolanum (Roman Milan) and was paved and flanked by a series of porticoes. All you can see today from that time are archaeological remains (the Basilica of St. Nazarius), as the atmosphere surrounding the street and the area near it is working-class one.

Before going onto this street, it's worthwhile to stroll around **Piazza Sant'Alessandro**, dominated by a 1600s Baroque church of the same name, and opposite that, Palazzo Trivulzio. Its high façade is topped by the crest of the ancient Trivulzio family, which produced two great figures of Italian history: the military leader Gian Gia-

como, who conquered Milan in 1499 for the French, and the far more patriotic Cristina Trivulzio Belgiojoso, fascinating but unappreciated supporter of the Italian Risorgimento. Near the square, there are a couple of well-known restaurants: Alla Collina Pistoiese (Via Amedei 1, www.allacollinapistoiese.com) specializes in meat dishes while Assassino

(Via Amedei 8) has a pleasant outdoor dining area, using the porticoes in the courtyard of an old residential building.

The main monument on the first part of Corso di Porta Romana is the very old **Basilica of San Nazaro Maggiore** (Basilica of St. Nazarius). It was founded by St. Ambrose in the fourth century and was renovated a number of times. The overall appearance of the exterior is Romanesque at the rear, while the façade is Renaissance, due to the work done by Bramantino between 1512 and 1550. This was done to add the Trivulzio chapel, which was an austere but scenic mausoleum for Gian Giacomo Trivulzio, whose tomb bears Latin inscription: *qui numquam quievit quiescit; tace* (he who never rested rests now: be quiet).

For the body and the mind

The narrow alley to the left of the basilica leads to Via Festa del Perdono, dominated by the building of the **State University**, erected in the 1400s as a state-of-the-art hospital for its time, both in its structure and its purpose. The inspiration behind the Ca' Grande (The Big House, as it was known) was, in fact, to create a structure where sick people could go to be healed, whereas hospitals, at that time, were simply places where poor and terminally ill people were taken to for comfort before they died. The

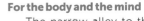

right wing of the building (the older side, going back at least to the 1500s) has maintained its original structure: a very large courtyard overlooked by the church and smaller courtyards, where the patients were separated by their illness (another new idea for the time), which avoided spreading of infection. The building was in use as a hospital until the mid-1900s, when the ownership passed onto the university.

On Via dell'Università and nearby streets, there are bookstores, photocopy shops, and several bars offering cheap snacks, mostly visited by students. There are also restaurants offering full meals. Two of these are upscale restaurants: La Rena (Via Festa del Perdono, 1, www.larenaristorante.it), whose specialties are lobsters, and La Dolce Vita (Via Bergamini 11, www.dolcevitaristorante.it), where dinner is accompanied by opera in a period decorated dining room.

> **"Porta Romana Bella" is the title of a popular song once sung in the prisons of Milan, and today, all the Milanese know it.**

In and around Crocetta

Coming back onto Corso di Porta Romana, you'll pass by Panarello (Piazza San Nazaro in Brolo 15, www.panarello.com), a shop run since 1930 by a family of confectioners, and get to the intersection of Via Santa Sofia and Via Francesco Sforza. This is part of a ring around the center of Milan, known as the *"cerchia dei Navigli"* (the Navigli ring). A little farther, Corso di Porta Romana runs into the square **Largo della Crocetta**, where you'll find the Carcano theater (Corso di Porta Romana 63), dating back to the time of

Napoleon, although it looks from the 1900s. In the past, this was used for operas and plays and, more recently, it has been a cinema and university teaching rooms. Over the past few years, it has been winning back its old reputation, with a quality playbill. Past the theater, turn left onto **Via Orti**, which has an unmistakable air of Old Milan about it, with typical houses with their long balconies and a large number of bars, trattorias, and restaurants. La bettola di Piero (Via Orti 17), a restaurant that is steeped with the atmosphere of a Milanese osteria from times gone by, is always full. Another successful establishment is Lacerba (Via Orti 4, www.lacerba.it), a wine bar, ideal for aperitifs, with elegant surroundings combined with a restaurant specializing in fish. The name comes from the futuristic magazine founded by Papini and Soffici in 1913, which explains why the walls are papered with copies of pictures and posters produced by

those legendary artistic pioneers. **The Roy** also offers excellent seafood in a bright and elegant setting (Via Benvenuto Cellini 2). Although not exactly around the corner, the menu variety and the freshness of the ingredients are definitely worth the walk. Also, live concerts here are not uncommon.

A walk out of town

At the end of the avenue is the **Porta Romana** (the Roman Gate), erected in 1598 to welcome Margaret of Austria, who had just become queen of Spain and therefore sovereign of Milan. Nowadays the structure stands at the center of the traffic-bearing Piazza Medaglie d'Oro, where a part of the Spanish wall, erected

in the 16th century, can still be seen. Right up against the ruin are the **Thermal Baths of Milan** (Piazza Medaglie d'Oro 2, www.termemilano.com), an elegant complex, including hydro-massage, saunas, Turkish baths, and other facilities for physical relaxation and beauty treatments.

From Piazza Medaglie d'Oro, turn into the lively Via Muratori and walk for ten minutes until you come to **Cascina della Cuccagna** (Via Cuc-

cagna 2, www.cuccagna.org). This is the Big Rock Candy Mountain farmstead, and it looks a little out of place in this context. It is actually a farmstead from the 1700s, a reminder of the time when the area was just fields. It has been renovated without changing its appearance and is now a social center, where they hold meetings, teaching workshops, and recreation for kids. There is even a workshop for cyclists, who are encouraged and helped by expert staff to repair their own bicycles. In front of a nice kitchen/garden, they have a bar-restaurant specializing in cooking bio products. There is also a zero-mile food store, supplied by the farms nearest the city.

THE CHRISTMAS CAKE

The panettone is one of the few foods that can be found on every Christmas dinner table all over Italy. It is a sweet bread made from flour, yeast, egg yolks , and butter, enriched with candied fruits, lemon peel, currants, and raisins. Simple but impossible to bake at home.

This invention of Milanese baking, which has become a national symbol of the most important festival in the Catholic world, is the object of various legends about its origin and its name.

The most common one says it comes from *"pan del Toni"* (Tony's bread), a worker in the kitchens of Ludovic the Moor, lord of Milan in the latter half of the 1400s. The duke's magnificent Christmas banquet was a success because Tony saved the face of the court baker, who burned the splendid cake he had spent days preparing. Panic was growing in the kitchen as the moment neared for the triumphant entry of the cake into the dining room. But Tony bravely took the place of the hapless baker and baked a new cake, using what he normally used at home; poor man's bread enriched with whatever he could find in the duke's pantry. A hybrid sweet was born, basically simple (sweet bread) but rich with secondary ingredients, and was a great success with the Moor and his court.

This legend is very popular with the Milanese, who think it highlights two aspects of their character, of which they are especially proud: enterprise and the ability to react to problems with a touch of genius. But unfortunately it's completely untrue.

The origins

Reading the oldest description we have of this cake (it is mentioned in a Milanese–Italian dictionary from 1606), it becomes clear that, even centuries after the time of the Sforza family, it was relatively poor in ingredients and taste, compared to what we eat today. The author, Cherubini, describes quite a plain loaf, which was baked for Christmas Eve, and the first slice was traditionally cut by the head of the family. It is not until 1839 that we find a description of a panettone similar to what is eaten today. Cherubini talks about "a wheat bread decorated with butter, eggs, sugar and raisins or sultanas." He also adds that in the country, the recipe was poorer because they used dough made from corn flour instead of wheat. Cherubini also reports that the bakeries of the period also made *panattonin* (minipanettoni), which were sold all year. So the panettone originated and spread from the Milanese bakeries, perhaps in the 1600s, but more likely in the 1700s or the beginning of the 1800s—a somewhat more prosperous times when people's diet improved considerably. The name certainly does not derive from *"pan del Toni,"* but from the word *"panetto,"* a term once used as a unit of measurement in bakeries and is still used for packs of butter.

In the 1800s, the panettone began to look like it does now. It changed from a flat bread into a light, spongy mixture, and from a sweet bread, it became a product of high-quality confectionery. A lot of the credit for that must go to Antonio Cova, an ex-soldier in Napoleon's army,

What makes the best panettone is the use of natural yeast, which makes it more tasty and more digestible. The best thing to add to the panettone is a cupful of custard. If you must have wine, let it be a dessert wine and not spumante, as is so often the case.

There is a Milanese tradition, which people still believe in, that a slice or two of Christmas panettone should be put aside until February 3, as protection against throat infections for the whole year. February 3 is the name day of St. Biagio, who is considered the protector of the throat.

who opened a confectioner's shop in 1817, next door to the La Scala theater (the shop with his name, Caffè Cova, still exists, but it has moved to Via Montenapoleone). A few years later, a confectionery shop specializing in panettone opened near Corso Magenta. This historic shop also still exists and bears the name of the family that bought it in the latter half of the 1800s: Pasticceria Marchesi, Via Santa Maria alla Porta 11. Another of the Milanese confectioners of that period that

has to be mentioned is Biffi della Galleria, a business that is still at its original location, although they stopped making their own confectionery some time ago. At the end of the 1800s, the form and packaging of the panettone began to take the shape of a hatbox, with the top of the cake puffing out of its wrapping, and this is now coming back into fashion with some producers.

Angelo Motta made the panettone famous on a national scale after the First World War, when he opened his confectionery business on Via della Chiusa and considerably improved the recipe. His mixture was so soft, it needed a paper wrapping to keep its tall, round shape, and nowadays all makers use paper wrappings for their panettone. He was so successful that he had to open more and more shops within a few

years, so he decided to invest in the first industrial scale production of panettone. His example was soon followed by another Milanese confectioner, Emilio Alemagna. Until the 1970s, these two shared the market, which now covered the whole country, and fought each other for market share with advertisements and publicity gimmicks.

Panettone is also used as a common metaphor in local football jargon. If the coach of one of the Milan teams starts the season badly, the fans in the city start to say he won't even get to eat his panettone— he'll be fired before Christmas.

The classic recipe uses candied fruit and raisins; many other variations also use chocolate and marron glacé.

MILANESE RECIPE

Veal cutlet is a very popular dish in Italy, but the variations found around the country are often quite different from the original "milanese" : a steak of veal, on the bone, fried in bread crumbs.

Seeing the similarity to Wiener schnitzel, some say the recipe comes from the time when the Austrians dominated the city. But they are wrong: the dish was actually mentioned in an account from Milan in the 12th century. In reality, it's more likely that the Austrians copied what they found in Lombardy. Evidence comes in a letter from the first half of the 1800s, written by the commander of the occupation forces, General Radetzky to Count Attems, where he describes the breaded cutlet as if he had never tasted it before. This is also conjecture, though, because there is quite a difference between the two dishes, especially the fact that the Austrian dish uses different meat: a slice of pork with no bone.

To prepare the dish properly, the nerves have to be removed and the skin cut before cooking, so that the meat doesn't curl. The cutlet should then be beaten lightly to tenderize it, but not flattened before coating both sides with a mixture of eggs and bread crumbs, which should stick well to the meat. The cutlet is then placed in a large frying pan, in plenty of sizzling-hot clarified butter and turned frequently to ensure a golden brown color on both sides. The meat should be served immediately and on a hot plate.

Despite this simple preparation, it's quite rare to find it cooked as it should be, especially in restaurants. Cooking on the bone may be more difficult, since the meat is not uniformly thick and may be undercooked in some parts and overcooked in others. It is also fundamental to fry it in clarified butter, which makes the recipe more costly than if it were fried in oil.

The cutlets may sometimes be sprinkled with lemon juice, but the dish loses its crispness. A better solution is to sprinkle with the butter from the pan.

ShowRestaurant

The excellence
of the mediterranean
cuisine

Via Benvenuto Cellini, 2
Milano
Tel. 02 5519 6786

ROBERTO PALUMBO,
A RESTAURANT ENTREPRENEUR AND LOVER
OF THE GOOD THINGS, HAS A CAREER HIGHLIGHTED
BY HIS LOVE FOR THE TRADITIONS. HE STARTED FORM CAPRI,
HIS MYTHIC LAND OF SUN AND SEA, AND FOR MORE THAN 15 YEARS
HE EXPERIENCED HIS PERSONAL GROWTH IN CATERING
AND RESTAURANT COMBINED WITH DEVOTION TO THE CUSTOMER
AND THE CULTURE OF HOSPITALITY.

LEVERAGING ON HIS BACKGROUND RICH OF SUN, NA- TURE AND CULTURE, HE CREATED ROY RESTAURANT SHOW IN VIA CELLINI 2. AN ELEGANT AND REFINED PLACE WHERE YOU FEEL IMMEDIATELY AT HOME WITH A FRIENDLY ATTITUDE AND A LOT OF FAMILIAR OBJECTS. A PLACE WHERE YOU CAN RELAX AND ENJOY VERY GOOD FOOD AND GREAT SERVICE.
THE KITCHEN IS DELIBERATELY MEDITERRANEAN, THE CHOICE OF INGREDIENTS CAREFULLY SELECTED FROM SICILY AND CAMPANIA, LAND ENRICHED BY THE MY- STERY OF FIRE THAT LIVE IN THEIR VOLCANIC TASTE. THE SICILIAN BLUEFIN TUNA, SHRIMP FROM MAZARA DEL VALLO, MOZZARELLA WITH THE STRONG FLAVOR OF CASERTA OR WITH THE MOST DELICATE TASTE FROM SALERNO ARE JUST A FEW OF THE SOPHISTI- CATED PROPOSALS.

AN INNER PRIVATE ROOM IS DEDICATED TO THE CLIENTS WHO WANTS ENJOY A CIGAR OR EVEN AN OLD BRANDY OR RUM WITH CHOCOLATE FROM MODICA: IT IS NOT A SMOKE ROOM BUT A SMALL WORLD OF PLEA- SURES RESERVED FOR WHO LOVES GOOD THINGS DONE WITH THE SUN AND WITH YEARS OF MATURATION.

THE FINE CELLAR INCLUDES FAMOUS AND IMPORTANT LABELS.

THE WORDS ARE ALWAYS APPROXIMATE AND CAN'T DESCRIBE THE RESULT OF YEARS OF EXPERIENCE. THE ATMOSPHERE AND THE WARMNESS OF THE NEW RESTAURANT EXPECT YOU THERE. ENJOY IT! A KITCHEN WORTH TO TRY IS WAITING YOU FOR AN EVENING AT ROY RESTAURANT.

AN ANCIENT RECIPE

The yellow risotto is the real icon of Milanese cuisine. It takes its flavor from the saffron, as well as its unmistakable color, and it probably goes back to the 1400s.

It doesn't take long to understand how important rice has been to the diet of the people who live in the Valley of the Po. Just travel a few kilometers from Milan, along the roads toward Turin or Genoa, and you see nothing but paddy fields of rice. Or try tasting a few of those marvelous dishes that are among the best food the area has to offer.

The best-known among them is saffron risotto. It is distinct because of the brilliant idea of adding saffron to the recipe, giving it a refined taste and a color that is unmistakable, warm, and

bright. The spice is obtained by crushing the stigmas of the crocus (Crocus sativus), a species of the flower that comes originally from Persia and has been spread around the Mediterranean world by the Arabs.

History and legend

According to legend, the use of saffron in the Milanese risotto is down to a chance discovery by a cook working for the Sforza family in the 1400s. He just happened to be passing by an enormous building site, which was the cathedral under construction, when he

noticed some workers pilfering a little of the precious powder used to color the windows. They were running the risk of serious punish-

The yellow risotto may be accompanied by various wines, from full-bodied reds to perfumed whites

ment, because the substance had already become very expensive. The cook realized that this must be something exquisite and decided to try it out in his recipes, leading to the stupendous invention of the yellow risotto.

It is quite possible there is some truth to the story, seeing that saffron was, in fact, used by master glaziers and so, there was always a supply available in Milan.

On the other hand, let's not forget that in the 1400s the city was already trading heavily with Spain, and saffron was widely cultivated and used for cooking there (it is still one of the main ingredients of paella Valencia, for example).

The tricks of the recipe

It is true that the yellow risotto is the pride and joy of the city's great chefs, but it can also be prepared at home by the average amateur. It takes time and loving care, but not necessarily the hand of a professional. Most important of all is to not choose the wrong raw materials. There are plenty of varieties of rice of different quality growing in the Lombardy-Piedmont river valley, but only two are really suitable: Vialone Dwarf rice and Carnaroli Superfine. The choice of butter used is also important, as a lot is used in the recipe.

Finely cut up some onions and heat it in a saucepan without letting it brown. The original recipe adds beef marrowbone to the onion, but a lot of people now prefer to do without it, to make the dish lighter and easier to digest. The rice is added and allowed to toast slightly before

When the yellow risotto is cooked at home, a little extra is often prepared and put aside for another recipe, which is typical of the Milanese tradition: the risotto al salto. The leftover risotto is put on a sheet of oiled paper and pressed into the shape of a small tart. Then it is put into sizzling-hot butter in a frying pan and left to fry until a crust forms on the bottom. At this point, it is turned over, taking care not to break it up, so that it becomes crisp.

gradually pouring in the beef stock, a little at a time, letting it evaporate before adding more. The stock has to be

kept hot while being poured in gradually, so that the rice stays at the right cooking temperature and turns out well cooked but firm, essential for a well-prepared dish.

The saffron should be dissolved in a little stock and not added until the rice is almost cooked. Otherwise it loses its aroma. Once the cooking is complete and the heat turned off, the crucial, final touch is to add butter and grated cheese, to give the risotto that all-important creamy consistency. What makes the dish is its creaminess, and this must not be due to the stock but entirely due to the butter and cheese.

The risotto alla milanese can be eaten as a first course or is excellent together with osso buco in gremolada, a dish of stewed meat. This is a way of cooking veal shanks, which should be cut exactly halfway up the muscle, where there is a perfect balance between the amount of meat and the amount of marrow in the bone— essential to flavor the dish and give it its typical appearance. The preparation is called "in gremolada" because of the addition of a mixture of lemon peel, parsley, anchovies, and crushed garlic. Observing the tradition of Lombardy, the cooking includes a little tomato sauce, to add color to the dish, rather than flavor.

MASTERS OF FINE LIVING

The great Milanese chefs are famous personalities across the country, thanks to which the metropolis is considered the capital of Italian haute cuisine.

It is the belief of many that modern Italian cuisine was born with Gualtiero Marchesi, the great Milanese chef who, in 1968, was the first to obtain the legendary three Michelin stars (he was also the first to renounce them in disagreement of selection criteria). An octogenarian, Marchesi is still actively at the helm of his restaurant, **Marchesino**, located in the most prestigious ambients that the city has to offer: the ground floor of the La Scala Theater. On the other side of the narrow Via Filodrammatici is the restaurant **Trussardi alla Scala**, where, for some time, one of its most talented students, **Carlo Cracco**, has acted as consultant. Cracco is the most well-known chef in the country, thanks to a popular television show and bestselling cookbook that bears a witty if not original title (*Se vuoi fare il figo usa lo scalogno*, loosely translated as "If you have liver, use scallion"), which is quite coherent with the character. His kingdom is the restaurant Cracco, where every recipe is an amazing invention of flavors and fragrances, presented with a compositional skill worthy of an artist.

A more classical taste can be savored at **Sadler**, well reputed for its fish dishes, and at **Luogo di Aimo e Nadia**, historic Milanese restaurant that has lived decades of transformation from Tuscan trattoria (in the 1960s most restaurateurs in Milan came from Tuscany) to a high-end restaurant.

Rising to heights, we see Andrea Aprea, chef of the restaurant **Vun**. Despite his age, Andrea, still young, has had many experiences abroad, setting out from his native Naples, and it emerges from his culinary repertoire, which combines international cooking flare with plates of regional Campanian tradition.

An outside-the-box character is Davide Oldani, very original figure of Italian haute cuisine, who is dedicated to promoting delicacies of excellence at reasonable prices far from the rumble of the city center at the restaurant **D'O** in Cornaredo.

The grand wining and dining scene of Milan also has a nook reserved for two "'foreigners" (the quotes are a must, since both Milanese can be deemed Milanese

by adoption): the Swiss Pietro Leeman at the restaurant **Joia**, one of the greatest interpreters of international vegetarian cuisine, and the Uruguayan Matias Perdomo, who introduced a touch of fantasy in one of the most historic restaurants in Milan, the **Pont de Ferr**.

Cracco
Via Victor Hugo 4,
www.ristorantecracco.it
D'O
Via Magenta 18,
San Pietro all'Olmo
(Cornaredo),
www.cucinapop.do
Joia
Via Panfilo Castaldi 18,
www.joia.it
Luogo di Aimo e Nadia
Via R. Montecuccoli 6,
www.aimoenadia.com
Marchesino
Via Filodrammatici 2,
www.gualtieromarchesi.it
Pont de Ferr
Ripa di Porta Ticinese 55,
www.pontdeferr.it
Sadler
Via Ascanio Sforza 77,
www.sadler.it
Trussardi alla Scala
Piazza della Scala 5,
www.trussardiallascala.it
Vun
Via S. Pellico 3
(Hotel Hyatt Park),
www.ristorante-vun.it

THE BITTER APERITIF OF MILAN

The Campari café—liquor store has been there since the Gallery was completed in 1876. It initially covered the display windows currently part of the Autogrill (highway rest area) in front of Camparino, which dates back to 1915.

Aside from being one of the loveliest bars in Milan, with its liberally styled furnishings designed by some of the most elite artists of their time, **Camparino** is certainly the most well-known, still bearing the name of late Gaspare Campari, to whom we owe the 1960s creation of the sweet-scented dutch-style bitter, a beverage consumed around world. While his wife, Letizia, sat at the cash register, the *sciur* (a term for "owner"), Gaspare, in the backroom of the shop, created and, over the years, refined an alcoholic aperitif with herbs, aromatic plants, and fruit extracts, spiced with cochineal, which gives the drink its nice, shiny red color. Enjoyed shaken, mixed with club soda, or as an ingredient for cocktails, it is the ac-

claimed symbol of the Milanese aperitif scene.

Important pages on the history of the city and beyond have been written in the Campari bar and Camparino. A sta-

ple hangout for top figures in Italian politics and culture, the two bars are the scene of many well-known events. For example: the brawl that broke out in 1909 and was captured in the famous *Rissa in Galleria;* almost a manifesto of futurist painting, by **Umberto Boccioni**, and kept at the art gallery of Brera.

Yet, Boccioni is far from being the only great Italian artist to have his name tied to Campari. As a matter of fact, the company's fame is also owed to the farseeing marketing strategy employed by the founder of the distillery, Davide Campari, Gaspare's son, who, in 1919, decided to industrialize his father's recipe for mass production.

A key figure in Campari's ad campaigns before World War II was the futurist painter **Fortunato Depero**: he designed countless billboards that have made the history of Italian graphic art, and he came up with the idea for the shape of the Campari soda bottle, now universally considered a classic of Italian design. The postwar years are especially notable for the creative endeavor of Bruno Munari, who chiefly worked on enhancing the company brand. Over the past decades, Campari has produced commercials that have become timeless artworks, turning to some of the most famous directors to shoot the ads, among whom was Federico Fellini.

HAPPY HOUR

In Milan, the brightest moment of the day, destined for company and conviviality after a hard day's work, corresponds to that of the aperitif, the most widespread of worldly rituals in the modern city.

The habit started in the 1920s, in venues that were becoming very famous right then, like the Camparino in the Gallery and, from the 1950s on, the Terrazza Martini (Martini Terrace) in Piazza Diaz (the premises only open for events and presentations nowadays). The idea of a predinner drink, to be enjoyed with a finger snack or two, underwent a radical change in form in the 1980s, when Milan the industrial city turned into a city of the service industry. Enterprising bar keepers tried

to fill their premises in what was then considered a dead moment (today, that period from 6:00 p.m. to 9:00 p.m. is the most profitable) by offering free food—small portions of hot and cold dishes—to accompany a glass of wine, a beer, or a cocktail.

Of the stronger alcoholic drinks, the classic is the **ne-**groni (similar to a red martini), made from one-third gin, one-third Campari bitter, and one-third vermouth. This also comes in lighter versions, such as the **sbagliato** (the mistaken), where the gin is replaced by prosecco, or **l'americano** (the American), made with soda water instead of gin. The Campari, a hot favorite for Milan, is based on oranges (with freshly squeezed orange), and often drunk neat, or possibly with a drop of gin or vodka, after a good shake. The spritz is very popular because it has low alcohol, being made with Aperol, prosecco, and soda, while the most chic of all is definitely the one made with fruit pulp in prosecco or, better still, champagne. It is called a **Rossini** if it's made with strawberries or a **Bellini** if it's made with peaches.

The aperitif ritual now involves every venue, in the trendy (and not so trendy) areas for the younger set, of all age ranges, and of every type of person imaginable: students, managers, companies inviting their foreign colleagues to a dip in the "drinking city," or even mothers with screaming kids.

For anyone looking for a well-known bartender, rather than the happy hour atmosphere, we would suggest, apart from the big hotels, five cocktail bars (below) in various areas of the city.

Bar Banco
Alzaia Naviglio Grande 46
Bar Martini
Corso Venezia 15
(inside D&G store),
www.dolcegabbana.com/martini
Café Trussardi
Piazza della Scala 5,
www.trussardiallascala.it
Nottingham Forest
Viale Piave 1,
www.nottingham-forest.com
Pravda Vodka Bar
Via Vittadini 6

THE MILANESE OUTDOORS

A short trip into the country to see nature, country houses, and trattorias. Or just coffee in Piazza Ducale in Vigevano, jewel of Renaissance Lombardy, which the great conductor Arturo Toscanini considered "a musical symphony."

Just a few kilometers west of Milan, along the main canal (Naviglio Grande), you meet a rural world that makes you think of picnics. You can get there on a bicycle, using a bike path along the canal bank, or with a motor (a motorcycle is ideal in the summer season) using the highway SS494, called the Vigevanese (Vigevano Road).

After just about 10 km, you come to **Gaggiano**, a place the Milanese love. Here ,there is one of the most historic restaurants in the immediate vicinity of the metropolis, Antica trattoria del gallo, where you can enjoy the décor and atmosphere of an Old World inn and upscale traditional food. Another 10 km or so farther on lies **Abbiategrasso**, a village distinguished by a very beautiful church, Santa Maria Nuova (New St. Mary's), built in 1497, the last work completed in Lombardy by Bramante. Then, only 3 km north of that village, there is another: **Cassinetta di Lugagnano**, which the noble families of Milan used as a resort in the 1700s. Their country homes stand on the banks of the canal, at the same spot as another historic address for Milanese outdoor eating. Antica osteria del ponte is the realm of top chef Fabio Barbaglini. But anyone looking for something a little more modest, also in terms of price, can carry on along the canal to **Robecco** and beyond, where period country homes alternate with homely trattorias offering fried frogs, a local specialty.

If you are feeling fit, or have a car or a motorcycle, it is absolutely worthwhile to venture a little to the west of Abbiategrasso, as far as **Vigevano**, just across the river Ticino.

Here, you can visit the imposing 1400s castle, which now houses the interesting Museo della Calzatura (Museum of Footwear), illustrating the trade for which the town is historically famous. The castle overlooks the broad Renaissance square, Piazza Ducale.

Bar Antica osteria del gallo
Vigano Certosino (Gaggiano),
www.trattoriadelgallo.com
Antica osteria del ponte
Piazza Negri 9,
www.anticaosteriadelponte.it
Museo della Calzatura
Piazza Ducale, Vigevano,
closed Monday,
www.castellodivigevano.org

TRADITIONAL AND MODERN

Rediscover the spirit of the inns of the past and find that lively atmosphere animating those time-honored venues.

The inn, or that kind of establishment called *"osteria"* in Italian, from bygone centuries, no longer exists in Milan. And it's a good thing, too. They were places where only men could set foot and were often just dens for all kinds of scum. The most familiar description of the Milanese inn of the past comes from the book *Promessi Sposi* (The Betrothed), when the hero, Renzo, is tricked by an innkeeper and the police. Once they had lost their roles as hotels, they became poor neighborhood dives that served wine and, in some cases, a simple meal when they were described as "with kitchen service". These are the places the not-so-young still have in their minds and in their hearts and which the revival of "the good old times" has tried to resuscitate in recent decades. Now, every corner in districts with a lively nightlife seems to have an old time Milanese inn. For the most part, they are poor imitations. So, to find the true spirit of the inns of the past, it's better not just to rely on a likely name, but look for places where the clientele are not averse to exchanging a bit of friendly banter with the next table, as they used to once do. The most surprising, because it has managed to combine traditional with modern atmosphere, is **Pont de Ferr** (Iron Bridge) on the Navigli. Here, they have a traditional décor and plain but attentive service, while the modern aspect comes from the top chef, Matias Perdomo, who has added the best innovations of modern cuisine and creates surprising dishes.

An equally pleasant atmosphere, with good wines at reasonable prices, can also be found at **Osteria del Treno** (Railroad Inn), which also offers a lunchtime self-service. Next to the dining room, which offers a seated-only service in the evening, there is a large open space, which was used in the past by off-duty railroad workers and is now a venue for various events.

In the heart of the most ancient part of Milan, where the city's Roman remains have been restored, there is **Taverna Moriggi** (Morrigi's Tavern), which has stood there for over a hundred years. The décor and the character of the premises are still the same as when they sold casked wine, but the cuisine is now more sophisticated, concentrating particularly on traditional recipes.

Osteria del Treno
Via San Gregorio 46,
www.osteriadeltreno.it
Pont de Ferr
Ripa di Porta Ticinese 55,
www.pontdeferr.it
Taverna Moriggi
Via Morigi 8

Lombardy Wine Tourism Movement

...ASSO FARM

...adition and the desire to re-ignite an ancient
...or grapevines, lie behind the activity of Sor-
...m, in the village of Domaso. Their grapes are
...the hillsides of Domaso, at the top end of Lake
...d they employ modern wine-making methods
...e wines with intense perfumes that recall the
...eir origin. Showing tenacity and profound
...n to work, essential prerogatives for anyone
...d to building a modern company, this winery
...given up on the philosophy of the pleasure
...g wine.

...aggio 1/Bis - 22013 Domaso (CO) - Tel. 0344 910022 - fax 0344 910849
www.sorsasso.com - info@sorsasso.com

GRUMELLO CASTLE

Grumello Castle towers over the village of Grumello del
Monte and its vineyards, in the heart of Valcalepio, an
area of hills stretching from Bergamo to Lake d'Iseo.
Since 1953, it belongs to the Reschigna Kettlitz family, from Milan, who have given new impetus to the
wine-growing tradition of the Grumello territory, producing top-grade wines, which can be tasted and purchased after a tour of the castle. Today, the Castle is
a member of the Association for Castles and Country
Homes open to the public in Lombardy and its wineries
are members of the Lombardy Wine Tourism Movement.

Tenuta Castello di Grumello - Via Fosse, 11 - Grumello del Monte (BG)
Tel. 348 3036243 - www.castellodigrumello.it

...RUGHERATA

...erata, owned by the Bendinelli family, is situated in Scan-
...e, an ancient, traditional wine-growing municipality, 7km
...rgamo, at the very heart of the area the Moscato di Scanzo
...d. The real symbol of La Brugherata is the Doge Moscato
...docg, a classic wine from the Bergamo wine-producing
...usive to the town of Scanzorosciate and certainly one of
...sweet Italian straw wines. Apart from the Moscato, they
...ome excellent white and red wines, a brut full of character
...also, a sweet, delicate extra-virgin olive oil.

Via G. Medolago 47, loc. Rosciate
24020 Scanzorosciate (BG)
Tel. 035 655202 - Fax 035 6590467
...w.labrugherata.it - info@labrugherata.it

PERONI MADDALENA DISTILLERY

Just a couple of steps from Lake d'Iseo and Lake
Garda, in the heart of the Franciacorta area, the
town of Gussago is the cradle of the Peroni family
and their namesake company. Here, pride in the
local typicalness keeps a place of honor also for
"her majesty" the grappa. They produce spirits characterized by superior quality. The Peroni
family guarantees the use of select vinasse from
the most representative vineyards, especially in the
monovineyards of Franciacorta and Lugana, Amarone, Pinot and Chardonnay.

Via Alcide De Gasperi, 39 - 25064 Gussago (BS)
Tel. 030 2770640 - www. distillerieperoni.it - info@distillerieperoni.it

...ELLI BERLUCCHI FARM

...erlucchi farm is unde-
...ambassador for Franci-
...the world. The owners
...storic 1600's winery,
...e oldest in the area, the
...cchi brothers, have kept
...mily name on all their
...d, with their production
...0 bottles of wine a year,
...oly the best restaurants
...bars in Italy, Europe,
...ndia and China.

Via Broletto, 2
Borgonato
25040 Cortefranca (BS)
Tel: 030-984451
Fax 030-9828209
www.fratelliberlucchi.it

AZIENDA AGRICOLA FRATELLI BERLUCCHI
FRANCIACORTA

TENUTA AMBROSINI

In the heart of Franciacorta, there where the lake
shores meet and mix with the foot of the hills, ma-
jestically exposed to the sunshine and fresh air,
there lies the municipality of Cazzago S. Martino,
one of the nineteen that constitute the geo-political
area that is protected under its production name
"Franciacorta". Here the Ambrosini family has,
since the mid-1900's, been passionately dedicated
to the cultivation of eight hectares of vineyard,
growing Chardonnay, Pinot Bianco and Pinot Nero grapes.

Via della Pace, 60 - 25046 Cazzago San Martino (BS)
Tel. 030 7254850 - fax 030 7254440
www-tenutambrosini.it - info@tenutambrosini.it

...TEDELMA ESTATE

...elma Estate in Valenzano in Franciacorta, a so-
...ed new winery in an aristocraticold village in the
...ranciacorta, offers quality wines, the fruit of a
...hi-tech research with the knowledgeable care
...ique characteristics peculiar to this generous soil.
...u taste our wines, you will discover the harmoni-
...formation of all the essential ingredients we have
...-grade selected grapes, care and attention in the
...king process, hi-tech with respect for tradition.

TENUTA MONTEDELMA di Berardi P.& P. Soc. Agr.
Via Valenzano, 23 - 25050 Passirano (BS) - tel./fax 030 6546161
www.montedelma.it

MANUELINA FARM

Manuelina Farm is situated in the
municipality of S.Maria della Versa,
in the heart of the Oltrepò Pavese
area. The farm owns 22 hectares of
vineyard, and grows the grapes and
produces and bottles its wine directly on its own
premises, using the most suitable grapes for quality wine-making. The farm owners are dedicated
to making the best product they possibly can and
always satisfying their customers.

Az. Agr. Manuelina s.s.a. - Frazione Ruinello di Sotto, 3/a
27047 S. Maria della Versa (PV) - Tel. 0385 278247
Fax 0385 278749 - www.manuelina.com

...I COMPANY, CASTELROTTO ESTATE

...ily-run Torti Company "Castelrotto Estate" is
...Montecalvo Versiggia, in a perfect position with
...imate, 300 meters above sea level, in the heart
...trepò Pavese area. The Torti family has owned
...s in these hills since the start of the last century
...ills are particularly suited to wine-growing, espe-
...ot Nero, Bonarda and Barbera. The Casaleggio
...odo Charmat/Martinotti spumante is obtained
...ot Nero grapes grown on the Casaleggio. The company's "Jewel" is the Pinot
...comes from a plot of land called "Borgogna".

Frazione Castelrotto, 6 - 27047 Montecalvo Versiggia (PV)
Tel. 0385 951000 - Fax 0385 951002
torti@tortiwinepinotnero.com - www.tortiwinepinotnero.com

COOPERATIVE WINERY OF QUISTELLO

The social winery of Quistello, ever since it was established in 1928, has always had clear vision and ambitious
plans. It has always been a landmark in the area, both for
the quantity and the quality of its Lambrusco Mantova-
no, and with its own IGP Quistello it has developed an
evolved version of Lambrusco, by making concessions
to modernity without betraying its traditional roots as
producers of highly digestible wines in the typical local
style of Quistello with an excellent quality/price ratio.

Via Roma 46 - 46026 Quistello (MN)
Tel 0376 618118 - fax 0376 619772
www.cantinasocialequistello.it

EXCURSIONS

TRAVEL IDEAS

**Twenty-six places—all at only three hours'
travel, at most—to enjoy the uncontaminated
nature and art of central-northern Italy
and Canton Ticino.**

1. Bergamo
2. Bologna
3. Canton Ticino
4. Cinque Terre
5. Courmayeur
6. The Dolomites
7. Ferrara

8. Florence
9. Genoa
10. Lake Como
11. Lake Garda
12. Lake Maggiore
13. Langhe
14. Mantua

15. Parma
16. Pavia
17. Pisa
18. Portofino
19. Ravenna
20. Rimini
21. Sanremo

22. Turin
23. Valtellina
24. Venice
25. Verona
26. Vicenza

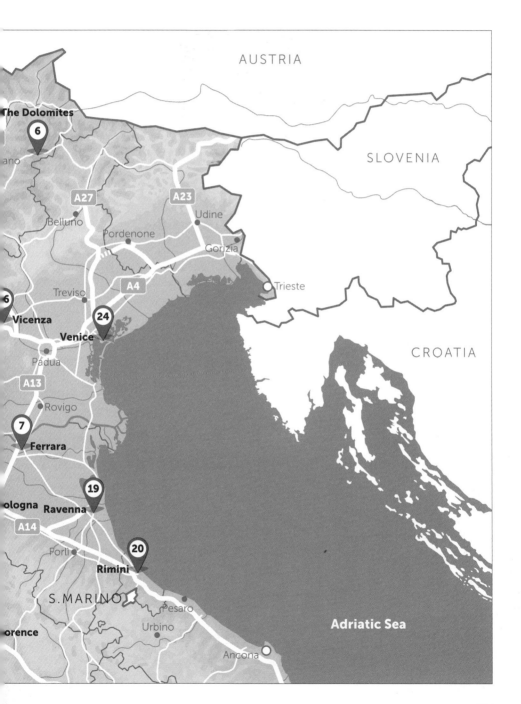

TWO SOULS IN ONE CITY

The modern part, fast and productive, lies on the flood plain, leaving the ancient heart of the city intact on its hill, lofty and silent, within its Venetian walls.

Located around 50 km east of Milan, it is connected by the A4 highway and regional trains leaving from Central Station. Orio al Serio International Airport is only 5 km from the city center, connected by a frequent shuttle-bus service.

The **Città Alta** (old town), almost completely traffic free, is one of the favorite places the Milanese like to go for a day out or for a romantic evening. You get panoramic views over the river valley and into the mountains beyond, and you can stroll through the charming medieval center, where narrow streets turn into wide, sunlit roads, and squares alternate with historic monuments.

There's a scenic ride up in a cable railway from the center of the city's newer part, which takes just a few minutes in a magic atmosphere and seems to take you on a leap back in time.

At the heart of the old town there is **Piazza Vecchia** (the Old Square), described by the great architect Le Corbusier as "the most beautiful square in Europe." On this square, there is the Torre Civica, the city's bell tower (Campanone, which tolled every evening, for the closing of the city gate), and the Palazzo della Ragione (Palace of Reason), the municipal administration building, with

the Venetian crest of the Leone di San Marco (Lion of St. Mark) in the middle of the façade, as a reminder of the time of Venetian domination.

From here, you can pass under the portico of the municipal building to **Piazza Duomo** (Cathedral Square), which is the location of the city's most outstanding religious monuments: the cathedral, the baptistery, and the Colleoni chapel (1472–1476), a jewel of the Renaissance and the mausoleum of the powerful warlord Bartolomeo Colleoni and his daughter, Medea. Next to the chapel is the Romanesque basilica, Santa Maria Maggiore, which is worth visiting, to see its magnificent Baroque decorations and the

Situated at the center of Lombardy, it is one of the historic cities closest to Milan, but for centuries it was part of the Venetian republic, traces of which are still visible.

inlays on the choir that were carved in the 1500s from designs by Lorenzo Lotto. Lotto was a genius in Bergamo during the Renaissance, who produced several altar pieces and private portraits.

You can visit the birthplace of the composer **Gaetano Donizetti** (1797–1848). The house is now a museum in Borgo Canale, a historic quarter of the old town that still has a rural atmosphere about it.

After the old town, the tour continues down the hill in the lower town (**Città Bassa**), which has a middle-class look. Enjoy a stroll along the famous boulevard, the Sentierone, with its old cafès looking on to the opera house dedicated to Donizetti. Art lovers simply must go to the Carrara Academy Museum, one of the most precious provincial art galleries in Italy. An unbelievable list of paintings in this gallery includes: Botticelli, Giovanni Bellini, Mantegna, Lorenzo Lotto, Titian, and Rubens.

The king of masks

Bergamo is the city of **Arlecchino** (Harlequin), the most famous character in the commedia dell'arte, an ancient form of popular theater,

which became an expression of "high"culture because of the work of professional performers who gave psychological depth to their masks. One in particular, the Venetian Carlo Goldoni, wrote the work, in 1745, that became the symbol of this kind of theater, *l'Arlecchino servitore di due padroni (Harlequin, servant of Two Masters)*. This play was first presented in the Piccolo Teatro in Milan and went on to enjoy success all over the world.

Harlequin, like many of his fellow countrymen, leaves his native land to look for work in Venice and finds employment as a servant. He is so poor that he cannot afford new clothes and has to make himself a jacket from old rags patched together. He is ignorant but curious, always hungry but happy, full of life and hope, and his heart is pure.

Perhaps this is why Harlequin has always been the best-loved mask from the commedia dell'arte. There are very few Italian children who haven't dressed up for Carnival in the Harlequin costume.

coined by Italians in the south to describe people from the north.

For centuries it was the only food available to the very poor, and they ate it without salt or seasoning, while the very rich acquired the habit of eating their polenta with cheeses and meats.

In the area around Bergamo, which was a hunting area, they created their own recipe. Here, they traditionally prepare a coarsely ground polenta and use it to accompany small spit-roasted game birds. The **polenta e osei** (polenta with birds) became such a typical dish in the area that local confectioners decided to invent a sweet version: a dome-shaped, cream-filled sponge cake covered with yellow marzipan (to look like polenta). Small birds of marzipan or chocolate were put on top as decoration.

Polenta

Corn was brought to Europe after the opening up of the New World and, in the Lombardy–Veneto flood plain, it became so widely used, especially in the 1700s, that it was the staple diet of the entire population there, cooked in the form of polenta. The derogatory terms *"polentone"* (polenta face) and *"mangiapolenta"* (polenta eater) were

A CHEERFUL, PLEASANT INTELLECTUAL TOWN

Full of historical buildings, and one of the capitals of Italian gastronomy, a lot of young people live here, attracted by its university.

Bologna lies about 220 km southeast of Milan, along the A1 highway. The high-speed Frecciarossa (Red Arrow) trains, departing every hour from the Central station, get there in about an hour.

Bologna lies on the edge of the flood plain of the river Po, a nerve center for communications between northern and central Italy; a city of more than 380,000 inhabitants, famous for its gastronomy, and with an old town center completely lined with **porticoes**.

To get to know the city, start from **Piazza Maggiore**, created in the 1200s to hold the market. It is still the beating heart of Bologna and the site of some of the most beautiful buildings, such as the **Palazzo del Podestà**, which was rebuilt in the 1400s on an existing site by the Bentivoglio family, lords of the city at that time.

Another dominant building in the piazza is the **basilica of San Petronio** (St. Petronius), the city's main church, started in 1390. Its sober façade has two magnificent bas-reliefs over the main doorway, the work of Jacopo della Quercia (1425–1438), from Siena, who

was a leading figure in gothic sculpting in the early 1400s. The church interior is full of frescoes and paintings, carried out between the 14th and 16th centuries by the best paint-

ers from Emilia, the likes of Giovanni da Modena, Lorenzo Costa, and Parmigianino.

Before leaving the square, art lovers should take a look inside the Palazzo Comunale (City Hall), also known as **Palazzo d'Accursio**, where they display the city art collection and the Museo Morandi (Morandi Museum), dedicated to Giorgio Morandi, a leading figure in Italian painting in the 1900s. To the left of the basilica is the entrance to the Archaeological Museum, which is of interest because of its large number of local exhibits, taken from the first Villanovan village, from the Etruscan city (Felsina,) and from the Roman city (**Bononia**). There is also an Egyptian collection, which is one of the most important in Europe. Piazza Maggiore connects to **Piazza di Nettuno**, opened in the 1560s and adorned immediately with its fountain. It is of Neptune,

in bronze, standing on a three tier base of angels, mermaids, and dolphins. The Palazzo di Re Enzo overlooks the square. The building got its name because it was the prison where King Enzio, the son of Emperor Federico II, was kept from 1249 until his death in 1272. It is decorated with crenellations and on the interior, it has a spacious 1300s gothic hall, where they hold exhibitions.

Walking south, passed the Archaeological Museum and under the arches of the portico del Paviglione, one of the best shopping areas, you come to the **Archiginnasio** (General University), in Piazza Galvani. It was built between 1562 and 1563 to house all the university's faculties, but its rooms were converted in the 1800s into reading rooms in the communal library. It's worth looking upstairs at the Teatro Anatomico (Anatomy Theater), from the 1600s but reconstructed after the 1944 bombings, where corpses were dissected for observation by anatomy students.

Farther on is the **church of San Domenico** (St. Dominic), built by Dominican monks between 1228 and 1238, which looks like a museum on the interior, with sculptures and paintings by artists from the medieval to the Baroque periods. Opening on the right of the nave, there is the chapel of San Domenico, with a fresco inside the dome of the apse, *Gloria del Santo* (*Glory of the Saint*), by the most important of Bologna's painters in the 1600s, Guido Reni. This chapel contains the famous **Ark**, which was started by Nicola Pisano and his workshop, and then enhanced in the 1400s. Niccolò dell'Arca added sculp-

Events that attract a lot of visitors are the motor show (an international automobile fair) and the Book Fair for Children.

tures and statues of patron saints of the city on the cornice, and Michelangelo added an angel and the statues of St. Petronius and St. Proculus.

If you go north from Piazza Maggiore and onto Via Rizzoli, one of the main arteries downtown, you come to the symbol of Bologna, the two **Leaning Towers**; the Torre degli Asinelli, 97 meters high and named after the Asinelli family around 1110, and the Torre Garisenda, also from the 12th century but only 48 meters high, because it was lowered to avoid collapse. Going to the top of the Torre degli Asinelli is not an experience you forget easily, partly because it has 500 steps winding up through trapdoors and tight stairways, and also because of the view over the city to the surrounding hills.

A group of monuments that is rich in history stands not far from the city's commercial center. The **basilica of Santo Stefano** (St. Stephen), also known as the **Seven Churches of Bologna**, is a complex of religious buildings—churches and chapels with their courtyards and porticoes, mostly built in the Romanesque period on a preexisting late antiquity site. The intention was to re-create in Bologna, for yjpdr who couldn't travel to the Holy Land, the sites such as the Cortile di Pilato (Pilate's Courtyard), the Chiesa del Crocifisso (Church of the Crucifix), and the Santo Sepolcro (Church of the Holy Sepulchre).

Of the other attractions, the **Pinacoteca Nazionale** (National Art Gallery) is not to be missed. It is in a 1600s building and contains masterpieces of the Bolognese school, from Vitale to Guercino and beyond. It also holds the famous *Estasi di Santa Cecilia* (*Ecstasy of St. Cecilia*), painted by Raphael for a noble lady from Bologna.

The **Santuario della Madonna di San Luca** (Sanctuary of the Virgin of St. Luke) is also worth a visit. To get there, to Colle della Guardia, you walk along a portico, flanked by the Cappelle del Rosario (Rosary Chapels). The sanctuary holds

names, in the 1700s, of Luigi Galvani and Alessandro Volta, spread rapidly through Europe.

Pasta with Bolognese sauce

Nothing is as typical of Italian cuisine as first courses of pasta, the prerogative of the national gastronomy and basis of the Mediterranean diet. There are two main variations: the Neapolitan version, with durum wheat flour and slow drying, and the Bolognese version, using a thin layer of 00 flour from common wheat, with egg but no water in the dough, rolled out by hand and used for fillings of meat or cheese with vegetables. The same procedure is used for lasagne, cooked with meat sauce or béchamel, and for tagliatelle, long strips of pasta, traditionally served with Bolognese sauce. This special sauce is prepared by lightly frying chopped carrots, onions, and celery, to which cubes of beef (there are variations using pork) are added, followed by tomato sauce and red wine. It should then be left to simmer for a couple of hours in a clay cooking pot, stirred with a wooden spoon, and the flavor softened with a little milk.

a revered icon of the Virgin Mary, probably from the 12th century, which was rumored to be painted by the evangelist St. Luke.

The mother
of the universities

Several Italian cities claim to be the oldest seats of university study: Salerno, which had an important medical school in the ninth century; Pavia had a law school; and Naples had the first public university. But Bologna's 1088, date established by historians in the 1800s, makes it the first in the Western world. In reality, the earliest documented date is 1158, when a constitution issued by Frederick I made university study independent of any outside influence. There is no lack of acknowledgments in the city regarding this cultural institution. One is on display in Piazza della Mercanzia, in the form of a 1400s stone with the inscription in Latin: "The privileges by virtue of which students must pay nothing for books and other materials, foodstuffs or clothes, neither for themselves, nor their fami-

lies." The study of law was the most ancient and illustrious, to which the so-called '"arts"were added in the 1300s, introducing students to philosophy, medicine, logic, and rhetoric. From then on, Bologna saw the most important figures of Italian literature, such as Guinizzelli, Dante, and Petrarch, either living or spending time there. The fame of the University of Bologna—the Alma mater studiorum (Nourishing Mother of Studies), to use its ancient motto—including the science and technology fields, which boasted the illustrious

Monte Generoso

1704 m s/m

Monte Generoso: the mountain with the finest panorama in Canton Ticino

The 1704 m high mountain top can be reached in 40 minutes by a small and comfortable cogwheel railway, which leaves Capolago, on Lake Lugano, at 274m above sea level, and winds its way through an unspoilt natural setting.

The Restaurant Vetta Monte Generoso, with its panoramic terrace, is the ideal place for a break during a fascinating excursion in the mountains. Here tourists can relax and enjoy a rich and traditional meal.

The mountain offers magnificent views over the Lake Region (lakes Lugano, Como, Varese and Maggiore), the city of Lugano and the Po Valley with Milan. The view ranges from the Apennines to the Alpine range, from the Gran Paradiso to the Monte Rosa, from the Matterhorn to the Jungfrau and from the Gotthard massif to the Bernina group.

- **Restaurant and panoramic terrace**
- **Conference room**
- **51 km of hiking trails**
- **27 km of mountain bike trails**
- **Moon and sun observations with experts at the astronomic observatory (themed evenings)**
- **Guided tours to the Bear's Cave**
- **Vintage train trips, with steam locomotive and panoramic carriage dated 1890**

> **visit our online shop for a wide variety of special offers !**

825 Capolago • Tel. +41(0)91 630 51 11 • Fax +41(0)91 648 11 07 • **montegeneroso.ch**

SWITZERLAND, THE ITALIAN WAY

The charm of its villages and the beauty of its panoramas make it a must as an excursion from Milan.

Lugano, a stop not to be missed on a trip to Ticino, lies about 80 km north of Milan, on the A9 highway (Autostrada dei Laghi), or on the A8, toward Varese–Stabio. Eurocity trains departing from Central Station get to Lugano in one hour.

The climate is mild, the vegetation is lush, and the little churches are the same as in the valleys around Como, but just 50 km north of Milan, you are in Switzerland, even if everyone speaks Italian. This is Canton Ticino, the part of the Helvetic Confederation that shared the fate of neighboring Lombardy, until the 1500s, borrowing its language, gastronomy, and customs.

The river Ticino flows through the territory, starting from the area of San Gottardo (St. Gotthard) and flowing into Lake Maggiore. The Canton is hilly in its southern part (the region of Mendrisiotto and Lake Lugano), but more starkly alpine north of the capital city Bellinzona and the smaller towns of Ascona and Locarno.

Lugano is the most important and most populous urban area in Canton. It lies on the northwest bank of Lake Lugano, has a population of about 60,000, and is known for its elegant urban development, streets lined with refined bou-

tiques, parks with subtropical plants, and the peaceful lakeside villages around the town. The city is the third largest banking center in Switzerland and a cultural interchange, but it has preserved its character as a livable city, where you can stroll along the lake shore or visit churches adorned with treasures, such as the church of Santa Maria degli Angioli (The Holy Virgin and the Angels), which has a wonderful

frescoed partition wall painted by Bernardino Luini. The excellent Museo delle Culture (Museum of Cultures) attracts a lot of visitors with its extraordinary pieces of non-European art and so does the Museo d'Arte (Museum of Art), which holds exhibitions featuring leading artists of the 20th century.

In nearby Melide is **Swissminiatur**, an open-air exhibition where visitors can walk among 1:25 scale models of the most famous Swiss monuments. The park is well laid out with plants, and equipped with kids' play areas. Visitors can admire 120 or so microbuildings with an extensive miniature railroad network running through them.

At the northern end of Lake Maggiore lies **Locarno**, a popular village resort of about 16,000 inhabitants, which has a picturesque lakeside promenade and an old town of narrow little alleys. At the heart of the village, there is Piazza Grande, teeming with cafés and small shops. It turns into a cozy movie theater during the Festival del Film, an internationally famous movie festival that turns the little town into a stage for the smart set.

It is worth visiting Castello Visconteo (Visconti Castle), built on the orders of the Visconti family, the lords of Milan who also governed here from the mid-1300s until the conquest of the Swiss Confederates in 1512. Inside the

castle, there is the Museo Archeologico, an archaeological museum with a valuable collection of Roman glass found in Ticino. Not far away, there is **Ascona**, a little village that is known for its panoramic views, a pretty town center, an inviting lakeside promenade, elegant stores, art galleries, and summer evening concerts.

One stop that should not be missed on a tour of Ticino is **Bellinzona**, a city situated in such a strategically important position that it was considered the "key to the Alps," when arriving from the south, or the "gateway to Italy," when arriving from the north. Between the 12th and 15th centuries, three castles were built to defend the city, and together with the massive defensive wall and a network of superimposed tunnels, they form a complex of extraordinary historical value, and was added to Unesco's World Heritage List in 2000. The oldest castle is the Castelgrande, built between the 1200s and 1300s, and later enlarged by the Sforza family.

Breathtaking views

An excursion in Ticino is a chance to get to amazing viewing points quickly and easily, thanks to major cable installations.

From the center of Lugano, from March through November, a funicular car ascends in just ten minutes to the peak of **Mount San Salvatore** (912 m), where a magnificent overlook opens up across the lake and the alpine chains (www.montesansalvatore.ch). Another funicular railway operates all year round from Cassarate, northeast of Lugano, rising 925 m up **Mount Brè** (www.montebre.ch). The panoramas

of Mendrisiotto can be seen from **Mount Generoso** (1701 m), connected all year round by a rack railway starting from Capolago (www.montegeneroso.ch).

Locarno also has a funicular railway, which, since 1906, has connected the town to the **Santuario della Madonna del Sasso** (Sanctuary of the Virgin of the Rock), built in the late 1400s following a miraculous appearance of the Holy Virgin. The sanctuary has been restored recently and is a destination for large numbers of pilgrims. The church and the

nearby Capuchin convent are a treasure trove of artworks and there is a platform in front of the façade that gives a stupendous view over the city and lake. A cable car designed by Mario Botta, an internationally famous architect from Ticino, goes up from here to the mountain station of **Cardada** (1329 m) and from there, a chairlift continues as far as **Cimetta**, to enjoy an inimitable 360° view that extends from Monte Rosa to the Dolomites on a clear day. It is necessary to continue on foot to reach

Mount San Giorgio (1097 m), which stands behind Méride. This mountain is included in the Unesco World Heritage List due to its abundance of geological and fossil treasures. An interesting collection of these exhibits is on display in the **Museo dei Fossili** (Fossil Museum) in Méride, which has been renovated and extended by Mario Botta.

Alprose, the chocolate factory

In Caslano, a few kilometers over the border on the road from Varese to Lugano, there is the Alprose plant, a company that has produced chocolate for more than 50 years. Even though it is not one of the most famous Swiss brand names, which are mostly in the French and German speaking cantons, it is still an interesting place to visit, to see the production processes of the product and to retrace the history of how cocoa became widely used in Europe after its discovery in America. A small historical exhibition contains old and ancient packages of chocolate, including brands that were quite famous in the past, together with a few oddities, like chocolate dispensers from the early 1900s. In the outlet at the end of the factory tour, Alprose products are on sale at discount prices. It is open every day, except December 24–26 and January 1 (www.alprose.ch).

The Ticino Discovery Card (www.cartaturisticaticino.ch) covers a visit to the Canton for 3 days for only 87 Swiss Francs, with visits and local transfers included.

BETWEEN SKY AND SEA

On the farthest eastern part of the coast of Liguria, there are five ancient villages, surrounded by uncontaminated nature and overlooking a marine protected area.

Lying about 230 km south of Milan, there are coastal roads leading here after exiting the A12 highway (Genova–Livorno). It is easier to use the Intercity trains, departing from Central Station and stopping at Riomaggiore or at Monterosso; local train services connect to the other villages.

Riomaggiore, Manarola, Corniglia, Vernazza, and Monterosso: five small villages connected to the world only since the late 1800s, thanks to a railroad that travels along a coastal stretch of rare beauty.

Starting from the east, the first village is **Riomaggiore**, with picturesque towerlike houses along the steep banks of the creek (Rio Maggiore) from which it gets its name.

From here, you walk along the famous Via dell'amore (Lovers' Path), a romantic walkway excavated on the cliffs about 30 m above the sea and is particularly striking in the early morning or at sundown, to get to **Manarola**. This colorful village clings high up on a promontory, with steep steps, called *arpaie* in Italian, leading down to the sea, where there is a small jetty for boats.

Corniglia is the only one of the five that doesn't face directly to the sea. In spite of this, its stretch of coast includes a beach with a lot of character, Guvano. It's used by naturists, and is a favorite marine area for divers, the so-called Franata di Corniglia (Corniglia Landslip),

home of lobsters, groupers, and moray eels.

Next is **Vernazza**, which many people regard as having the most character. It has its medieval fortifications, remains of a castle, an observation tower, and a harbor with a small 1200s church, Santa Margherita d'Antioca (St. Margaret of Antioch), built on the shore with its windows looking onto the sea.

The trail finishes at **Monterosso**, the biggest village and best equipped for tourism, with a large, sandy beach in front of the old town. The old part of the village, under the castle, is separated from the "new" part by a 1500s tower, Torre Aurora. In the "new" village, there is the Villa Montale, summer residence of the great poet Eugenio Montale, winner of the Nobel Prize for literature

Overlooking the sea on one of the world's best known coasts— steep, rocky, and rich in bays and coves— Cinque Terre were included in 1997 on Unesco's World Heritage List. Shortly afterward, a national park and a marine Protected area were established to protect this extraordinary territory, where nature and man stand together in harmony.

in 1975, who drew a lot of inspiration for his works from these "villages so barricaded between the cliffs and the sea."

Trails on the sea

This area is a paradise for hiking enthusiasts and offers a well-known trail, the **Sentiero Azzurro** (Blue Trail), used by tourists all year long. The hikers' trail is a series of one panoramic view after another, all overlooking the sea, and has been in existence since medieval times (only the Via dell'amore, was constructed in the early 1900s), and was, for centuries, the only land route that connected the villages. From the trail, there are a number of descents giving access to the sea, while donkeys labor up to the crest of the hills, cutting through cultivated terraces. There is an alternate trail, which is interesting in terms of history and nature, the Via dei Santuari (Sanctuary Trail). This is higher up on the hill, but still accessible, and it connects five churches, one for each village, which have been used for worship by the locals since ancient times. A third trail, not to be missed by the more athletic, is the Sentiero Alto (High Trail), 40 km along the crest between the coastal face and the inland face of the hills. It starts from Levanto, in the west, and runs as far as Portovenere, another jewel in the area around La Spezia, which is linked by its name (Port of Venus), and not by chance, to the goddess of beauty who arose from the sea foam.

The impossible vineyards of Cinque Terre

Over the centuries, generations of tenacious growers have shaped the landscape of

The Cinque Terre wine label goes back about five hundred years, but the area was already populated in the Middle Ages.

Cinque Terre, forming terrace *fasce*, or strips, with dry-stone walls on the steep, sea-facing hillsides. The large, very steep steppes also have water channels to enable the cultivation of olives and grapevines.

Their ancient labors have provided an extraordinary white dessert wine, the **Sciacchetrà**, enjoyed by Dante and Boccaccio. The wine is produced from Vermentino grapes, left to dry in the shade for a few months on mats, and then matured in the bottle for at least two years.

The low yield and the limited space for the vineyards—small lots cut from the terraces facing the sea—make this a rare, precious wine. It is not to be drunk with meals, but rather to accompany cakes without cream or with a piece of strong cheese.

AT THE GIANT'S FOOT

With an exclusive and elegant mountain village resort, and an unchallenged position on the slopes of Monte Bianco, which towers over it from its full height of 4,807 meters.

Located 220 km northwest of Milan, you get here on the A4 highway for Turin, taking the connector for the A5 highway for Turin–Aosta–Courmayeur. Intercity coaches leave from the Lampugnano subway station and take around three and a half hours to get there.

Courmayeur sits in a lush green bowl at an altitude of 1,200 m above sea level, right at the head of the valley of the Dora Baltea, the river that flows down the whole of the Aosta Valley and into the left bank of the river Po. The views from its panoramic balconies are some of the most beautiful in the whole of the Alps. Above the town, there are two more splendid valleys: Val Ferret, gateway into Switzerland, and Val Veny, on the French border. Two mountain streams pass through these valleys and into the Dora Baltea.

The area was discovered by tourists as long ago as the 1600s, when its thermal springs rose to fame. In the latter half of the 1700s mountaineers also started to come here.

Once a rather isolated mountain resort, a favorite of Piedmontese royalty and aristocracry in the 1800s, Courmayeur was turned into a tourist destination when the Monte Bianco tunnel opened in 1965, which connected it to France. The highway was completed in the Aosta Valley from the south, right up to the village. Nevertheless, even if it is now full of welcoming hotels, trendy venues, and luxury boutiques, it has not lost its alpine atmosphere. Some of its local districts, for example, still have all the charm of little

mountain communities with houses in stone and wood: La Saxe, Entreves, Dolonne, and Prè-Saint-Didier, to name a few. The latter is renowned as a health spa, because of its therapeutic waters.

It is worthwhile to take a ride on the **Monte Bianco cable car**, rising 2,000 m from the village, up to Punta Helbronner (3,462 m). From this vantage point, there is an exhilarating 360° view over the granite peaks of the Monte Bianco massif and, in the distance, Europe's 4,000-m-high mountains: Cervino (Matterhorn), Gran Paradiso, and Monte Rosa. In the summer, the cable car passes over a glacier as long as the Aiguille du Midi (3,842 m) and connects to Chamonix-Mont Blanc on the French slopes.

The Courmayeur ski resort is open all year. The **Veny valley**, punctuated with mountain shelters and bivouac areas, is a privileged starting point for spectacular excursions on the glacier, with its hidden lakes. The other valley, **Ferret valley**, wider and not so steep, has pastures and Larch forests and can be comfortably explored on horseback or on bikes.

Lovers of trekking can enjoy the unique experience of the Tour du Mont Blanc (the Mont Blanc tour), a 170-km tour around the Queen of the Alps, passing through Italy, Switzerland, and France.

There are also the white waters of the Dora Baltea, with stretches of rapids, ideal for adventurous canoeing, kayaking, or rafting.

Winter visitors have plenty to choose from, ranging from relaxing routes in Val Ferret, ideal for cross-country skiing or walks with snowshoes and poles, to free-riding. For experts, the Vallée Blanche (White Valley) stretches from Punta Helbronner to Chamonix across the **Mer de Glace** (Sea of Ice) glacier, a distance of 24 km that make it the longest

The 24-kilometer-long slope of Vallée Blanche is considered one of the most challenging free-riding routes of the Alps. It ends in Chamonix and passes through the Mer de Glace glacier.

free-ride in Europe. But there is no shortage of slopes for skiers of all abilities—around 30 in all, from the open slopes of Chécrouit to the pine woods of Val Veny, all overlooked by the majestic White Giant.

The peaks that made history

The massif of Monte Bianco, studded with peaks over 4,000 m, is considered the cradle of mountaineering. The first men to conquer the summit from the French side

were Michel-Gabriel Paccard, a famiy doctor from Chamonix, and Jacques Balmat, a collector of crystals. Their historic exploit was on August 8, 1786 and marks the birth of modern mountaineering. The first ascent from the Italian side was not made until almost a century later, August 6, 1864, by the geologist Felice Giordano.

For some fascinating insights into the great exploits of mountaineering, it is worth visiting the **Alpine Museum, Duca degli Abruzzi**, in the Casa delle Guide (mountain guides' center) in Courmayeur, which displays collections of documents, memorabilia, and climbing equipment.

The mountain wine

The vineyards on the terraced slopes overlooking the river Dora Baltea are not valuable just for their scenic beauty but also for the quality of the grapes that grow there. These are all native species, such as Petit-rouge, Fumin, and Prié rouge, or from neighboring areas, such as Piedmont's Nebbiolo and Moscato. Some others originate from the Swiss canton Vallese (Petite Arvine grape) or from France (Chardonnay, Gamay, and Pinot Nero grapes). All these varieties are selected because of their suitability for growing at high altitudes. In this area, the lowest vineyards are 300 m above sea level, while others go up to 1,200 m. These are in the vicinity of Morgex and are among the highest in the world since grapevines do not grow at higher altitudes.

Apart from the quality of some of the labels, Valdostano wines (from the Aosta Valley) are also appreciated for their variety, which is surprising for such meager, mountainous growing conditions. They range from fresh, aromatic whites, like Chardonnay, to whites with a more intense flavor (the most renowned is Blanc de Morgex) and full-bodied reds, such as Torrette, the Valdostano wine produced in greatest quantity.

THE PALE MOUNTAINS

The Dolomites have some of the highest peaks in Europe and make up such a unique chain of mountains that they have been included on the Unesco World Heritage List.

To get to the Dolomites, take the A22 Modena–Brennero highway from Verona. Otherwise the A27 Venezia–Belluno highway takes you to Cadore, la Marmolada, and Cortina d'Ampezzo. There are trains from Milan to Trento, Bolzano, Ora, and Bressanone. Local bus services operate from there.

The Dolomites cover a vast area, from Friuli to Veneto and to Trentino Alto Adige, and they are distinguishable from other Alpine chains because of their unusually **pale-colored stone**, Dolomia. At dawn and sunset it lights up with pink, red, and violet highlights. The rock was studied at the end of the 1700s by the French naturalist Dèodat de Dolomieu, who gave it its name. It started to form around 250,000 years ago, out of a buildup of seashells, corals, and calcareous algae.

These mountains have a varied landscape, rocky peaks alternating with serene valleys of broad pasture land, conifer woods, and small lakes, which make them ideal for tourists, both in summer and winter.

In the summer season, the valleys of the Dolomites are filled with tourists riding either motorcycles or bicycles (these roads are an essential part of the testing stages of

Giro d'Italia, so they are a part of history of Italian cycling), but they also offer plenty of alternatives, in hikes or quiet walks to suit everyone. Maybe the greatest satisfaction is reserved for mountaineers, though. No less than ten **Alte Vie** (High Routes), partly equipped and often above 2,500 m, lead into the heart of

the Dolomites. To name just two: the legendary Numero Uno (Number One), the first trekking route established in the "pale mountains," taking you from the banks of Lake Braies to almost as far as Belluno, or the Alta Via dei Silenzi (High Route of Silence), winding for 190 km among the springs of the river Piave.

In winter, these mountains are a skier's paradise, with hun-

dreds of kilometers of slopes, while enjoying a constantly changing view. From a scenic point of view, there is nothing to equal the **Sellaronda**, 40 km of slopes, with modern ski lifts, that run around the Sella massif, touching four of the most celebrated passes in the Dolomites: Pordoi, Gardena, Sella, and Campolongo.

There is no shortage of runs for expert skiers, as is proven by the runs used for the World Skiing Championships: The Gran Risa, at La Villa, is where they hold the Giant Slalom; the Saslong, in the heart of Val Gardena, used for the downhill; and the Olimpia delle Tofane, the venue for the women's competitions.

Lovers of spectacular ski slopes simply have to go up to the Marmolada, known as the "Queen of the Dolomites" because of its altitude of 3,342

meters. The ski lifts take you to within a few meters of the peak of the glacier, and from up there you can see across the whole Dolomite range.

For those who go to the mountains for something other than uncontaminated landscapes and sporting prowess, the Dolomites also boast some pleasant village resorts. Cortina d'Ampezzo is the catwalk of the international jet set, while Madonna di Campiglio, in the area of the river Brenta, has been renowned since the 1800s, when the nobility of the Hapsburgs era used to go there.

Under a blanket of stars

To enjoy a truly unique experience, you have to spend a night surrounded by the silences of nature in one of the Dolomites' many mountain shelters. Often, these are mountain huts or true chalets, which, despite being a long way from the chaos of the city, are still capable of offering the comforts of home. The shelters at higher altitudes are a little more spartan, as they are intended more for the High Route users, but lower down, you may find actual hotels, equipped for all needs, including those of the little ones. They all share a cheerful, wel-

coming atmosphere and the flavor of good mountain food.

On the wine route

The slopes of the Dolomite mountains are lands of picturesque ancient castles and fine wines, both in the Italian-speaking area and the German-speaking area, where the western face of the Adige valley is almost entirely given over to wine producing.

On the 40 km of road between Appiano/Eppan, a village near the regional capital of Bolzano, and Salorno/Salurn, one village after another has the German words "*an der Weinstrasse*" ("on the wine route") included in its registered name, and each village has a wine producer—you can taste and buy famous local wines. The most typical wines of this area are the Gewürztraminer and the Lago di Caldaro, a light, perfumed red wine that goes well with bacon, which is another local speciality.

In the town of Caldaro/Kaltern, in the tithe basements where they used to collect the dues that the farmers had to pay to their landlords, they have set up the **Wine Museum** (www.suedtiroler-weinstrasse.it), as an educational attraction and to display antique equipment used in winemaking.

RENAISSANCE SPLENDORS

The old center of this ancient little capital is a treasure trove of antiques, handed down intact to modern times.

Located 260 km southeast of Milan, you get here on the A1 as far as Bologna, then the A14 toward Ancona, linking to the A13, toward Padua, as far as the Ferrara exit. The train takes you here in just over two hours, with a train change in Bologna.

It is no coincidence that Unesco should have included Ferrara's center, an intact and shining example of the Renaissance, in its World Heritage List. In that period, Ferrara, now a dynamic provincial city of around 130,000 inhabitants, was the seat of the **highly refined court** of the Este family.

At the end of the 1400s, Duke Ercole planned a premature but eventually very successful urban project, the so-called Ercolean extension. A famous architect, Biagio Rossetti, was hired to fill in the Giovecca canal, which enclosed the northern part of the city, to make room for a new extension to the original medieval center, with streets and squares in a regular plan, based on perspective views.

The city has always been loved by artists, and during the

Renaissance, it was a hub for European painters. Ludovico Ariosto, a major figure in Italian literature and author of *Orlando Furioso* (*The Frenzy of Orlando*), spent his last years here, writing poems and creating sets for theater. More recently, Giorgio De Chirico, the great metaphysical painter, immortalized the castle square with his emblematic painting *Le Muse Inqietanti* (*The Disquieting Muses*).

The city has a lively, varied cultural life, with plenty

of events. These include the *Palio di San Giorgio* (*Palio of St. George*), a traditional medieval re-creation, and the **Busker Festival**, at the end of August, which attracts musicians, acrobats, clowns, and jugglers from all over the world.

The river Po flows past not far from the city and creates striking landscapes, especially where it starts to widen into its delta and form a park that has been included in the Unesco World Heritage List. A visit to this city means walking around the welcoming streets and squares in peace and quiet. Ferrara is a no-traffic zone, and people get around on bikes.

The massive, turreted **Este Castle** stands at the center of the oldest part of the town, surrounded by its moat. It was built as a defensive fortress in 1385, with underground prison cells, but it was later turned into a luxury residence, decorated with frescoes.

Not far away is the **Cathedral**, a jewel of the local Romanesque style. It was started in 1135, and the exterior opens out in a series of loggias and small arcades. Above the central portal, there is a bas-relief by Nicolaus, one of the great masters of Romanesque sculpture, of St. George and the Dragon. The Cathedral Museum is also worth visiting. Among its exhibits are some 12th-century marble panels, depicting the months, as well as the doors from the organ in

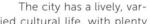

by their scenes of craftworks, the triumphs of Pagan deities, and astrological symbols. The work was carried out for Borso d'Este, around 1470, who had commissioned leading local painters, the Ferrarese workshops of Cosmè Tura, Francesco del Cossa, and Ercole de' Roberti.

Delicacies of the lagoon

A stay in Ferrara can also offer the chance for a quick visit to the attractive lagoon area created by Italy's biggest river, the Po. The most interesting place in the part of the delta near Ferrara is **Comacchio**. Not only does it have an unusual atmosphere as a city on the water, divided up by canals, but it also provides an example of typical, somewhat refined, cuisine.

Eels are a local specialty, smoked in oak and beechwood, and then marinated in vinegar, salt, a laurel leaf or two, and a little water.

A short distance from Comacchio, where the Po reaches the Adriatic, there is another area that's just as well known to gourmets: **Sacca di Goro**, a bay formed by the delta around the port of Goro. It is one of the richest areas in Italy for shellfish breeding, and it's the place to find firm, meaty clams, mussels, and even some oysters.

the ancient cathedral, which were painted in 1469, in an agitated style, by Cosmè Tura, pioneer of the Ferrarese school.

The **Palazzo dei Diamanti** (Diamond Palace) is well known, both for its marble-covered exterior, covered with small marble blocks carved to look like diamonds, and for the art exhibitions held there. It was built between the 1400s and 1500s and is now the home of the Pinacoteca Nazionale (National Art Gallery), with masterpieces by the Ferrarese school and other Renaissance painters.

Off for the "delights"

In Ferrara and the surrounding area, you can visit more than 30 mansions, built between the 1300s and the 1400s by the lords of the city. These aristocratic residences, the **Este Family Delights**, were places of pleasure and

are elegantly inserted into the landscape. **Schifanoia Palace**, in the center of Ferrara, should not be missed. Albert V d'Este wanted it to "dodge the boredom" (how he described the tedious nature of political life). On the interior, in the Salone dei Mesi (Hall of the Months), you can admire one of the most intriguing cyclical frescoes of the whole Renaissance, made intriguing

THE CRADLE OF THE RENAISSANCE

The city of art, without a doubt, is driven by a contagious vitality, tangible in every corner.

Florence lies 300 km southeast of Milan by taking the A1 highway. The fast trains departing from Central Station cover the distance in one hour and 45 minutes.

It would be a pity to come to Italy and not spend at least one day in Florence, the city that, with its art, has done more than any other to make Dante's Belpaese (Beautiful Country) famous in the world.

With 360,000 inhabitants, the **capital of Tuscany** is laid out like an amphitheater along the banks of the river Arno. Its center is one of the most beautiful in the world and one of the first national sites to be included in the Unesco World Heritage List.

As far back as the 1200s, when it began to stand out above the other Tuscan cities and internal struggles were raging between Guelphs and Ghibellines, Florence was enjoying a period of political power, economic prosperity, and intensive construction. During the 1300s, the city walls were extended and Gothic buildings erected, both civil and religious, such as the Palazzo Vecchio, the Palazzo del

Podestà, the Basilica di Santa Croce, the Basilica di Santa Maria Novella, and the Campanile di Giotto. At the start of the 1400s, the Renaissance was budding, a conscious new way of conceiving man's role in the universe, as exemplified by the invention of perspective.

Between the 1400s and 1500s, Florence enjoyed its greatest splendor, under the dominion of the Medici family, patrons who sponsored the work of the greatest talents, such as Michelangelo, Leonardo, and Galileo. Under

the Medicis, Florence became the wealthy capital of a small state, with banking headquarters and branches spread all over Italy and Europe.

A tour should start at the **Piazza del Duomo**, the spiritual heart of the city and a complex of extraordinary monuments. Here to welcome you is the cathedral **Santa Maria del Fiore**, undisputed symbol of Renaissance Florence, by virtue of its majestic dome, which has always attracted special admiration. In the words of Leon Battista Alberti, "such a large structure erect in the sky above, enough to cover all the peoples of Tuscany."

The building was started in 1296 by Arnolfo di Cambio, one of the best Gothic architects and sculptors, but the dome, 45.5 m in diameter, was not put on until the early 1400s. The design and "overseeing the work" was the responsibility of Filippo Brunelleschi, a leading figure

during the Renaissance. At the same time, the façade was enriched by statues in antique style, created by Ghiberti, Nanni di Banco, and Donatello. These works can be admired today in the nearby **Museo dell'Opera del Duomo** (Museum of the Cathedral Works).

Giotto's Campanile stands next to the cathedral. The artist died three years before work started on his project, and he only ever saw the first tier of his structure. Clad with the same red, white, and green marble as the cathedral, the campanile boasts a cycle of splendid reliefs, explaining how medieval man saw himself, his work, and the story of the Salvation.

In the center of the square, the paleo-Christian **baptistery** stands out. It is embellished, since the 1400s, by three beautiful bronze doors. The main one, opposite the cathedral, is adorned with stories from the Old Testaments,

The best-known architectural symbols of Florence are the Renaissance cupola of the duomo, designed by Brunelleschi, and the medieval Palazzo Vecchio, the city hall.

so gracefully chiseled by Lorenzo Ghiberti that it has been admired as "the most beautiful work in the world" and described by Michelangelo as the "Door to Paradise" (the original doors are kept in the Museo dell'Opera del Duomo).

The political center of the city since medieval times has always been **Piazza della Signoria**, an open-air museum and one of the favorite meeting places for the people of Florence, easily reached from the cathedral along the busy Via de'Calzaiuoli. The square is dominated by **Palazzo Vecchio**, one of the tallest examples of Gothic civil architecture, which was erected as a fortress, designed by Arnolfo di Cambio, between the end of the 13th and the start of the

14th centuries. It was originally intended to house the Priors of the Arts (representatives of corporations, which governed the city in that period) and, it was an emblem of the pride and independence of the people of Florence. Today, it houses the municipal administration, but can also be visited, to admire lavishly decorated interior.

At the entrance to the palazzo, you meet the majestic marble statue of Michelangelo's **David**. What you see in the square is actually a copy; the original is protected from the weather in the **Galleria dell'Accademia** (Accademia Gallery), together with other paintings and sculptures, including a set of Michelangelo's *Prigioni* (*Prisoners*). The

southern side of the square is closed by the **Loggia della Signoria**, built to hold public assemblies and official ceremonies of the republic, but used as early as the 1500s as a scenic exhibition area. There are some famous statues from the 1500s on display under the Gothic arches, including Cellini's bronze *Perseus* and *Ratto delle Sabine* (*Rape of the Sabine Women*), sculpted by Giambologna.

Around the corner is the **Galleria degli Uffizi** (Uffizi Gallery), a museum that cannot be missed. In the mid-1500s, Duke Cosimo I, at the height of his powers, had a whole medieval quarter cleared to make way for a building that was to house the "uffici," or offices of the magistrates. Designed by Giorgio Vasari, his trusted architect, and completed by Buontalenti, this large building gave birth to modern Europe's oldest museum, with a gal-

lery of paintings and sculptures, which was open to viewing by request.

You need a few hours to see all the rooms, where one group of masterpieces follows another, such as Botticelli's *Primavera* (*Allegory of Spring*) or *Nascita di Venere* (*Birth of Venus*), Leonardo's *Adorazione dei Magi* (*Adoration of the Magi*), Michelangelo's *Doni Tondo* (*Doni Madonna*), and Caravaggio's *Medusa*.

Thanks to Vasari's ingenious design, the duke could leave Palazzo Vecchio unrecognized, by using the **Vasari Corridor**, which passed through the Uffizi and over the **Ponte Vecchio**, then into **Palazzo Pitti** (Pitti Palace) on the opposite bank of the river Arno. Even without using the upper passage, which can only be visited upon request, it is worthwhile to cross the river on this most striking bridge, which was spared by the Second World War bombings and is known for its charming little goldsmiths' shops. On the other side, you come to Palazzo Pitti, built in 1458 and the biggest building in Florence that now houses the **Galleria Palatina** and the **Galleria d'Arte Moderna** (Palatine Museum and Modern Art Gallery).

Rising above the palace are the **Boboli gardens**, an Italian-style landscaped park, laid out

during the 1500s and 1600s and littered with statues, grottoes, and fountains.

Staying on the other side of the river, it is worth strolling around the fascinating little streets of Santo Spirito, a district where there are still a number of little handcraft shops tucked away. The square of Santo Spirito, opening out in front of the Augustinian basilica designed by Brunelleschi, is one of the liveliest in the Tuscan capital. In the morning, it is enlivened by the market, and in the evening, it is lit up by a number of nightspots. Near here, in the **Chiesa del Carmine** (Church of Crimson), there is the Brancacci chapel, frescoed by two masters, Masaccio and Masolino da Panicale, working in tandem on the scaffolding between 1424 and 1428—a jewel not to be missed by enthusiasts of Renaissance painting.

Back on the other side of the Arno, it's worth taking a look at the **Basilica di San Lorenzo** (St. Lawrence's Basilica), another inspired work

by Brunelleschi. It was built with the patronage of the Medicis, who, from the mid-1400s, lived in their palace just a stone's throw from here (on Via Larga, now called Via Cavour, where you can still admire the **Palazzo Medici Riccardi**, a prototype of a Renaissance nobleman's residence, designed by Michelozzo).

Inside the basilica, the **Sacrestia Vecchia** (Old Sacristy), where the elegant modular architecture of Brunelleschi is in tune with Donatello's sculptures, vies for attention with the **Sacrestia Nuova** (New Sacristy), a masterpiece completed by Michelangelo in the 1520s. This is the burial complex of the Medici family, where the triumph of the dynasty is represented in the mausoleums of Lorenzo the Magnificent and Giuliano and by the allegories of the four parts of the day: the statues of Aurora (Dawn), Giorno (Day), Crepuscolo (Twilight), and Notte (Night).

After admiring the sacristies, there is more Michelan-

Ponte Vecchio, the city's oldest bridge, dates back to the mid-1300s, and crosses the river Arno near the main square, Piazza della Signoria. Since the 1500s, the two rows of little shops lining the bridge are used exclusively by goldsmiths.

gelo architecture to see in the nearby **Biblioteca Laurenziana** (Laurentian Library), or a shopping break can be enjoyed in the city's main market, which goes right around the basilica and is crowded with tourists looking for souvenirs, especially leather goods.

There are a lot more buildings, churches, and museums to see in Florence. It would certainly be a pity to miss the **Santa Maria Novella**, a Gothic Dominican church with a superb façade in inlaid marble, designed in 1457 by the architect and essayist Leon Battista Alberti. The church boasts a very large number of treasures inside, such as a *Crocifisso* (Crucifix) painted by Giotto, a *Crocifisso* in wood by Brunelleschi, and the fresco with the *Trinità* (Trinity) by Masaccio, one of the most famous pieces of the Renaissance in terms of its rigorous application of perspective.

Another stop should be made at the number-one church for the Franciscans, **Santa Croce** (Holy Cross), started at the end of the 1200s by Arnolfo di Cambio. A lot of illustrious men are buried here (Michelangelo, Alfieri, Galileo), and in the chapels, frescoed by Giotto and his followers, the triumph of Gothic painting is on show.

Having had a fill of masterpieces, it would be best to view the sunset over the city and the Arno from high up, looking out from the vantage point of **Piazzale Michelangelo** or from the nearby churchyard of the Romanesque church of San Miniato al Monte.

On the tracks of Dante

Over the centuries, Florence has played a leading role

in the formation of the Italian identity, not least because it is the **birthplace** of the father of the Italian language, Dante Alighieri. It was his *Divine Comedy*, one of the greatest masterpieces of literature that laid the basis of Italian. Suffice to say that his work contained about 90 percent of the words currently in use.

Strolling through Florence, some familiar haunts of the supreme poet may be tracked down, starting with his **birthplace**, in the heart of the town, where a museum now retraces his life and works. Close by, in the **church of Santa Margherita de' Cerchi**, the very young Dante met Beatrice, the daughter of Folco Portinari, a woman that he only saw fleetingly but loved

all his life, choosing her as a guide through the paradise of *Divine Comedy*.

Florence also has some portraits of Dante, done by painters who had probably met him. His face appears in

the frescoes from the 1300s in the **chapel of the Bargello Palace** (the ancient Palazzo del Popolo or People's Palace, which now houses the important National Museum). His face is also very much on show in the Strozzi chapel inside **Santa Maria Novella**, among the chosen ones in *Giudizio Universale (Judgment Day)* painted by Nardo di Cione in the 1300s, following Dante's description in his novel.

Chianti

The most famous Italian wine in the world takes its name from the hills where it is produced, a splendid area of land between Florence and Siena.

It is a perfumed, dry, red wine, a typical table wine to go with almost any dish in Italian cuisine, and in some cases reaches extraordinary peaks of quality. It has good body, even when it is young, but when refined, it releases intense perfumes and truly noble complexity. The label was put under copyright too late in relation to the spread of its fame, so the real Chianti is, unfortunately, tainted by wines that carry its name without having its virtues. That is why the Chianti label is not in itself a sufficient warranty of quality, but needs to have the word "Classico" on it. There should also be a seal on the neck of the bottle bearing the image of a black rooster, a symbol in use since 2005, identifying all the Chianti producers. If left to mature for at least two years, including at least three months of refining in the bottle, the wine can acquire the superior denomination of "Chianti Classico Riserva."

THE SUPERB LADY OF THE SEA

Tales and images of a rich and lively past, an invitation to discovery.

It lies about 140 km south of Milan, taking the A7. Intercity trains departing from Central Station get to Genoa Principe Station in an hour and a half.

The name Genoa evokes the idea of Janus, a divinity from the Roman-Italic pantheon with two faces, much like this city, which faces the sea and the mountains. Another association could be from **ianua**, Latin for "door"; an uninterrupted passage, again between land and sea, for people from everywhere, which Genoa has always been, thanks to its port, one of the first in the Mediterranean. It was independent for a large part of its history, a feared **maritime Republic** during the Middle Ages and returned to glory during the 1500s. It is even known as the **Superb**, since Francesco Petrarch described it in the 1300s as "a regal city, backed onto an alpine hill, superb for its men and its walls, whose appearance alone indicate it as a lady of the sea."

Genoa is a regional capital, with a population of more than 600,000, and stretches into a shape of an amphitheater for 30 km at the center of Ligu-ria's coast. It nestles between the mountains and the Golfo Paradiso (Gulf of Paradise), and along the coastline it has a famous Riviera on each side.

It is an important industrial and commercial hub, but it's also a valuable city for art. It is surprising how many treasures there are here, what a lively cultural life it has, and how many attractions it holds. All this, together with its neighboring seaside towns, make it a pleasant holiday resort. Every October, an enormous number of boating enthusiasts come to the city for the **boat show**, one of the world's main fairs for pleasure boats.

A city tour has to start from the fascinating **medieval old town**, woven from a labyrinth of narrow alleys called **"caruggi,"** full of slopes, steps, and lively little squares. As Renzo Piano, a famous Genoese architect, puts it, Genoa does not seem to be made of streets along which houses have been built, but rather houses, from

which the streets have been carved with a sharp knife. Every corner brings a surprise. It may be a doorway sculpted in marble or black stone, a painted newsdealer's, the façade of a building from the 1500s, a portico, a courtyard, or a church.

The heart of the ancient part is the cathedral, dedicated to **San Lorenzo** (St. Lawrence), with a façade locked in between two bell towers and enlivened by two splendid Gothic doorways. Construction started in 1098 and went on to the 14th century and beyond. The black-and-white stripes on the outside walls are reflected in the columns and arches on the interior.

Another association with the city's medieval affairs comes from the nearby square, **Piazza di San Matteo** (St. Matthew Square), which is linked to one of the most prestigious Genoese families, the Doria family. Martino Doria had the church built in 1125 and dedicated to the saint who was a tax collector, like his family. The same combination of marble and slate that characterizes the cathedral had also been used for this church, equipped with a cloister from the 1300s, as well as for the residences of the old noble families in the neighborhood. The most famous member of the Doria family was Andrea, who was nominated Father of the Country after he protected the independence of the re-

public by forming an alliance with Spain. He had a splendid residence, overlooking the sea, built by Perin del Vaga, Raphael's pupil. This residence, the **Villa del Principe** (Prince's Mansion) is now a museum full of treasures.

Doria's idea was later copied by the city's wealthiest and most aristocratic families. During the 1500s and 1600s, they constructed a collection of splendid residences, in similar styles. These houses were called Rolli, because they were entered on official lists, or **"rolls"** (*"rolli"* in Italian), which were then used to select a property for honored guests of the republic of Genoa. They grew up along Via Garibaldi and Via Balbi, on the edge of the medieval urban area. Walking along these sumptuous streets seems to revive the splendor of Genoa's "golden century." In 2006, it was included on the Unesco World Heritage List. These properties have preserved important fresco decorations, and many of them are occupied by public institutions. Three of them—**Palazzo Bianco** (White Mansion), **Palazzo Rosso** (Red Mansion), and **Palazzo Tursi** (Tursi Mansion)—are occupied by the Musei di Strada Nuova (New Street Museums).

There is no shortage of fascinating collections for art enthusiasts. A little to the south of Strada Nuova is the **Galleria Nazionale di Palazzo Spinola** (Spinola Mansion National Gallery), which holds works by two prominent 1600s artists: Rubens and his pupil Van Dyck, both painters of unforgettable portraits of the aristocracy of Genoa. Then, going back up Via Balbi, there is the **Museo Nazionale di Palazzo**

Reale (Royal Palace National Museum), with a gallery in the sumptuous rooms on the second floor.

The **Palazzo Ducale** (Ducal Palace) is another prestigious location, one of the symbols of the city and the heart of the cultural life. Construction started in the late 1200's and the medieval structure's Torre del Popolo (Tower of the People), known as the **Grimaldina**, still stands. In 1339, it became the residence of the Doges, the ruling dukes, elected heads of the republic, and it was renovated in the late 1500s.

Before leaving the old town, stop by the nearby

Porta Soprana, the old main gate and the best preserved of all those that opened on the 12th-century city walls. Near this gate is the site of the **house of Christopher Columbus**, Genoa's most illustrious son. What stands there now is a building from the 1700s, reconstructed on the ruins of the house where the navigator was born.

Nobody can say they have visited Genoa until they have been to the **Porto Antico** (Old Port), the city's largest square, which opens onto the Mediterranean. Here, the urban fabric was transformed in 1992 for the celebrations of the 500th anniversary of Columbus's voyage to the Americas. Renzo Piano's revolutionary but respectful redesign triggered a metamorphosis in this part of the city, which the architect restored in relations to the old town. Today, modern structures stand next to renovated ancient edifices. The painted Renaissance façade of the **Palazzo San Giorgio** (St. George's Palace), headquarters of the city's main bank and the fulcrum of commercial and maritime life for centuries, overlooks Piazza Caricamento

(Waterfront Square) amid the port warehouses. Its presence creates a dialogue with the futuristic creations of Piano; in particular, the panoramic elevator called the **Bigo**. In the distance, the **Lanterna** (Lantern) can be seen, the 117-m-high lighthouse that is the city's emblem and has guided ships into the port since the 12th century.

The magic world of the port

The Columbus celebrations rejuvenated and enriched the old port of Genoa and made it an exceptional tourist destination. In place of partly disused wharfs, there is now a remarkable multifunctional leisure complex, tailored particularly for the younger generation, including, in winter, an ice-skating rink to bring life to Piazza delle Festa (Festival Plaza). Old cotton warehouses have become the Magazzini del Cotone multiscreen movie theater and also the home of an exhibition of scientific games for kids, the **Città dei Bambini** (www.cittadeibambini.net). Two interesting new museums have been created: the Galata (www.galatamuseodelmare.it), which retraces the history of the sea, with displays of all kinds of boats,

from galleys to steamboats; and the Antarctic Museum, **Museo dell'Antartide** (www.mna.it), illustrating the expeditions to the frozen continent. Part of an old port structure, called the Millo building, houses an upscale gastronomy/slow food center, **Eataly** (www.genova.eataly.it), with shelves full of Ligurian specialties (and much more), which can be enjoyed at the center's bars or in the excellent restaurant Marin, under the same roof. The jewel in the crown of the old port is the **Acquarium** (www.acquariodigenova.it). With 71 tanks and over 10,000 creatures from 800 different species, it is one of the biggest in Europe. Excellent reconstructions of various underwater environments show the creatures of the sea, but also those of the rain forests or from freshwater; from dolphins to sharks, from turtles to penguins and from seals to brightly colored jellyfish. Some of the animals can almost be touched, in 19 "open" tanks

specially set up in a converted merchant ship called *Nave Italia* (*Ship of Italy*).

Focaccia and pesto

Even though they have a lot of sophisticated recipes, Ligurian cuisine is especially associated with these two remarkably simple icons of popular cooking. The classic version of the Ligurian flatbread, whose local capital is Recco, a small seaside resort just outside Genoa, is made from two layers of dough mixed from wheat flour, white wine, olive oil, and a little salt. The layers are filled with a thin coating of soft cheese (Italian Crescenza or stronger-flavored Stracchino are used by Ligurians) and put in the oven until crispy.

The quality of the oil is fundamental for the focaccia, but no less important for success is the pesto, a sauce whose fame has traveled beyond the Italian border. Traditionally, there should be seven ingredients: extra-virgin olive oil, a mixture of two grated cheeses (Parmigiano-Reggiano and Sardinian Pecorino), Genoese basil, pine nuts, garlic ,and sea salt. These should all be ground up together using a wood pestle in a marble mortar.

NATURE AND HIGH SOCIETY

The lake has been frequented for centuries by international high society, artists, and intellectuals.

Como lies 50 km north of Milan, along the A9. You can get here in less than one hour by train, departing from Central Station or Cadorna station (Ferrovie Nord railroad line).

Lake Como is an upscale tourist destination, internationally renowned for its picturesque landscape, luxury mansions, and a mild, healthy climate. It is the third largest in Italy in terms of surface area, but the deepest of all. It is completely encircled by hills and mountains with dense vegetation and has the form of three long branches, looking like an upside-down Y. The three branches are named after their lakeside towns: to the southeast is Lecco, the southwest is Como, and the one to the north is Colico. The best thing to do is a boat tour of Larius (the name of the lake in Latin), using the efficient network of small boats and ferries connecting all the lakeside villages and the Comacina, the lake's single island. Coming from Milan, the starting point

on the lake is **Como**, which was founded more than 2,000 years ago by the Romans, and is one of the most historical cities in Lombardy. It has a population of just over 80,000 people and is the major Italian center for silk, since the duke of Milan, Ludovico Sforza,

forced the local peasants to plant mulberry trees in the 1400s. The old town, lying in a little basin at the eastern end of the lake, is still partly enclosed within the medieval walls and enriched by a number of historical buildings. In particular, there is the cathedral, started in 1396, and two famous Romanesque basilicas: the church of Sant'Abbondio (St. Abundius) built in 1013, and San Fedele (St.Fidelis), founded in the tenth century and reshaped in the 1500s. From the town, it takes just a few minutes by funicular to climb to **Brunate**, a little village that was much loved by the aristocracy of Milan.

The first town on the western bank is **Cernobbio**, known mainly for Villa d'Este, once the residence of the aristocratic Este family and now a luxury hotel where politicians, Nobel Prize winners, and experts from all over Europe meet every year to discuss the world's economy. It dates back to the 1500s and stands in a delightful Baroque garden.

Moving north, to the Punta di Balbianello (Balbianello Point) at **Lenno**, there is another magnificent residence of a noble family, Villa Arconati. This is the starting point of an enchanting stretch of landscape, especially where the lake widens at the union of its two southern branches. Here, in this particularly panoramic postion is **Tremezzo**, where

cow's restaurants" for 35 million euros.

The *"crotti"* of Valchiavenna

Going up to the northern tip of Larius, near the valley of Valchiavenna, the scenery is sterner than on the lake shore nearer to Como. This valley, which is decidedly alpine in its upper reaches (it leads to Malesimo, one of the most popular ski resorts in the Valtellina area), is famous because of the "crotto." This is a sort of natural cellar found in the hillside, where a constant temperature between four and eight degrees Celsius is maintained by a continuous breeze, called the Sorèl in French, circulating inside.

The "crotti" have been used as wine cellars or eating places, which are especially pleasant in the hottest summers. They are a traditional meeting place for the locals, but since the expansion of tourism, some have turned into restaurants, although others still maintain their simple nature, a place where you can drink a glass of red wine with cured meat or cheese.

you can visit Villa Carlotta (Villa Charlotte), built by Marquis Giorgio Clerici, and bought in 1856 by Princess Marianne of Prussia for her daughter Charlotte, who gave it its name. It is not to be missed, with a splendid garden and an art collection, including paintings by Hayez, friezes by Tordwalsen, and Canova's sculpture *Amore e Psiche* (*Psyche Revived by Cupid's Kiss*), one of the most famous masterpieces of neoclassical art.

The best-known village on the east bank of the lake is **Bellagio**, lying on the northern tip of the promontory dividing Larius into its two southern branches. Bellagio has a classic old town, with welcoming porticoes, framed by lush vegetatio, and elegant, historic mansions, embellished by enchanting gardens, such as Villa Serbelloni, which has been converted into one of the most luxurious grand hotels, and Villa Melzi, which has a fine botanical garden.

Celebrity spotting

Over the last few decades, word of the views to be enjoyed from the lake, and of the lake, has spread over the world, especially to Hollywood. Its most beautiful views have featured as locations for famous movies, from George Lucas' *Star Wars*, partly filmed in Villa del Balbianello, to *Casino Royale*. The most publicity, however, has gone to George Clooney, after he bought his mansion, Villa Oleandra in Laglio. Another residence well-known to the paparazzi is Villa Fontanelle, in Moltrasio. The mansion belonged to the Versace family, who often had celebrity guests, such as Madonna, Julia Roberts, Sharon Stone, and Michael Douglas. In 2008, it was sold to Arkadij Novikov, the "king of Mos-

A LITTLE SEA BETWEEN THE ALPS AND THE PLAIN

Italy's largest lake lives in contrast—the soft expanse of deep blue water with the hard backdrop of the mountains.

Peschiera del Garda, on the southern bank of the lake, is located around 140 km east of Milan, beside the A4. After Peschiera, the state road SS 249 runs along the eastern bank of the lake, the SS 45 bis along the western one. By train you can get to Peschiera in one hour and ten minutes.

Lake Garda, or Benaco, nestles between Lombardy, Veneto, and Trentino and is the holiday destination for millions of Europeans, especially Germans, every year. With an area of 370 sq km, it is the largest lake in Italy. The landscape changes at different areas of the lake. To the north, in Trentino, it looks like a fjord, locked between the Mt. Baldo chain and the Ledro Alps, while to the south, the waters widen, and the landscape is dotted with green moraine hills.

The villages around the lake are full of atmosphere and ancient tales and make for an interesting cultural tour. Starting from the south, the first obligatory port of call is **Sirmione**, celebrated in a famous ode by the Latin poet Catullo and renowned for the remains of a Roman villa and a medieval castle. Continuing to the west, on the Brescia shore, you come to Salò, which lies on an enchanting bay and is embellished by elegant Renaissance residences. A little farther on is Gardone, a hillside estate, which contains the extensive monument known as the **Vittoriale**, a shrine to Italian victories. This complex was conceived by Gabriele d'Annunzio, the most famous intellectual in fascist Italy, who retired there in 1921 until his death in 1938, and it includes the Priora (Priory), a majestic mansion-monument, icon of a period, and the museum with memorabilia and relics of the famous "armed poet."

Venturing on in Alto Garda, the upper part of the lake, it is worth stopping at Limone, with its pleasant citrus groves, and then at **Riva del Garda**, at the foot of the Brenta Dolomites. Riva has some important examples of ancient architecture, including La Rocca (the Fortress), the Apponale Tower, and the Pretorian Palace.

Coming back down the eastern coast, the first stop is **Malcesine**, with its castle built on top of a sheer rock on the lake. From this town, there is a cable car that goes up to **Mount Baldo**, called "the Garden of Europe," because of the rare species of plants growing there. Moving south, you come to Garda, which has a medieval center, with

Along the 158 km of shoreline, with alternating creeks, beaches, small bays, and steep cliffs, there is the ideal environment for every kind of amusement.

an English-style park in Villa Albertini and the Camaldolese Hermitage, from the 1600s, open only to males. The nearby Punta San Vigilio (St.Vigil's Point) is one of the most romantic panoramic spots along the whole shoreline.

The lake has become a resort in high demand because of the many sporting options available around its shores. There are various centers equipped for water sports: sailing, windsurfing, fishing, and swimming. The sheer rocks, directly on the water, make it an ideal challenge for climbers, while the mountains along the shoreline have an abundance of trails. Hang gliders and paragliders can launch from the top of Mt. Baldo or Tremezzo.

There are also plenty of fun parks for children, or for the young at heart. There is **Gardaland**, the largest park in

Italy, and Caneva World, with a water park.

Everyone down to the beach

A stay at Lake Garda in the summer is every bit as good as a holiday at the sea. The best beaches are along the western and southern shores. **Peschiera del Garda** has its beaches, the Lungolago Mazzini or Cappuccini. The waters of the upper part of the lake attract thousands of fans of windsurfing and sailing. The area has become the venue for major international competitions in these sports, one of which is the Centomiglia del Garda, a regatta over a distance of 100 miles.

Franciacorta

The area between Brescia and Lake d'Iseo, just to the west of the Garda area, is the land of the noblest of Italian spumante—white wines based

on Chardonnay and Pinot Bianco grapes, with the aroma of freshly leavened bread. These wines often achieve excellence, particularly the most select, called Satèn, identifiable by its very fine, but lasting, bubbles, created by the fermentation in the bottle. The

name that is given to this wine, resembling the word "satin," tends to highlight the nobility of its effervescence.

However, apart from being the land of great wines, Franciacorta is also an area of great natural beauty, and it was the favorite resort of the richest families of Brescia. Places to visit are Rodengo Abbey, the castle in Passirano, and the town of Erbusco, which has preserved its medieval buildings. In **Erbusco**, you can also find one of the most famous restaurants in Italy, l'Albereta (www.albereta.it), dominion of top chef Gualtiero Marchesi.

ARISTOCRACY ON THE LAKE

Here the great patrician families of Milan have taken their vacation for centuries.

Arona, the ideal base for a tourist trail around the lake, lies 65 km northwest of Milan, taking the A8, then the A26. By train, the journey takes about one hour, departing from Central station or from Porta Garibaldi station (Ferrovie Nord railroad line).

Lake Maggiore stretches along a glacial valley formed at the mouth of the river Ticino valley. With a total area of 212 sq km, it is the second largest in Italy after Lake Garda. Its beauty was praised long ago by the ancient Romans, who called it Verbanus Lacus, which is still its official name. (The correct Italian name is **Verbano**. Maggiore simply means the "Greater Lake.") It is enclosed in an area among Piedmont, Switzerland, and Lombardy, with a varied landscape becoming more starkly alpine at the northern end, but generally adorned by abundant vegetation and picturesque villages, either along the shore or clinging to the first spurs of the mountains.

The **Piedmontese bank**, to the west, is better known for its historic residences with lush gardens, its mansions, and its Belle Epoque hotels. This part of the lake was modeled by

the Borromeo family, one of the most influential Milanese dynasties, who arrived on Verbanus in the 15th century and held both civil and ecclesiastical power there in the 1500s and 1600s.

Arona, first stop on a tour going north, was the birthplace of San Carlo Borromeo (St. Charles Borromeo), archbishop of Milan, who has a 35-m-

high copper statue dedicated to him, known locally as the *Sancarlone* (*Big Charles*). A stroll along the lakeside is recommended here, with a stop at the pedestrianized center, which has important historic buildings, such as the Collegiata dei Santissimi Martiri (Collegiate Church of the Holy Martyrs), or the Palazzo di Giustizia (Law Courts), built by the Visconti family.

The jewel on this bank is undeniably **Stresa**, which was discovered by the Piedmontese aristocracy in the 1800s. Then, at the start of the last century, luxurious hotels sprang up, particularly the Regina Palace Hotel and the Grand Hotel des Iles Borromèes, which turned the area into a famous resort. It has always been a favorite of the elite and is today a center for important events, like the Settimane Musicali (Music Weeks), with

symphony concerts, chamber music, and instrumental and vocal recitals.

Opposite to Stresa, the lake widens into the scenic Golfo Borromeo (Borromeo Bay), where there are three famous islands that can be visited by boat: **Isola Bella** (Beautiful Isle) and **Isola Madre** (Mother Isle) were "designed" by the Borromeo family, who built mansions and gardens there. **Isola dei Pescatori** (Fishermen's Isle) is an attractive lakeside village, complete with restaurants.

A cable car ascends from the lake shore in Stresa to the top of Mt. Mottarone (1,491 m high), a natural viewing balcony between Lake Maggiore and nearby Lake Orta (but on a clear day the view stretches to the snow-covered peaks of Monte Rosa and all the lakes in the province of Varese). Mottarone is a ski resort in winter.

There are also plenty of attractive resorts on the eastern **Lombardy shore**. The main center on this bank is **Luino**, which is almost on the border with Switzerland and attracts many visitors, particularly on Wednesdays, when it holds the open-air market, a tradition dating back to the time of the Emperor Charles V, who granted its concession in 1541. Moving a little farther south, is

The parks and gardens of Lake Maggiore are famous for their elegant buildings and even more for their long period in bloom, from Sspring to late fall—a display of azaleas, rhododendrons, camellias, magnolias, hydrangeas, and many other plants.

Laveno, a village in a small, natural bay at the foot of the Sasso del Ferro (Iron Rock). The village boasts a spacious, well-equipped lakeside marina.

One of the most fascinating places on the whole lake is the **hermitage of Santa Caterina del Sasso** (St. Catherine of the Rock), which is perched on a spur of rock in the vicinity of Leggiuno. The hermitage was erected in the 12th century, as an offering to a divinity, by a rich merchant, Alberto Besozzi, who survived a shipwreck on the lake waters. The monastic building also has an oratory dedicated to St. Catherine, a spacious loggia, and chapels with Renaissance frescoes.

with its garden, laid out in the 1600s by Count Vitaliano. This park, one of the best examples of an Italian Baroque garden, is shaped like a cut-off pyramid with sloping terraces. It is well-stocked with exotic plants and contains a lot of obelisks, statues and fantasy animals, particularly the unicorn, the emblem of the Borromeo family.

Leaving Stresa, there is another park waiting at **Villa Taranto**, in Verbania, with botanical assets equaling thousands of plants, imported from all over the world and planted in various scenic layouts. It was created in 1931 by a Scotsman, Captain Neil McEacharn, who believed that "…a good garden does not need to be big, but has to be the realization of your dream, even if it is only a couple of square yards on a balcony."

Hillside delicacy

The best-known gastronomic specialty of the Verbanus area comes from Ossola, the area between Lake Maggiore and the two Swiss cantons of Ticino and Vallese. The specialty is a cheese called **Bettelmatt**, made from milk taken from cows that graze on the pastures of the alpine hills around the valleys of Formazza and Devero. Its German name reminds us that this is an area populated by the Walser, or Walliser, a German-speaking people who migrated to the southern slopes of Monte Rosa during the 13th century. It is a golden-yellow or straw-colored cheese, with a firm but soft consistency, and it bears the name of the hillside it comes from, stamped on the rind with a hot iron. Bettelmatt is produced from June to early September and is matured for two months.

Last but not least is **Angera**, the town that dominates the southern end of the lake and is famous for its Rocca (castle), which also deserves a visit. First built by the Romans as a lookout tower, the castle was fortified by the Lombards. The structure then passed to the Visconti family in the 1200s, who left frescoes that can still be seen in the Sala della Giustizia (Law Room), and finally to the Borromeos, who became the feudal rulers of the whole lake area in the 15th century. The Rocca houses the Museo delle Bambole e dei Giocattoli (Museum of Dolls and Toys), one of the most important of its kind in Europe

Enchanted gardens

On the western bank of the lake is a series of gardens, which light up with color when the roses, camellias, azaleas, hydrangeas, and rhododendrons come into full bloom.

The area around Stresa has a large number of gardens. At the entrance to the town, there is the park of Villa Pallavicino, an English-style garden laid out in the late 1800s around the eclectic, lordly residence. The

park features lawns and centuries-old trees, with llamas, deer and goats roaming free. If you take the cable car from Stresa, up to Mottarone and get off at the midway station at Alpino, apart from a good view of the area, there is also a botanical garden, the **Giardino Botanico Alpinia**, dedicated to typical mountain flora.

Then there is the island, **Isola Bella**, a paradise for botany enthusiasts (and others), which looks like a ship on the lake with the graceful building of Palazzo Borromeo, together

Ready
for
boarding!

MAGGIORE
GARDA
COMO
AMAZING LAKES!

ARCH'S COMUNICAZIONE

navigazionelaghi.it

IN THE ROLLING HILLS OF BACCHUS

Dotted with charming villages, it is considered a paradise for gourmets.

Prime destination for an itinerary in the Langhe is Alba, located 150 km southwest of Milan. Take the A7, then the A21 until the Asti Est exit, followed bythe main road SS231. A three-hour train ride with transfers in Turin and Ba is another comfortable solution.

Located in southern Piedmont, among the provinces of Cuneo, Asti, and Alessandria, this land of exquisite sights is not to be missed, especially in autumn, when the hills are tinged with warm hues and caressed by a frosty azure mist. The term *"langa"* in the local lan-

guage, indicates the crest's hill range and the scenery—especially in the Bassa Langa—is a series of hills with vineyards and dominated by castles that stand high above the villages, protected at their bases.

The main town is **Alba,** full of historic buildings and medieval towers, which grant the town an unmistakable skyline. There is also a Gothic cathedral and a Baroque parish church dedicated to St. John the Baptist. The town comes alive especially between October and November, when it hosts the annual truffle fair, with the humorous Palio degli asini, preceded by a procession in medieval fashion. The area has seen the emergence of large-scale businesses, such as Ferrero, a prestigious

multinational confectionery business that was born in Alba in 1946, and Slow Food, an international association committed to the defense of biodiversity and the promotion of "good, clean, and fair" food, founded by Carlo Petrini in 1986 in neighboring Bra.

Another village nestled in the hills of Barolo and Barbaresco is **Grinzane Cavour**. The great Camillo Benso, Count of Cavour, was mayor of the town from 1832 to 1849. The count appointed expert French winemakers to select vineyards, and he was the lord of the city's stronghold, where you can visit the Langhe Museum, dedicated to agricultural heritage, or taste wines bottled in the 'Enoteca Regionale Piemontese. The Winery promotes an annual international truffle auction, which takes place in connec-

tion with two satellite locations abroad.

Let us not forget nearby **Cherasco,** a fine 18th-century town that houses an elegant Visconti castle, and **Monforte d'Alba**, which was the center of the Cathar heresy in the Middle Ages and now hosts the Jazz festival of Monforte.

Take a trip to **Serralunga d'Alba** and the estates of Fontanafredda, with Casa di Caccia della Bela Rosin, the lovely commoner who caught the fancies of felled King Vittorio Emanuele II, who wanted her as a "morganatic" wife (without any rights, for herself and for their children, over the securities and property of her husband). There is even a castle here: a 14th-century fortress that has guarded the hill from the village.

Literary connoisseurs should stop at **Santo Stefano Belbo**, in the Alta Langa. The town boasts the remains of the Romanesque abbey of San Gaudenzio and was home to Italian literary giant Cesare Pavese, whose birth house is now a museum. Pavese wrote in *La luna e i falò (The Moon and the Bonfires)*: "One needs a town if not only for the pleasure of leaving it. A town means not knowing loneliness, having the certainty that something of yourself is in the people, plants and soil, which awaits you in every moment."

His Majesty the truffle of Alba

The hills of the Langhe guard a treasure: the underground mushroom with the intoxicating scent known as the Alba white truffle *(Tuber magnatum Pico)*, the most valuable and rare among truffles. Aided by patiently trained scent hounds, the legendary *trifulau* (truffle) is sought in autumn nights. Even the ancient Romans deemed it the food of the gods, but it was not until the 18th century that this "fruit of the earth" was acknowledged as one of the finest foods in the European courts, so as to be compared by Giaocchino Rossini as the

"Mozart of mushrooms," or by Alexandre Dumas the "Holy of Holies of the table." Promoted among the powerful men of the world, this delicacy still kindles the dreams of the most discerning palates as it is sliced over two fried eggs; on a carpaccio of veal; or on a plate of tajarin pasta, which are thin, homemade egg noodles at the base of one of the most typical Piedmontese dishes.

Barolo and his brothers

Communication difficulties—the fruit of common country dweller distrust—have long prevented the Langhe wines from gaining the proper international recognition. In this regard goes the story of

the famous producer who refused to adopt the use of a phone so as not to be bothered by customers. The new generations of winery owners have quickly changed the scenario, and now there is probably not a wine expert who does not know the virtues of aged Langhe reds.

The crown is born by Barolo wine, which is made with Nebbiolo, Michet, Lampia, and rosé grapes that grow in the area around the town of the same name. This wine must be aged three years (five in the case of reserve) and goes well with stuffed pasta and meats. An aromatic variant, known as Barolo chinato, also is well fancied. The other great local red is Barbaresco, made with the same grapes as the Barolo, and requires a minimum aging of two years; four for the reserve. More delicate and finer than Barolo, a full body comes with aging.

In addition to Barolo and Barbaresco, the area produces other reds that are usually less demanding, but reveal signs of excellence, such as Barbera, Dolcetto, and Nebbiolo. They all carry the name Alba to distinguish them from products of the same denomination but vinified in other areas.

THE PEARL OF THE PLAIN

The Renaissance architecture of Mantua is on the Unesco World Heritage List, but the city is also a pleasant destination for a culinary holiday and nature tours.

Lying 160 km southeast of Milan, you get to Mantua by taking the A1, then the A21 toward Piacenza–Brescia, and after Cremona, the divided highway SS10. The train takes around two hours by direct regional train, departing from Central Station.

Mantua (population 50,000) lies in the middle of the river Po Valley, conveniently placed on the borders of three regions: Lombardy, Veneto, and Emilia Romagna. It is served by the river Mincio, which flows into the three lakes that surround the city before passing into the nearby river Po.

The historic town center is small and can be visited on foot. A tour would start from the **Piazza delle Erbe**, the ancient marketplace where the main medieval attractions can be found. The Palazzo della Ragione dates from the 1200s and was the seat of power

when Mantua was a free municipality. The 11th-century Rotonda di San Lorenzo church, was modeled on the Holy Sepulchre in Jerusalem and was built for Matilda di Canossa, one of the most enterprising and charismatic women of the Middle Ages.

The other places worth visiting go back to the time when Mantua was the capital of the Gonzaga domain, one of the most illustrious small Italian city-states in the Renaissance period. Their main residence was the **Ducal Palace**, which was made up of

buildings from various periods and contains many art masterpieces. A list includes remaining traces of frescoes showing scenes from a horse tournament—the work of Pisanello, who was an inventive exponent of Gothic painting; tapestries from the 1500s, woven by hand in Flanders, following cartoons by Raffaello, on display in the *appartamento degli Arazzi*; and the celebrated **bridal chamber**, *camera picta*, which was completely frescoed between 1465 and 1474 by Andrea Mantegna. Marquis Ludovic brought Mantegna to Mantua in 1460, and he stayed there until his death, working as an artist to the duke's court and becoming one of Italy's most famous painters. Ludovic was a cultured philanthropist and lover of antiques, and other leading Renaissance figures also worked for him, including Leon Battista Alberti, famous for his *Chiesa di San Sebastiano* and the **Basilica of St. Andrew**, where, as legend would

have it, the relic of the Blood of Christ is kept.

Palazzo Te is another magnificent architectural structure. It was designed and decorated by Giulio Romano, between 1524 and 1534, for the leisure of another Gonzaga, Frederick II. The artist, who was a favorite pupil of Raffaello, also decorated the interior of the palace with spectacular illusionist frescoes. The best example is in the Giants' Room, where enormous figures seem to move on the walls.

Rigoletto

Very few Italian operas are so closely linked to a city as the masterpiece composed by Verdi in 1851, which tells the tragic story of Gilda, the daughter of Rigoletto, who was a jester in the despotic, libertine court of the duke of Mantua. This has been illustrated again, recently by the worldwide success of the film version by Marco Bellochio, filmed on location in the most spectacular parts of the city, with Placido Domingo starring in the role of Rigoletto. This success is due to the director, the stars, and the sublime music, enriched by well-known arias such as *La donna è mobile* and *Bella figlia dell'amore*.

Renaissance on the table

The best-known local dish is the **sbrisolona**, a dry, crunchy cake that goes well with a glass of Lambrusco wine. It is plain but tasty and easy to make at home, using wheat flour, corn flour, butter, egg yolks, almonds, lemon, and vanilla. **Ravioli stuffed with pumpkin** is another famous Mantuan speciality, which is more complex in its preparation and content, with contrasting flavors. This is a sweet-and-sour recipe, with pumpkin, mostarda Mantovana, macaroons, Parmesan cheese, and melted butter, making a difficult but delicious combination. Most people now think this is an unnatural mix of flavors (repeated in one of the ingredients, mostarda, which is a pickled fruit), but it goes back to Renaissance cuisine, when the Mantuan school of gastronomy became famous for its "scalch" (as they called their great chefs at the time).

The city, which gave birth to Virgil, one of the greatest Latin poets, celebrates for five days every September the Festivalettura—an international cultural event with shows and concerts, as well as meetings with the world's top writers.

THE ANCIENT CAPITAL OF GASTRONOMY

The hometown of Verdi gives its name to the classic Italian cheese, Parmesan, as well as the most delicious ham, Parma ham.

Lying 125 km south of Milan, you get to Parma by taking the A1. The Frecciabianca train, departing from Central Station, takes around one hour.

Parma is a medium-sized city on the edge of the broad Po River Valley, very close to the foot of the Appennine Hills. It is a first-class tourist destination, because of its pleasantly provincial atmosphere and also because it boasts some major sights, a reminder of its prosperity during the Middle Ages. In the countryside to the northwest of Parma, there is the village of Roncole di Busseto, where Giuseppe Verdi, the Italian composer, was born on October 10, 1813.

Parma is also the base for the European Food Safety Authority, the European Union agency that oversees the quality of food sold in its member countries.

On arrival in the city, proceed directly to the central cathedral square, **Piazza del Duomo**, where there are two fine examples of medieval architecture and sculpture: the cathedral and the **baptistery**.

The latter is seen as among the best of Italian art in the 1200s, with statues and bas-reliefs on its interior and exterior by Benedetto Antelami (worth noting, the cycles of the signs of the zodiac, the seasons and the months). The **cathedral** also has a masterpiece by Antelami, the bas-relief of the deposition from the cross. In the dome of the cathedral, there is also a fresco showing the scene of the Assumption of the Virgin, painted by one of Parma's outstanding painters, Correggio, between 1526 and 1530. Lovers of Correggio go from here to the nearby church of San Giovanni Evangelista (behind the apse of the cathedral), to admire the frescoes he painted there between 1520 and 1523.

Parmigianino is another glorious local exponent of painting, who also lived in the first half of the 1500s. Some of his work can be seen inside the Renaissance church, Chiesa della Steccata, and in the nearby **National Gallery**, where his best-known painting, *La Schiava Turca*, and his self-portrait, *Autoritratto*, are displayed. This gallery also has some Correggio masterpieces: a young girl's head, attributed to Leonardo da Vinci; and Hans Holbein's *Portrait of Erasmus of Rotterdam*. The gallery's lobby is actually the old Teatro Farnese, the historic local theater, built entirely in wood in the first half of the 1600s.

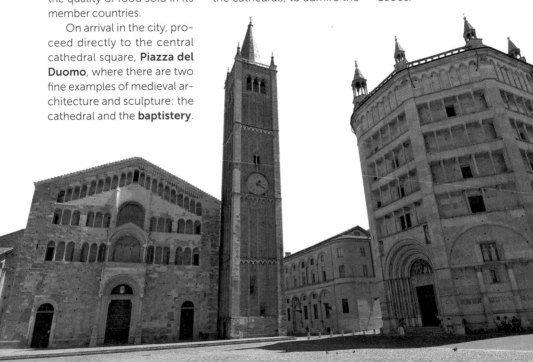

Just north of the center, going toward the highway, there is the monastery where Stendhal's hero, Fabrice del Dongo, shut himself away. This was in the writer's most famous novel, *The Charterhouse of Parma* (1839), which was largely set in Parma.

Musical melodrama

It may have been because it was the only way to communicate for illiterate people who spoke different languages (the situation in most of Italy before the 1900s); it may have been because talented people in a country that was divided and practically enslaved had nothing else to do; or it may have been simply a

natural gift of talent. We don't know why, but the fact is that the art of beautiful singing was born, and it became world famous as being typically Italian. So much so that even today, the world of opera continues to use Italian as a common language. And opera is still vibrant everywhere in Italy. Out of Italian cities, Parma is where popular enthusiasm for musical melodrama has remained more a part of the city.

The city of Verdi and Toscanini has two opera theaters: the Farnese, which puts on shows during festivals, and the Regio, one of the stages that singers aspire to (and fear) the most. The love of opera is also felt outside this prestigious theater, where you can listen to singing competitions, associations, bands, and choirs.

Parmigiano-Reggiano

This is one of the most nutritious and balanced foods that Italian gastronomy has to offer. It is also the most copied, and in vain. You only have to look at the number of unlikely Parmesans that are sold almost all over the world. The true Parmigiano-Reggiano is a hard, grating cheese, protected by a brand of authenticity, and it can be produced only in the area between Mantua and Bologna. Each wheel of cheese must weigh between 24 and 34 kg. It has an age classification: "new" is sold in the same year it is produced; "old" goes on sale after 18 to 24 months, and "very old" means it is over two years.

Its origins certainly go back a long way, seeing that

Boccaccio recounts in the Decameron that Calandrino believed there were mountains of Parmesan cheese in the country of Bengodi.

Parmigiano-Reggiano is one of the easiest cheeses to digest, despite being rich in protein, vitamins, and minerals.

A QUEEN AMID THE PADDY FIELDS

A city of art in the heart of a rich, fertile plain, boasting an ancient college, which, for centuries, was the university of the Milanese.

Pavia lies 45 km south of Milan, first along the A7 toward Genoa, as far as the exit for Bereguardo—Pavia Nord, then the A53 to the exit for Pavia—Via Riviera. Intercity trains departing from Central station get to Pavia in about 20 minutes.

Guardian of an eventful past, Pavia, with its 70,000 inhabitants, lies in the fertile Po River flood plain, where the Ticino flows into the Po. It is a provincial capital, and everyone associates it with its vineyards and paddy fields that stretch out in the area where medieval monks tamed the impassible marshes, but its urban fabric has preserved the heritage of an important past. In the seventh century, the Lombards chose it as the capital of their kingdom, and the Visconti family, dukes of Milan, founded one of the first universities there in 1361. Many students still choose to study there, particularly in the renowned faculties of medicine and law.

The same Visconti family also built the **castle** that stands in the heart of the city, which is embellished by frescoes and equipped with an excellent library. Today, the castle

houses the Musei Civici (Civic Museums), which are worth a visit to see the important collection of Lombard and Venetian Renaissance paintings in the Pinacoteca Malaspina (Malaspina Art Gallery).

A tour of the old town, on foot—passing through narrow alleys, medieval towers, and cozy little squares—you simply must take in the most important churches. Starting near the castle, there is

San Pietro in Ciel d'Oro (St. Peter in the Sky of Gold), a church founded, according to legend, in the eighth century by Liutprand, king of the Lombards, to hold the remains of St. Augustine, which he had paid its weight in gold to buy from the Saracens in Sardinia. The present structure of the church, from the 12th century, holds the ark with the saint's remains over the main altar.

Moving south on Strada Nuova, one of the busiest streets, overlooked by the historic university buildings, you come to the cathedral, with its large, octagonal dome. The first design for this was done by Donato Bramante, one of the greatest architects of the Italian Renaissance.

The city's most important religious building is the **Arcibasilica Reale di San Michele** (Archbasilica of St. Michael Major), founded by the Lombards and

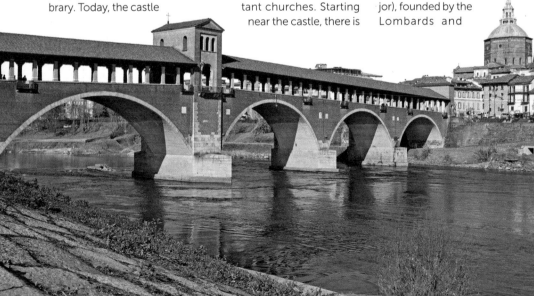

rebuilt in Romanesque style between the 11th and 12th centuries. It has a splendid façade (extending above the roof level), which features bas-reliefs of curious symbolic figures. The basilica was used for the coronations of a number of royal heads, including Frederick Barbarossa in 1155.

After this, Strada Nuova proceeds down to the river Ticino, crossed by the hump-backed bridge **Ponte Coperto** (Covered Bridge).

Ten km north of the city, there is one of the most beautiful monuments in Italy, the **Certosa** (Carthusian monastery). Gian Galeazzo Visconti, the duke who sponsored the construction of the cathedral in Milan, had the Certosa of Pavia built in the late 1300s as a mausoleum for his family. The main core of the complex goes back to the subsequent century and the beginning of the 1500s, when an illustrious group of sculptors completed the multicolored marble façade and the body of the church. The interior, which is resplendent in frescoes, contains the burial monuments of Beatrice d'Este and Ludovic the Moor (sculpted by Cristoforo Solari in 1497). The two cloisters from the 1400s have a particularly striking atmosphere: the smaller of the two is distinguished by its elaborate earthenware tiles while the larger one overlooks the monks' cells.

The ancient towers of Italian cities

Pavia was called the city of 100 towers because that was the number of towers on the skyline in the 12th and 13th centuries when it was a commune. They were slen-

der and up to 50 m tall. They were not militaristic, but symbols of prestige for the families they belonged to. The most powerful families usually erected one on the birth of their first child. It seems that Filippo Maria Visconti, lord of the city, had one built upside down to celebrate his son's graduation. It was knocked down in the 1700s to avoid collapse, but it was an engineering masterpiece—it got wider as it rose and had broad balconies.

Rices and frogs

Of all the strange things that Italians put on their dinner tables, frogs are the tastiest. They are a typical dish of northern Italy and are a tender meat with a delicate flavor. Gone are the days when sellers walked the streets with large baskets of frogs they had caught in nearby holes. But a traditional dish typical of Pavia from that period still remains: risotto with frogs. It is not complicated to prepare, although the cleaning of the frogs may be for someone who is expert. Once the insides have been removed, together with the head and legs, the frog must be skinned and rinsed with water and then put into boiling water for a few minutes. Then, it is relatively easy to separate the meat of the thighs from the bone, which then has to be crushed up with a pestle and mortar and then boiled again (this time in salted water). The resulting liquid is filtered and used as a stock for the risotto, which is prepared in a pan in the same way as a Milanese risotto (but without saffron!). In the meantime, the frogs' legs are cooked in a pan, with some butter, parsley, and a little oil (garlic may be included, but has to be removed as soon as it starts to change color); it is important not to let the meat turn into a pulp. The meat should be added to the rice, just before it is completely cooked. The dish is best served with a sprinkling of chopped parsley.

THE ANCIENT SOVEREIGN OF THE SEAS

Today it is a small university town, but it was rich and powerful between the 11th and 13th centuries, as its famous monuments testify.

It lies 280 km southeast of Milan, and you get there first along the A1, then the A15 toward La Spezia, then onto the A12 toward Firenze–Livorno, and finally the A11 to Pisa Nord. By train, you get there in about four hours with the high speed train Frecciabianca (White Arrow), departing from Central Station.

Pisa enjoyed its golden age around the year 1000, when it was a powerful Maritime republic and its fearsome fleet crossed the Tyrrhenian Sea, even managing to defeat the Muslims at Palermo. To demonstrate their gratitude to the Virgin Mary for this victory, the people of Pisa laid the first stone of the cathedral and thus started the biggest Romanesque complex in Europe, the Piazza dei Miracoli (Square of Miracles).

The city is a provincial capital with 85,000 inhabitants, a major university campus, and it is an important manufacturing center. It lies along the Arno River, not far from its mouth (at the time of the maritime republic, the coast was a lot closer).

The Lungarni (Along the Arno) roads run along the riverbanks, flanked by majestic buildings, fortifications, and medieval churches, including **Santa Maria della Spina** (St. Mary of the Thorn), a jewel of Gothic architecture. The charm of these riverside roads is best enjoyed on the Notte di San Ranieri (Eve of St. Rainerius), the city's patron saint. On the evening of June 16, 1,000 tea lights illuminate the houses and bridges in a ceremony called the Luminara (Illumination). Events on the occasion of the saint's festival also

include the Gioco del Ponte (Bridge Game), a historical recreation where the various districts of the city compete against each other, and the closing event is the famous regata on the river Arno.

The cathedral square, universally known as the **Campo dei Miracoli**, is bordered by a square wall, inside of which there are lawns and majestic marble monuments that have been on the Unesco World Heritage List since 1987.

The oldest building is the **cathedral**, founded in 1063,

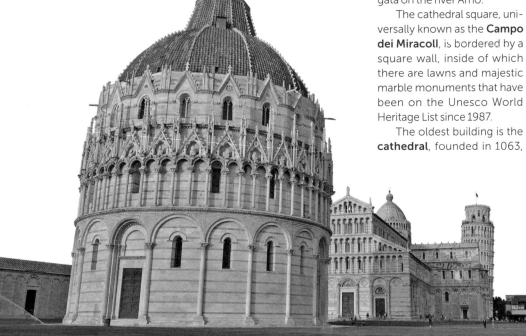

in a fusion of elements from classical, Norman, Byzantine, and Arabian traditions). It is characterized by the horizontal black-and-white marble stripes on the faces of the walls and by the open galleries in the façade, distinctive features of Pisan Romanesque style. The numerous treasures inside include the marble pulpit, by Giovanni Pisano, a high point of Gothic sculpture.

Opposite the cathedral is the imposing, round **battistero** (baptistery), in white marble and topped by an original dome, started in 1153 by Diotisalvi and completed in the Gothic period. Inside, it contains the Pulpit (1260) of Nicola Pisano, Giovanni's father, who was an ingenious architect and sculptor and founded a specifically Italian Gothic language.

The most well-known monument is the **Leaning Tower**, started in 1173. The ground gave way beneath it at an early stage of construction, which caused it to lean

The monumental cemetery in the Campo dei Miracoli is built around a shipload of soil brought from Golgotha in 1202. At that time, Pisa was a flourishing maritime republic.

so famously. In reality, the bell tower is quite stable, because the vertical axis of its center of gravity is over the foundations. So nobody has to worry about climbing the 294 steps inside the tower to reach the top! One of the most famous sons of Pisa, the scientist Galileo Galilei went up there to test his theories of gravity.

The "miracles" are completed by the **Camposanto** (**Holy Field**), the cemetery where the crusaders brought

a shipload of sacred soil from Golgotha. When the frescoes, badly damaged by the 1944 bombings, were taken down, they exposed their underpaintings, which are now kept in the Museo delle Sinopie (Museum of the Underpaintings).

A timeless two-wheeler

In Pontedera, not far from Pisa, motorcycle enthusiasts can visit the **Piaggio Museum**, in a warehouse of the company that is mainly famous for its production of the Vespa. The world's most famous motor scooter, which entered the collective imagination of the world through famous movies, such as *Roman Holiday*, was first produced in 1946 and immediately cornered the market. Since then, the company has kept faith with the original, innovative design by its inventor Corradino D'Ascanio, and the pleasant, reassuring lines that have made it an icon of Italian design. A series of new models have followed and customized versions have been created as one-offs. The permanent collection in the museum retraces the history of the motor scooter and in-

The Vespa has been defined as the most ingenious means of transport invented in Italy since the biga chariot of the ancient Romans.

cludes some rare examples, such as the Vespa with Salvatore Dali's autograph.

Tuscan soups

Without denying the goodness of our pasta, tourists in Dante's "Beautiful Land" of-

ten feel the need to try a dish of soup, something that is missing from Italian tables. There is no shortage of soups, but what is usually described as such on the menu is, in most cases, a very thick and very rich recipe (fish soup or onion soup come to mind, as examples).

But we have an exception in Tuscan cuisine, where one of the most common specialties in summer is **vegetable minestrone**. It can be served hot or cold, with pasta or with rice, very thin or a little thicker, but it is always quite a typical dish. There is no exact recipe, since the choice of vegetables depends on their availability at the time, but it should always include onion, celery, tomato, chard, and carrots.

The winter version is called the **ribollita** (the name literally means "reboiled" soup), adding pieces of bread and using seasonal vegetables, such as Tuscan kale and dried beans. Both minestrone and ribollita can be seasoned with a good "cross of oil," preferably from the region—Tuscan extra-virgin oil is usually full-bodied and has a sharp flavor that goes well with vegetables.

THE JEWEL OF THE GULF OF TIGULLIO

Surrounded by lush Mediterranean Maquis, Portofino is one of Italy's most renown hot spots for seaside vacations.

Located 170 km south of Milan, take the A7 for Milan–Genoa, and then the A12, as far as the Rapallo exit and follow the road SP227. Intercity trains depart from Milan's Central Station to nearby Santa Margherita Ligure, which has bus links to Portofino (for timetable: www. atpesercizio.it).

"There, out of nowhere, a hidden inlet appears, lined by olives and chestnuts. A little village, Portofino, extends like a crescent moon around this serene bay." This is how the French writer Guy de Maupassant described his approach to the village in 1889, which pans out like an amphitheater in a headland inlet between Paradiso Gulf (to the west) and the Gulf of Tigullio (to the east). The pedestrianized town stands out for its picturesque tall, narrow, and vibrantly colored buildings and is framed within an inimitable natural panorama: rocky cliffs that plunge into the sea, rugged Mediterranean fauna, and an intense rapport between sky and sea.

The area also offers a great deal for **underwater** enthusiasts. In particular, the underwater cliff along the headland, from Punta del Faro to Punta Chiappa, help create a sea bottom of stupendous naturalist wealth that boasts spectacular sea fans and a rich fauna.

Pliny spoke of the location as the ancient Port of the Dolphins (perhaps referring to the large numbers of dolphins of the Gulf of Tigullio at that time). The small farming and fishing village began to take on the role of **internationally renowned resort** in the latter half of the 1800s, when the first foreigners arrived. Its rise to fame is likely attributed to the British consul to Genoa, Montague Yeats Brown, who transformed the fort of Portofino into a splendid residence, still visible at the top of the headland. In the 1950s and 1960s, the village became a luxury tourist resort, a catwalk for Hollywood stars and the "place to be" of the elite. None of this, however, has altered the morphology of the village, which retains its original size and layout.

Vibrant in the summer, when the small central square, **La Piazzetta**, teems with tourists, and the harbor hosts fleets of yachts flying the flag of every nation, this tiny town of less than 500 resumes its sober, seafaring atmosphere in winter as only local fishing ships moor off the jetty.

An uphill walk from the the square leads to St. George's church, set on the ridge of the headland, that offers a sensational **panoramic view** across the bay and open sea. From here, you can get to Brown's Castle, also known as St. George's fortress, and continue, nestled in pine trees, to the farthest point of the headland, where the lighthouse stands.

Lovers of outdoor excursions find a wide range of

pathways—of all levels of difficulty and open all year—to explore one of the most striking stretches of the Ligurian coastline. Several footpaths, enjoying priceless views over the Gulf of Tigullio, lead up to Mt. Portofino, a natural park where broad-leaf woodlands stand alongside the maquis. Moving eastward takes you to the picturesque inlet of **Paraggi**, with its turquoise waters and a quaint beach that is sought after by summer sunbathers from early in the morning, and then on to the elegant, charming town of Santa Margherita Ligure.

One excursion not to be missed, either on foot or by boat, is a visit to the tiny village of **San Fruttuoso**, which can be reached only by sea or by way of a steep footpath. The village frames the little harbor and stands below an ancient Benedictine abbey and an imposing 16th-century observation tower. The monastery contains the ashes of St. Fruttuoso, a third-century bishop, and a crypt with the remains of seven members of the powerful Doria family, under whose influence this community reached its peak during the 13th century.

The mariner patron

In the bay overlooked by the abbey of St. Fruttuoso, the bronze statue of the **Christ of the Deep** sits on the sea bottom, 17 m below the surface, where it has protected mariners since 1954 and has become, over time, a world-famous symbol of the passion for underwater exploration. Many divers go down to see it in person, while in the summer months, small boats shuttle back and forth from the jetty,

enabling non-divers to view the sea bottom and the statue from the surface. In August, there is a popular ceremony in the bay, in memory of all those lost at sea, involving the blessing of the waters, a torchlight procession, and divers going down to place a laurel wreath on the head of the Christ.

Sea and mountains

Ligurian cuisine is considered among the best in Italy, as it combines typical hillside flavors with a wide variety of seafoods. A typical lunch may start with vegetable-filled ravioli, such as the fried Gattafin of Levanto, followed by a fish course, which means squid or, especially, local Monterosso anchovies, eaten raw, with their firm flesh and bright color, or octopus, often used as a base for a patè mixed with capers, olive oil, and black pepper and then spread on slices of bread. This meal may often finish with a slice of chestnut bread pudding (called "castagnaccio"), made with chestnut flour, raisins, and pine nuts, and served with ricotta cheese.

The combination of seafood with inland ingredients is even more surprising when it is found in the same dish. The best-known example of this is a dish called "**cappon magro**," which was supposedly created onboard the Genoese galleys as a high-protein meal for the rowers but was then transformed in the 1800s into a sophisticated dish. It is made up of various layers of ingredients, ranging from plain ship's biscuit, to vegetables (artichokes, green beans, cauliflower, beetroot, mushrooms pickled in oil, carrots, and celery) and various fish (best of all sea bass and scorpion fish). In its most sumptuous version, it may be topped with shellfish and oysters.

THE GOLDEN TWILIGHT OF THE ROMAN EMPIRE

Ravenna provides valuable evidence of the late Roman era, when the city was the capital of the empire.

Ravenna lies approximately 290 km southeast of Milan. Take the A1 as far as Bologna, then the A14.
By train, you can get there in about three hours, on the intercity trains leaving from Central Station for Bologna, continuing with the regional trains.

Ravenna is a dynamic city of around 160,000 inhabitants, and lies a few kilometers from one of the busiest stretches of the Adriatic coast, popular because of the long, sandy beaches here. It is also close to the delta of the river Po, with a unique landscape of pine woods and flooded forests.

In the summer, it goes international, when they hold the **Ravenna Festival**, and the city turns into a stage for performances of classical music, jazz, theater, and dance, involving the world's top orchestra conductors and plenty of big names from modern music and theater.

Stands in the southern part of the city, the **Mausoleum of Galla Placidia**, sister of Emperor Honorius, who moved the capital of the western Roman Empire to Ravenna in 402 AD. On the outside it's a plain little brick-clad edifice, but the interior sparkles with mosaics, including the unforgettable

starry sky in the vault, with a golden cross in the center. Not far on is the **Basilica of San Vitale**, the most magnificent one in Ravenna, with a well-structured interior embellished with mosaics and marble slabs. It was financed by Giuliano Argentario, a rich banker from Ravenna, and consecrated in 547 by Maximian, the city's first archbishop under Byzantine rule. The monument was given the blessing of Emperor Justinian, whose image stands

out beside the bishop, with guards and dignitaries—in front of his wife, Theodora, and her court—in a mosaic next to the altar.

Walking on through the old city center, where you can see the tomb of Dante Alighieri (the illustrious author of the *Divine Comedy* died in Ravenna in 1321 during his long exile from his beloved city of Florence), you come to another jewel, the **church of Sant'Apollinare Nuovo**. This was built by the king of the Ostrogoths, Theodoric, who occupied the city in 493, and boasts a stupendous cycle of mosaics on three strips in the central nave. The best-known scenes are that of the palace, with the court figures—who were covered by curtains when the church changed from the Aryan (the Goths) to the Catholic religion—and

The paleo-Christian monuments in Ravenna have preserved the most valuable inheritance of mosaics from the fifth and sixth centuries.

surrounded by symbols of the Evangelists, a magnificent Transfiguration, highlighting the abstract tendencies of the refined Byzantine art.

a bird's-eye view of Classe, Ravenna's port in that period.

A city tour cannot overlook two important monuments outside the city walls: Theodoric's mausoleum, to the northeast, and the **Basilica of Sant'Apollinare**, in Classe, 8 km from the center.

Theodoric's mausoleum, inspired by Roman models, is constructed on two floors and closed by a single block of stone. According to legend, the Ostrogoth king died there while taking shelter from a storm, being struck by lightning which passed through a cross-shaped hole in the roof.

The **Basilica of Sant'-Apollinare** was built with marble brought from Asia and consecrated by Maximian in 549. In the apse, above the figure of Sant'Apollinare with a flock of sheep, there is a cross studded with gems,

The city of mosaics

The ancient technique of mosaics involves the use of small tiles of stone, marble, and pate de verre. The smaller the tiles, the richer the image in terms of detail and coloring effects. In the period when

No less than eight of the city's monuments are part of the World Heritage, an extraordinary example of fusion of Western and Byzantine art.

the masterpieces that made Ravenna world famous were produced, the surfaces to be decorated were prepared with a layer of mortar and then of plaster, where they could sketch the preparatory drawings. Then the mosaic workers positioned the tiles, paying attention to the inclination, to get the best reflection of light.

In the church of San Nicolò, in the center of Ravenna, the Tamo exhibition area has been set up, which retraces the history of mosaics through themed displays, with the help of interactive and multimedia setups. The city also organizes **Ravenna Mosaics**, the first in-ternational festival of contemporary mosaics, and Mosaico di Notte (Mosaics by Night), an event during the summer months involving the opening of some of the more important monuments in the evenings, with free guided tours.

The piada romagnola

The real icon of gastronomy in this region is not the Sangiovese red wine, but a dish that it traditionally accompanies, a round flatbread cooked on a flat pan and filled with cured meats and cheese. The dish is called the piada, or piadina, and for the Italians, it's a symbol of the quick, tasty bite, which is often associated to happy memories of summers spent on the beaches of the Riviera. There are various ways of making the dough; some mix the flour with water, others use milk; some add lard, others don't; some use yeast and others use baking powder. There are also different options for the cooking pan, even though a clay pan is preferable to stoneware or metal pans, because it absorbs more humidity from the dough and leaves the bread drier.

In Ravenna, there is a real institution of the piadina. This is the **Ca' de Vèn** (Via Corrado Ricci 24, www.cadeven.it), literally the "house of wine," a typical trattoria/wine bar that specializes in this extraordinary example of popular cuisine. It is served with its classic extras and also in the way that is typical of the area—in Brisighella olive oil, an excellent extra-virgin oil produced from rare, top-quality olives that grow in the hills around Ravenna.

Franciacorta:
wine, a land that convey a dream

e land itself, the landscape, the ysical makeup of the growing area: all these have a richer story to tell than quick glance may reveal. At first, they naze, then, increasingly, they intrigue e visitor, exciting a whole series of notions and thoughts that infuse with sh meaning every new thing seen. anciacorta, lying on the banks of the go d'Iseo, just a few minutes from lan, is distinctive for this evocative ocess, recounting in this way the story its traditions, of its people, of a land rich in art, culture, and natural beauty. anciacorta wine is the flawless, thentic expression of this "universe," t simply a nonpareil sparkling wine t an elegant interweaving of past d present that will intrigue and gage anyone willing to savour its utter tinctiveness.

anciacorta was Italy's first bottle-fermented sparkling wine to granted, in 1995, DOCG enominazione di Origine Controllata Garantita) status, and in the same ar, recognition of the Franciacorta oduction Code, the world's most orous for this wine type. Long left hind is the term spumante: the bottle pel reads simply Franciacorta; the only her examples in Europe are Spain's va and France's Champagne. anciacorta is Franciacorta, oresenting a unique case in Italy: little more than 50 years, thanks to e collective passion and commitment its producers, Franciacorta has cended to become one of the most estigious ambassadors of Made in ly across the globe.

is a wine increasingly sought-after, t just for special occasions but for any

moment during the day, and for enjoying throughout the meal, since its range of styles makes it a great partner to almost anything, from traditional Italian dishes to the most exotic international cuisine.

Expo 2015 will offer a splendid opportunity to bring to the attention of the world this wine and its magnificent growing area, both with a priceless heritage that has never ceased to amaze visitors, with its marriage of a prestigious wine, Franciacorta, and the stupendous

beauty of the nature that produces it, Franciacorta.

For this important event that will attract to Milan millions of visitors from everywhere in the world, it is crucial to prepare ourselves, by learning "their language," trying to decipher, from examining their behaviour, their needs and the desires that bring them here among us; we must welcome them with the best resources we have, help them to achieve a unique experience that they will cherish as the ne plus ultra, no matter where else they go.

Certainly not a simple task but one where Franciacorta can make its own

contribution, offering uncommon opportunities plus the excitement of an area increasingly united in its determination to develop and protect this growing area and its products.

This is a land that is awaiting Expo 2015 as a precious opportunity to showcase its magnificence and to enchant those who love the good and the beautiful, be they aficionados of fine wine and dining, of nature, art and culture, or of sports, photography, or of the good life.

Franciacorta's is a quality that fears no rivals, oriented as it is to sustainability in full respect for its environment.

Feeding the planet, energy for life, the theme of the Universal Exposition, beautifully complements the theme of Franciacorta, Passions. United. For it is only through sharing and uniting together our passion for life, for beauty, and for our origins that we can find new paths and energies to offer to an always-evolving world. Franciacorta is already hard at work, and now awaits "the world" so that it can eloquently communicate its dream.

Franciacorta
Unione di Passioni

info@franciacorta.net - www.franciacorta.net

ART AND HISTORY NEXT TO THE BEACH

Right behind the coastal symbol of Italian summers lies an admirable, ancient city.

You get there by traveling 330 km to the southeast of Milan, along the A1 as far as Bologna, and then the A14 toward Ancona. Direct Frecciabianca (White Arrow) high-speed trains, departing from Central Station, get to Rimini in three hours.

Rimini is the most well-known resort on the Riviera of the Romagna region, has 145,000 inhabitants, and extends for about 15 km along the Adriatic coast, on the delta of the river Marecchia. It has long been a tourist center, owing its fortune especially to its well-developed beach resorts. The first bathing establishment—the idea of a physiologist who specialized in thalasso-therapy—opened in 1843 and combined leisure and therapy. Vacationers, including many foreigners, know they can find hospitality and amusements on these soft, sandy beaches. The evenings are lively, too, especially around the harbor and the promenade, but also in the heart of the old town, behind Vecchia Pescheria (fish market).

Families with children like Rimini because of its shallow

water and the leisure parks in the area, such as: Italia in Miniatura, a miniature model park with 272 scaled-down reproductions of the nation's major monuments; the Aquafan water park; the Delfinario dolphin park; the Parco Tematico dell'Aviazione (aviation museum), with 40 vintage air-

craft; and Fiabilandia (Fairy Tale Land), a whole park dedicated to two to three years olds.

Major historical sites make Rimini also a leading art destination. The first thing is to retrace the story of Ariminum, the ancient Roman colony, through its visible remains, such as the amphitheater, the bridge of Tiberius, and, especially, the imposing **Arco di Augusto** (Augustan Arch). The last mentioned is an elegant city gate, built at the end of the Via Flaminia, the Roman road that connected Rome and Rimini. The arch was consecrated in 27 BC by Emperor Augustus, who is shown riding a four-horse chariot in a bronze statue on the structure. A recent archaeological discovery was opened to the public in 2007, the **Surgeon's House**, which came to light right in old town. It is a third-century residence containing the most complete set of surgical instruments from the Roman world.

The city enjoyed a period of great splendor during the Renaissance, when the court of the Malatesta family flourished, one of the liveliest of the period and a hub of activity for artists who left some undeniable masterpieces. The most famous complex is the cathedral, known as the **Tempio Malatestiano** (Malatesta Temple), a masterpiece of the great architect Leon Battista Alberti. There are several things to see in the interior of the temple,

which was transformed into a Renaissance form on the orders of Sigismondo Pandolfo Malatesta, lord of the city from 1432 to 1468. Agostino di Duccio completed some sculpted reliefs; Piero della Francesca left a fresco, showing Sigismondo Pandolfo Malatesta praying; and there is also a crucifix by Giotto, who had frescoed the preexisting Franciscan church in the early 1300s.

In the middle of Rimini, the center can be seen of Sismondo Castle, a defensive structure with six turrets that Sigismondo had built by leveling a wide area of the city close to the more important medieval square. Today, the castle is often used for exhibitions.

A historical-cultural tour cannot overlook the **Museo della Città** (City Museum), in 1700s Gesuit college. Its rooms make it possible to retrace Rimini's past, from the archaeological section (including a fine Roman lapidary) to the art gallery, where works from the 1300s Rimini school stand out, together with some important Renaissance paintings.

On the streets of Amarcord

Although he never shot even a meter of film in his native city, Federico Fellini often recalled people and places of his beloved Rimini in his movies. The Italian director, who made the biggest mark on the history of the movie world, winning five Oscars, was born here in 1920 and spent his youth here until 1939, when he moved to Rome. In particu-

lar, in the movie *Amarcord*, produced in 1973 at the peak of his career, he relives his Riminese past: Piazza Cavour, Piazza Tre Martiri and the Fulgor Cinema, where, as a boy, Fellini earned his ticket by doing portraits of the stars of the movie on the program. The beach and its cabins appear in *Città delle Donne*, while the harbor and the *palata* (a jetty that stretches 200 meters into the sea and is perfect for romantic strolls or thoughtful moments, disturbed only by the sound of the waves) were the favorite meeting places for the boys in *I Vitelloni*, a movie that can be considered Fellini's farewell to his provincial and adolescent life.

The more nostalgic fans of Fellini can treat themselves to a night at the Grand Hotel, in the maestro's favorite suite, which is now named after him.

The triumph of fish soup

The fish dish most typical of this area is **brodetto** (light broth), a very rich soup, which derives from the dish they used to prepare on the fishing boats. Its strong, lingering flavor, due to the seasoning of black pepper, garlic, and wine, combined with the abundant use of tomato sauce, make this an exception to the cookbooks of the Emilia Romagna region and more like the dishes served in the neighboring areas of central–southern Italy. Various fish can be used, depending on availability in the market. The most commonly used are mackerel and red mullet, but the richer variations of the recipe also add a little cuttlefish, small turbot, and even mantis shrimps or crabs.

RIVIERA OF FLOWERS AND NOTES

The well-known resort hosts the Italian Song Festival every February.

Sanremo is located 266 km southwest of Milan, taking the A7, exiting onto the A26 for Genova–Ventimiglia and then the A10 toward Ventimiglia, and then exiting at Arma di Taggia, and finally taking the state road NSA306. Intercity trains departing from Central Station take less than four hours.

A town of about 56,000 inhabitants, near the border with France, Sanremo is located in a river blessed with a temperate climate throughout the year and is famous for floriculture. The town saw an important increase in buildings at the turn of 1900, when nearly 200 villas, 25 hotels, and the impressive casino were built in only a few years, all in an elegant Art Nouveau style, which has indelibly marked the face of the city. At the time, Sanremo was already an international tourist destination, having hosted crowned heads of state, such as Empress Maria Alexandrovna, in the past decades. It is to the Russian community, which flocked to Sanremo, thanks to the empress that we owe the Orthodox Church, built in 1913 in imitation of St. Basil's Cathedral in Moscow and dedicated to the Redeemer and St. Catherine, and still open for worship. The **Sanremo promenade**, fulcrum of the town's Art Nouveau zest, is dedicated to the wife of Tsar Alexander II.

A stroll along the promenade leads to the **casino,** built in 1905 and still the heart of the worldly life. At the time of its construction, the Riviera was the winter-spot getaway for many Russians, Germans, and English, these last enchanted by the elegant dwellings of the **Corso degli Inglesi** (English Avenue).

The two most prestigious villas are located on the Corso Felice Cavallotti: Villa Nobel, in Moorish style, which was inhabited between 1890 and 1896 by the Swedish scientist and, now a museum, and Villa Ormond, which excels for its park that is ornate with fountains, exotic plants, and a miniature Japanese garden.

To unveil the ancient visage of Sanremo, the visitor must delve inward where the medieval village, the **Pigna**, clings to the hills , compact within the walls, with towers and edifices made of stone, rich with carved portals. The hamlet is presided over by the Baroque sanctuary of Madonna della Costa, from where the visitor can take in a vast panorama. At the foot of the ancient hamlet is the 12th-century **cathedral of St. Siro**, restored to its original clean shapes after a major restoration of the early 20th century.

In summer, the city, which boasts two marinas, Porto Vecchio and Portosole, offers a wide variety of **beaches** and is a great starting point for sailboat excursions. Sailing past Capo Nero toward France offers the chance to take in the fabulous Balzi Rossi cliff faces.

Only a few miles in the hinterland of Sanremo lies **Bussana Vecchia,** a village de-

A resort with a great tradition, it was a destination for elite tourism at the start of the 1900s.

stroyed by an earthquake in 1887 and revived in the 1960s by an international community of artists who have occupied the ruins with laboratories and homes. Still heading inland, the visitor should head to **Dolceacqua** and its magnificent ruins of the Doria castle, the village of **Taggia** with its 16th-century palaces, and **Triora** with its all crisscrossing *caruggi* (alleyways), under vaults and arches carved into the rock, renowned for its 16th-century witch trials.

Heading along the coast offers endless itineraries: Ventimiglia lies west while Genoa lies opposite. Then there are the famous coastal resorts, such as **Alassio,** a beachgoer paradise, or **Albenga,** with its charming old town, which also boasts an early Christian baptistery.

The festival most loved by Italians

Since its first edition in 1951, the name of Sanremo is invariably associated with that of its *Italian Song* Festival. The show was first broadcast on radio and then took to television in 1955, immediately acquiring huge popularity. Protagonists of those early years were unforgettable singers, such as Nilla Pizzi, Claudio Villa, and Domenico Modugno, who in 1958 won the festival with a song destined to become the anthem of Italian music thoughout the world: *"Nel blue dipinto di blue,"* better known as *"Volare."* Since then, the best-loved artists on the national and international scene found in Sanremo include da Celentano (*Ragazzo della via Gluck*, 1966), Toto Cutugno (*L'Italiano*, 1983), Vasco Rossi (*Una vita spericolata*, 1983), and Zucchero Fornaciari (*Donne*, 1985).

The festival manages to stir a buzz at each edition for its presenters, dancers, international music celebrities, and, above all, Italian musicians: those already established that participate in the competition as well as new talents just taking to the scene. The festival brings a special spark of life to the town: The crowd anxiously awaits the singers in front of Teatro Ariston, while journalists and paparazzi invade the streets, premises, and hotels that host the stars of the festival.

Olive oil

Many regions of Italy produce excellent extra-virgin olive oil. Ligurian oil is particularly prized for its sweetness and is considered ideal for raw condiment dishes with a delicate taste. Comparable to other northern olive oils (that of Garda is just as famous), Ligurian extra-virgin olive oil is produced mainly in the hills between Sanremo and Imperia.

No one knows who brought the olive tree to these lands—perhaps the Romans, perhaps the Crusaders returning from the Holy Land—but what is certain is that the extensive use of the plant for the production of oil is the work of the Benedictine monasteries in the Middle Ages.

This also holds true for the diffusion of the Taggiasca olive, which is still considered the most valuable among varieties grown in western Liguria and one of the best in Italy. Small, dark, and slightly curled, it is delicious served in brine, but is also used for the production of the finest types of extra-virgin olive oil.

THE GRANDEUR
OF AN ANCIENT CAPITAL

It lies about 130 km west of Milan, taking the A4. Intercity trains departing from Milan's Central Station get to Turin in one hour.

The first capital of unified Italy is a noble, austere city, with distinguished buildings and an orderly urban layout.

Turin is the capital city of the wealthy Piedmont region, and has 900,000 inhabitants and a solid industrial tradition, especially in the automobile industry. It also plays a leading role in publishing. Several publishing houses started here, including Utet, the oldest in Italy, and the country's main publishing exhibition, the Salone del Libro (Book Fair), is held here every year. Another of its major exhibitions, the Salone del Gusto (Food and Drink Fair)—plus the presence of the largest outlet in Italy of the food chain Eataly—make it a reference point for Italian gastronomy. It gains an extra specialness from its imposing backdrop (the city lies at the foot of the Alps) and the presence of the river Po, which flows right through its center.

Any tour should start from **Piazza Castello** (Castle Square), with elegant porticos on three sides and a large palace, **Palazzo Madama** (named after Madama Cristina). In 1584, when the Savoy family, the reigning dynasty in Piedmont and the kings of Italy after 1861, reconstructed the square, there was already a castle there from the 1200s. Later again, in the 1700s, this underwent a major restyling at the hands of Filippo Juvarra and acquired a magnificent Baroque façade. The palace's rooms house the collections of the Museo di Arte Antica (Museum of Antique Art), with

masterpieces, such as *Ritratto d'uomo* (*Portrait of a Man*) by Antonello da Messina.

Next, visit the **Palazzo Reale** (Royal Palace), designed in the late 1500s and joined to the castle in the early 1600s by the Grand Gallery. It was the ruler's palace until 1865, when

the capital of Italy was moved to Florence. The rooms have a series of Baroque ceilings and lavish furnishings.

Back at the square, there are other major buildings to see, such as the Teatro Regio (Regio Theater), the **Armeria Reale** (Royal Armory), one of Europe's most important collections of arms, and the **Biblioteca Reale** (Royal Library), which holds Leonardo's *Autoritratto* (*Self-Portrait*), kept in the basement for reasons of preservation.

Behind the Palazzo Reale is the **cathedral**, dedicated to St. John the Baptist, the patron saint of Turin. It was built in the late 1400s, while the Cappella della Sindone (Chapel of the Holy Shroud), a highly original creation of Guarino Guarini, was designed in the 1660s to hold the precious relic.

The streets spread out from Piazza Castello and are partly pedestrianized. Via Roma leads into Piazza San Carlo, a large, elegant square lined by symmetrical buildings and boasts two of the city's principal cultural institutions: **Museo Egizio** (Egyptian Museum) and **Galleria Sabauda** (Savoys' Gallery). Museo Egizio is full of ancient sarcophagi, mummies, and papyruses, all priceless relics that make the museum second of its kind in the world, after the Cairo Museum. Apart from the artistic value of the exhibits, the museum is particularly renowned for its theatrical layouts. A visit to the Galleria Sabauda is also compelling, as it displays the works of Italian, Fleming, and Dutch masters.

Returning toward Piazza Castello, you can cut through the elegant iron-and-glass passageway of the Galleria Subalpina, with its fine Art Nouveau decorations, and come out in front of Palazzo Carignano, a large building that housed the first Parliament of unified Italy and today houses the Museo Nazionale del Risorgimento (National Museum of the Risorgimento).

From here, you can move on to the **Mole Antonelliana**, whose towering spire is the symbol of Turin. It dates from 1862 and was designed as a synagogue by Alessandro Antonelli, who it is named after. Today it houses the **Museum of Cinema**, where visitors are absorbed by the fascinating display created by the Swiss architect François Confino. A trip in the elevator, up to a height of 85 m, gives a wide view across the city rooftops as far as the snow-covered peaks of the alpine chain.

Thanks to the Winter Olympics, which it hosted in 2006, a lot of the city's treasures have been restored to their former splendor.

Walking toward the river Po, you come to Piazza Vittorio Veneto, a very large, porticoed, pedestrianized square, much loved by the Torinese. You can walk along the riverbank to **Valentino Park**, where there is a 1200s castle. The edifice was rebuilt in the 1600s, on the orders of Maria Cristina of France, along the lines of the castles of the French Loire area. Legend has it that the duchess met her lovers there and then threw them into a well.

In the park, there is also an attractive re-creation of a medieval village, erected for the Universal Exhibition of 1884 and used today for short-term exhibitions. Then, farther along the river, south of Valentino Park, there is the **Automobile Museum**. It holds a large number of vintage and old vehicles, including the first Fiat, built in 1899.

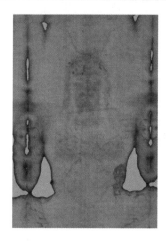

There are also excellent attractions outside Turin. A rack railway climbs up the **Superga hill**, where there is a monumental basilica. It's also possible to enjoy a trip to one of the Corona di Delizie (Crown of Delights) attractions. These are the out-of-town residences of the Savoy dynasty, all included on the Unesco World Heritage List. The most beautiful are the **palace of Venaria**, now restored to its former splendor, and the smaller, hunting **palace of Stupinigi**.

A sheet shrouded in mystery

Turin is the guardian of the **Holy Shroud**, one of the most revered relics of Christianity; but also for non-believers, one of the world's most analyzed and famous artifacts. It is an ancient linen sheet, over 4 m long and 1.10 m wide, bearing the impression of a double image of a martyred man. Blows from a whip, marks from a crown of thorns and from crucifixion are all visible. Legend has it, although not unanimously accepted, even by Catholics themselves, that this is the shroud, mentioned by the Evangelists, that was wrapped around the body of Jesus in his tomb.

The first documentaed evidence of the relic goes back to the 1300s, when the French knight Geoffroy de Charny deposited it in a church in his estate near Troyes, France. In the 1400s, the shroud started wandering around Europe, until it arrived at the court of the Savoys, who bought it in 1453 and placed it in the chapel of the castle of Chambéry, France, capital of their state at the time. A fire broke out there on Decenber 4, 1532, and the shroud was badly damaged. This damage is still partly visible, even though swift repairs were made. Then, in 1578, it was taken to Turin by Emanuele Filiberto, giving rise to a long history of stately showings, especially in the Baroque period, after the construction by Guarino Guarini of the Chapel of the Shroud inside the cathedral.

Since the 1990s, the relic has been subjected to extensive diagnostic examination by an international commission, appointed to develop the best means of protecting it, especially in the aftermath of a 1997 fire in the chapel. Since then, the shroud was repaired in 2002 and placed, spread out (not rolled up), inside a special cabinet protected by state-of-the-art technology. In the spring of 2010, the shroud was on display for 44 days, the first showing in the third millennium, which attracted an incredible influx of pilgrims to Turin—more than 2.5 million visitors, including Pope Benedict XVI, who used the occasion to define the relic "an icon of the mystery of Holy Saturday."

Eating Italian style

Eataly opened in 2007 in Lingotto, a district of Turin that was once highly industrial. It is inside a former warehouse that used to house the factory of the Carpano liqueur company.

This outlet offers the best Italian gastronomic specialties, with special attention paid to those from Piedmont. There are also bars for enjoying quick snacks or more complex dishes, or for tasting glasses of wines. This was the first premises of a chain that has now gone intercontinental, with renowned outlets in New York and Tokyo. Eataly in Turin includes a bookstore specializing in gastronomy and a center offering courses on dietary education and cooking lessons, sometimes with the participation of top chefs.

Eataly, Via Nizza 230
www.torino.eataly.it

What does Federturismo Confindustria do?

Federturismo Confindustria, the national travel and tourism Federation, represents the companies operating in the different areas of the tourism industry. It belongs to the Confindustria system and currently includes 20 sector associations, 11 company members (directly associated) and several local associations.
Established in 1993 on the initiative of 18 founding members, Federturismo Confindustria was recognized as an Industry Federation by Confindustria in 1995. The President of Federturismo Confindustria is a member of the Confindustria Council.
— The sector associations represent all areas of tourism business. Members include all the major players in the market and in some case 100% of the companies in the business area (hotels, villages and resorts, tour operator and travel agents, airlines, thermal resorts, convention centers, transportation and car rentals, sailing, marinas, beach resorts, amusement and theme parks, museums and museum services, ski lift operators, real estate agents, hotel laundry services, entertainment).
— Federturismo Confindustria officially represents the tourism industry in labour relations.
— The national labor contract for the member companies was renewed in July 2010.
— A Federturismo office in Bruxelles handles relations with the European Union and with the representatives of the tourism industry at the European level.

Represents tourism industry interests in economic policy and labour relations

Provides information regarding tourism policy and legislation

Represents members within and outside the Confindustria system

Promotes entrepreneurial values and sustainable tourism

Promotes training opportunities to further business culture and quality

Provides information and communication about initiatives and activities of interest to members

Develops and promotes relations with similar organizations in other countries and provides assistance to members participating in international events

Conducts research, analysis and debates about tourism supply and demand, and tourism legislation at national and European levels.

Federturismo Confindustria
Viale Pasteur, 10 - 00144 Roma
Tel. +39 06 5903351 Fax +39 06 5910390
segreteria@federturismo.it www.federturismo.it

IN THE HEART OF THE ALPS

The Milanese love this area so much, they have studded its villages with expensive holiday homes and go there for the exceptional facilities it offers for skiing enthusiasts.

Morbegno, at the mouth of the valley, lies 113 km north of Milan, along the SS36 divided highway to Nuova Valsassina, then the SS38 from Colico to Stelvio. By train, you get to Morbegno in one hour and 40 minutes departing from Central Station.

Valtellina, in the Italian province of Sondrio, is an important connecting route between northern and southern Europe. It has been carved out by the river Adda, from the Retiche Mountains, to its north, and the Orobie, to its south, and stretches for 200 km between Lombardy and the Swiss Canton of Grigioni on the Italian–Swiss border. From the gently sloping lower valley, the ground rises to become majestic mountain landscapes, framed by glaciers and high peaks, topped off by Mt. Bernina, 4,021 m high.

Coming from Colico, at the northern end of Lake Como, and entering the alpine valley, the first center you come to on the broad base of the valley is **Morbegno**, a small town that flourished over the centuries thanks to trading between the leagues of the local Grigioni and the republic of Venice. People crossed

by the nearby San Marco Pass, using the Via Priula, the "salt road," to avoid paying duties to the duchy of Milan.

From here, it doesn't take long to get to **Sondrio** (about 25,000 inhabitants), the largest and most economically

important town in the Valtellina area. It is surrounded by terraced hillside vineyards, which provide a remarkable example of transforming the territory by rural engineering. The heart of the town is Piazza Garibaldi, which is especially lively on market day on Saturdays. It is worth taking a look at the ancient *Collegiate Church of Saints Gervasius and Protasius,* founded in the 12th century and rebuilt in the 18th century, or the fine collections in the Valtellina Museum of History and Art. North of Sondrio you enter the valley of **Valmalenco**, known to climbers because of two fearsome faces called the Disgrazia and the Bernina, but appreciated by walkers because of its net-

work of high-altitude trails and cozy mountain shelters.

Around Sondrio, there are picturesque little villages, including **Chiuro**, the main center for the grape harvest, which is enhanced by elegant country houses, such as the Palazzo Quadrio–Pontaschelli, a family mansion from the 1700s. Another village, **Ponte in Valtellina**, is also worth a visit to see the Parish Church of St. Maurice, with its Renaissance treasures inside. These include the altarpiece, which was carved and gilded by Giacomo del Maino, an important sculptor in wood in the 1500s and the presbytery, renovated in 1498 by Tommaso and Jacopo Rodari. There is also a scenic road that climbs a few kilometers up the hill to **Teglio**, a resort where you can visit the Palazzo Besta, an ancient castle, decorated with frescoes and enhanced by 16th-century furnishings.

The next stop is **Tirano**, which has always been a crossroads for people and cultures, since it stands at the mouth of the Swiss valley of Poschiavo, leading over the Bernina Pass to Engadina, Switzerland. Tirano boasts an important Santuario (Sanctuary), on the spot where the Virgin Mary appeared in 1504. It is also the terminal station of the Trenino Rosso (Little Red Train) of Mt. Bernina. This railroad is on the Unesco World Heritage List and connects Tirano to St. Moritz, Switzerland, by the world's most beautiful rail route. Not far away, near **Grosio**, is the Parco delle Incisioni Rupestri, a park where you can see prehistoric rock carvings left by the first inhabitants of the valley.

By now, you are in the area of the Upper Valtellina, one of the most famous tourist areas in the Alps. Here, you have a wide range of resorts: **Livigno**, **Bormio**, **Santa Caterina Valfurva**, **Valdidentro**, **Aprica**, and **Madesimo**—all offering incomparable ski slopes, hospitality areas, and state-of-the-art ski lifts—that also host major sporting event. There is plenty to do in the summer, too: mountain bike trails, trekking trails, and relaxing thermal baths (in Bormio), as well as shopping in Livigno.

The national park of Stelvio

This large park was established as early as 1935 and covers a vast area, partly in Lombardy and partly in Trentino–Alto Adige, featuring mountain grasslands, fast flowing rivers, and majestic peaks. In the north, it borders with the Swiss national park, and in the south, with the regional park of Adamello. To see the wonderful range of

bird and animal species (it is home to deer, chamois, ibex, squirrels, and golden eagles) you have to take a trip into the parka. The botanical side can be appreciated just by staying in Bormio and visiting the Rezia Botanical Garden. Also worth seeing is the Centro di Documentazione Aree Protette, in Sondrio, an information center with audio visual displays of the world's parks, using material collected each year during the Sondrio Festival, an international festival of documentaries on natural parks.

**From the hillsides
to the table**

The wealth of cultural traditions in the Valtellina area is well reflected in the wide range of local wine and food products, as illustrated in the six gastronomy tours in the guides Strada del Vino (Wine Road) and Sapori di Valtellina (Flavors of Valtellina).

Bresaola, salted and matured beef sliced and eaten raw, is the typical product of the valley. The name of this cured meat, which is nutritious and low in fat, probably comes from the name of the braziers used to heat the rooms where

Valtellina gastronomy is among the best in the Alps, thanks to its excellent products, like Bresaola, and its superb wines.

the meat is matured, or possibly from the word "*brisa*," which means "salted." The bresaola from Valtellina is guaranteed by strict standards, checking the choice of meat (the tip of the haunch is best, but rump or similar cuts may be used) and each stage of production, to enable the granting of the PGI (Protected Geographical Indication) brand. The Bresaola Festival, held in Chiuro every July, is a good occasion to get to know this product, which we recommend tasting on its own, or maybe accompanied just by a slice of good rye bread.

The trademark Valtellina dish is **pizzocheri**, tagliatelle made with buckwheat and seasoned with plenty of butter, cabbage, potatoes, and local cheese, like Casera or Bitto. In Teglio, they have set up an academy to safeguard this excellent example of plain cooking, and every year, from July through September, they organize two delicious events; the Pizzoccheri Festival and the Golden Pizzocchero.

This dish absolutely must be eaten with a glass of one of the great local **red wines**, mostly made from Nebbiolo grapes. Top of the scale is the Sforzato (or *Sfursàt* in the local dialect), obtained from grapes left to dry on mats, inside well-aired attics, and lofts.

UNIQUE IN THE WORLD

It grew as a miracle on the lagoon and, as if shrouded in a dreamy atmosphere, it has kept intact its highly original urban structure, where you can only get around on foot or afloat.

Venice lies about 280 km east of Milan and you get there on the A4. Frecciabianca (White Arrow) trains, with frequent departures from Central Station, get there in two hours and 35 minutes.

Peggy Guggenheim, a key figure in art in the 1900s, who introduced emerging American talent to Europe at the first Venice Biennale in 1948 and bought a building in Venice to transfer part of her extensive art collection, had this to say about the charm of the city: "Living in Venice, or just visiting it, means falling in love and in your heart there remains no room for anything else."

Venice was pulled out of the water and built up on more than 100 little islands, linked by more than 400 bridges, sections of canals, and canals. It is now the **capital of Veneto**, one of the wealthiest regions of Italy. The heart of the city (with less than 60,000 inhabitants) seems to follow its own time in the middle of the lagoon, unaware of the frenetic rhythms of dry land. Founded in the sixth century on marshlands, by Venetians from inland seeking protection from the Lombard invasions, it established itself over the centuries as a strategic center on the Adriatic. As a glorious **maritime republic**, self-proclaimed *Serenissima* (Most Serene Republic), it acted as a bridge between east and west, especially after the fourth crusade, when it played a decisive role in the conquest of Constantinople. It enjoyed a period of splendor between the 1300s and 1500s, when it became ever more powerful, thanks to trade and shipping. In this period, it enriched itself with splendid civil and religious buildings and saw its school of painting grow to be famous all over the world due to its incredible chromatic values and masters, such as Giovanni and Gentile Bellini, Giorgione, Titian, Veronese, and Tintoretto.

To savor the beauty of Venice, you could simply wander around and lose yourself in the streets. It is like an open-air museum, pervaded by a suspended atmosphere. An experience that is no less unique is to take a ride on one of the water buses (called "*vaporetti*," meaning "little steamers") on the **Grand Canal**, Venice's main street. Drawing a reversed *S*, the canal cuts the city into two halves, connected by four bridges, the most famous of which is the Rialto, which crosses the canal at its narrowest point.

The city is a prestigious university campus and holds two major cultural events: **the Biennale**, one of the main international exhibitions of contemporary art, and **the Venice International Film Festival**. Some centuries-old events also let you relive the old glories of the Most Serene Republic: Carnival, for instance; or the Regata Storica (Historic Boat Race), preceded by

(Golden Pall) altarpiece. The magnificent building we see today, gleaming with marble, based on the design of a Greek cross and with five Asian-looking domes, was rebuilt in the Romanesque period, after a fire. Over the course of time, it has been embellished by an incomparable mosaic cycle, around 8,000 sq. m, completed mostly between the sixth and 13th centuries, interwoven into a golden background, with the color of gold symbolizing the light emanating from the divinity. On the interior, there are cycles depicting the stories of the New Testaments, but also events from the life of Virgin Mary, St. Mark, and other saints particularly revered in the lagoon, such as St. John the Evangelist, St. John the Baptist, and St. Isidore. The mosaics from the 1200s in the atrium, some of the richest in anecdotal details, are dedicated to the Old Testaments. Another place worth visiting is the Museo di San Marco, which holds several treasures. The splendid basilica, which has been the cathedral only since the 1800s, previously functioned as the Doge's chapel and was closely linked to the

a spectacular procession of boats from the 1500s, led by the Bucintoro, the Bucentaur, or state galley, of the Doge; the Sensa (the name refers to the Ascension of Christ, the day of the celebration), a splendid celebration of the sea; or the Redentore (Saviour), on the third Sunday every July, the main religious celebration.

Piazza San Marco, closed into a horseshoe shape by the elegant buildings of the Procuratie (Procuracies), is one of the most splendid open-air sitting rooms in the world, especially early in the morning or in the evening. You can stop by one of its sophisticated historic cafès, such as Florian, pop into the Museo Correr to see its collection of paintings, or admire the Renaissance clock tower, with statues of Moors who strike the bell every hour. It is worthwhile to go up **St. Mark's Campanile**—from a height of 98.6 m, you have a fantastic view over the piazza and the lagoon. Built in the 12th century and renovated in the 1500s, it collapsed unexpectedly in 1902 and was then rapidly rebuilt, in about ten years, and an elevator was installed to take visitors up to the viewing platform.

The queen of the square is **St. Mark's Basilica**, founded in 829 to house the relics of St. Mark the Evangelist, purloined from Alexandria, Egypt, and still kept inside the high altar, near the priceless Pala D'Oro

nearby **Palazzo Ducale**, the headquarters of the Doge, or chief magistrate of the republic. The palace is a masterpiece of Gothic civil architecture, all a lacework of pink-and-white marble. It can be visited internally, either by following the traditional route, which passes through magnificent state rooms, or by passing along the "secret paths," visiting the *stanza della tortura* (torture room), the *piombi* (leads, or prison cells, under the roof, for less serious crimes), or the terrible cells of the *pozzi* (pits, the cells for more serious crimes). Evidence of these long-past matters of prison regimes is preserved also in the **Bridge of Sighs**, where the moans of the condemned were once to be heard. This bridge passes over to the bank called the "bank of the Schiavoni."

After the visit to the heart of the city, there is a plethora of choices. One of the most popular paths leads to the Rialto Bridge, by way of little shops of the **Mercerie**, the main shopping area. Those who prefer a sea view to that of the streets can stay a bit longer in the little square next to St. Mark's, where two 1200s **columns** stand out, one topped with the statue of St. Theodore and the other with the winged lion of St. Mark, symbol of the Most Serene Republic. Wonder at the St. George's Island and the Giudecca canal, before strolling along the Schiavoni bank to the *sestiere* (district) of Castello, where there are Biennale gardens and the **Arsenal**, with its Museo Navale (Naval Museum).

On foot or by water bus, from St. Mark's, stop at the **Gallerie dell'Accademia**, the city's best-known art gallery, which delineates the whole development of Venetian painting, from the 1300s through the 1700s, with a series of masterpieces, such as several altarpieces by Giovanni Bellini, *The Tempest* by Giorgione, *The Feast in the House of Levi* by Veronese, and *The Miracle of Saint Mark* by Tintoretto. From here, you can move on to the Punta della Dogana art center (former customs house) and stroll through one of the most romantic parts of the city, before coming to the **Peggy Guggenheim collection** (one of the most prestigious international collection of contemporary art) and the Basilica della Salute (St. Mary of Health). The basilica is a masterpiece of Venetian Baroque architecture and was designed in the 1600s by Baldassarre Longhena, who imagined it as a "crown for the Virgin Mary." Inside the church, there is a revered icon of the Virgin Mary.

If visiting Venice in the warmer months, do not miss the chance to take a boat trip on the lagoon to discover some of the charming islands. The tour takes in, especially, **Torcello**, where the roots of Venetian culture can be traced in the ancient buildings, but also colorful Burano, well-known for its lace work, and Murano, where all the furnaces needed for glass working were transferred in the 1200s, to reduce the risk of fires in the city, and which is still the home of the master glass blowers.

In the ten days before Lent, the city enjoys the magic of Carnival. It is one of the most famous in the world, because of its long history and its procession of splendid costumes.

Carnival

Venetian documents talk about the festival of Carnival as early as the end of the 11th century, but it was in 1296 that it acquired the honor of a public festival, much awaited because in the days that pass—from the opening of the dancing until midnight on Mardi Gras—anything can happen. In the workshops of the *mascherari*, the mask makers, Carnival never finishes, though, because these skilled craftsmen make costumes all year long. They make masks in painted gesso, with a wide variety of faces, or even the more simple kind, such as the *larva*, a plain white mask worn by men together with a black cloak, the *tabarro*, and a three-cornered hat, or, for women, the **Moretta**, an oval mask in black velvet. The peak of splendor for Carnival was the 1700s, the century of Giacomo Casanova. With Venice occupied first by the Austrians, then the French, by the start of the 1800s, they no longer celebrated Carnival and it was not until 1979 that it was reintroduced. In recent years, it seems to have regained some of its old glory, now enriched with cultural events, such as exhibitions, theater shows, and concerts.

Amid the bàcari in the city of shadows

Anyone looking for a livelier Venice than the one you encounter along the dazzling museum city trails, should drop into some of its traditional inns, called *bàcari*, a strange name that possibly comes from the name of Bacchus, the pagan god of wine.

There are still plenty of these "temples of Bacchus" tucked away in the narrow streets and alleys, which still preserve the color and genuineness they once had. They offer simple snacks (but sometimes anchovies, shellfish, and seafood too) to be eaten only standing at the bar, washed down with a glass of wine called *ombra* (shadow). Even today, in and around Venice, this strange description is commonly used. It goes back a long time, to when the kiosks of St. Mark's Square offered protection from the sun, to those clients who would stop to take a drink. Another version, although quite similar, has that the term comes from the fact that the street sellers of wine in the square moved around the Campanile to stay in the shade and keep their products cool.

BETWEEN ITALY AND EUROPE

City of Art, Verona has always been the "gateway of Italy" from the German world.

Verona is located about 170 km east of Milan on the A4 (toward Venice). Fast trains, departing frequently from Central Station, reach the location is just an hour and 20 minutes.

Populated by about 270,000 inhabitants, and the capital of one of the most productive provinces of Italy, Verona is known throughout the world not only for the wealth of its cityscape, included in the Unesco World Heritage List, but also for its lavish operas held in the Roman arena. Of course, Verona is also the city of Romeo and Juliet.

A visit to the old town must start from Piazza Bra', site of the **Roman arena**, a spectacular legacy of ancient Rome and a city icon. With its grand elliptical construction (140 x 110 m) and the three tiers of concentric seats, it is one of the best preserved and third

largest amphitheaters of antiquity. Built in the first century to house gladiator fights, it then became the scene of competitions and performances of all kinds—tournaments, games, circuses, bullfights—until its rise to opera temple.

Walking down Via Roma leads to **Castelvecchio**, an imposing mansion built between 1354 and 1356 as a residence and fortress by Cangrande II della Scala, member of the powerful family that ruled the city for 125 years. The castle was used as a residence throughout the 14th century, even when the Carrara (lords of Padua) and Visconti (lords of Milan) struggled for dominion of the city, while the Venetians— who conquered the city in 1404— made military use of it, establishing the Accademia Militare della Serenissima (Military Academy of Venice) there in the 18th century. Barracks during the Napoleonic era, the building radically mutated in the 20th century and took on the role of main city

museum. The "historic" layout was designed by famous architect Carlo Scarpa in 1958 and still manages to exhaust the importance of the masterpieces here, safeguarded in all their purity.

The Ponte Scaligero (Scaliger Bridge) stretches out from the castle and over the Adige River. This work of military engineering has three battlement arches and once allowed for a hasty and secure retreat in times of assault.

After visiting Castelvecchio, you can work your way toward the two central piazzas: **Piazza delle Erbe**, which is located on the site that housed the forum during ancient Roman times and is now surrounded by buildings that span the many historical ages, such as the Casa dei Mercanti (Merchant's Dwelling); **and Piazza dei Signori**, with its buildings that herald the ancient powers of the city: those of the municipality and Region from the 12th century, that of the Capitanio from the 14th century, the ancient palace of the Scaliger family that now serves as the prefecture and the 14th-century Loggia del Consiglio.

A brisk walk from this spot leads to one of the city's most

The city's treasures range from the remains of the Roman past to testimonials of Scaliger Gothic dominion Scalas.

suggestive spots: the Square of the Scaliger family tombs. It is a monumental complex in the shape of a baldachin, and temples capped with stone portraits of the ancient rulers of the city, which are considered a peak in 14th-century Italian sculpture (some of the original statues are preserved at the museum).

An itinerary that focuses on the monuments of the city cannot overlook some of the more significant cathedrals: the Romanesque cathedral, with its solemn porch façade, decorated by Maestro Nicolò; the Gothic cathedrals of San Fermo and Sant'Anastasia, both richly adorned with the frescoes of Pisanello, refined painter of the 15th century; and Santa Maria in Organo, with its Renaissance marble façade.

The cathedral of **San Zeno Maggiore**, a jewel of the Romanesque Padano Plains is worth a visit, with its wooden doors of 24 superb bronze panels from the 12th century

that capture tales of St. Michael and St. Zeno (first bishop of the city) and whose interiors preserve an important Altarpiece (1457–1459) from the work of Andrea Mantegna, key patron of northern Italian Renaissance.

The always rich season of the Arena goes from June to September. Calendar of events on www.arena.it

The more romantic spirits can't miss **Juliet's balcony**, heroine of Shakespeare's timeless drama, which faces Via Cappello from its medieval tower abode. The entrance hall, flanked by two panels that daily collect countless writings and love notes, leads to the courtyard of the house where the bronze statue of the unfortunate lover stands.

Opera under the stars

The imperial amphitheater, better known as **Arena di Verona**, is open every day, all year round, and has hosted a lavish opera season since 1913, which comprises about fifty evenings from June to September dedicated not only to opera but also to other musical genres. Up to 20,000 spectators can attend these shows, attracted by the picturesque setting and spectacular event designs. In particular, this unique, scenic space lends itself to grand melodramas of superb choral musicality, such as the famous *Aida* and *Nabucco* by Maestro Giuseppe Verdi, as well as *La Gioconda* by Amilcare Ponchielli.

Amarone

Unexpected kin. The genesis of one of Italy's most appreciated wines is rather curious. We are talking about Amarone, a superfine red delight produced in Verona. Ancient tradition heralds this land as the cradle for fine ruby-red wine of medium intensity, a melange of three vineyards: rondinella, molinara, and corvina grapes. It's also called Valpolicella, a name that dates back to Roman times: *vallis polis cellae,* which in Latin means the "valley of many cellars." It sits only a few months in barrels, and its own sweetness is the most appreciated feature. It was not considered a wine suitable for aging until one day, a winemaker forgot about a few bottles in the cellar for several years. This is how the amiable and delicate Valpolicella magically mutated into that wonderful dry nectar (*amaròn*) that is rich and well structured.

Amarone is used in the preparation of rice and masterfully accompanies cheval platters, typical of the local cuisine, as well as aged cheeses produced in the foothills of the Venetian territory.

cagliari,
make it yours

liari offers everything that you are looking for.

looking the magnificent Golfo degli Angeli (Bay of Angels), Cagliari is
gateway to the whole of Sardinia. Enjoy this great city and experience
rue Italian lifestyle for yourself. Here, white limestone buildings rise
of the sea and reflect the light from across the bay, while its hundreds
arrow streets are home to Mediterranean rhythms, Sardinian flavours
exciting modern art. In Cagliari, contemporary style lives in harmony
thousands of years of history.

UNDER THE INFLUENCE OF PALLADIO

At the foot of the Berici hills, Vicenza is rich and lively, enriched by the works of one of the greatest geniuses of Italian architecture.

Vicenza lies about 210 km east of Milan on the A4. Frequent fast trains from Milan's Central Station reach Vicenza in less than two hours.

A bustling provincial capital of about 115,000 inhabitants, and an important industrial center renowned for textiles, agriculture, and jewelry—and at the heart of VicenzaOro, one of the world's leading trade fairs in this field—Vicenza is a city that has preserved a harmonious and tight-knit old town within its original city walls. Beyond its ancient confines, stately homes and gardens stand in splendor as a celebration of the elite families of the republic of Venice, which reigned unrivaled from the start of the 1400s until 1797.

An artistic tour meanders amid the most important buildings erected by the celebrated architect Pietro della Gondola (Padova, 1508–Vicenza, 1580), known as Palladio, who molded the cityscape with designs inspired by a classical ideal of majestic balance. Villa La Ro-

A large part of the old town center was included in the Unesco World Heritage List in 1994.

tonda, Teatro Olimpico, and the Palladian Basilica are just a few of the architectural sites (palaces in the old town center as well as stately homes on the outskirts, all examples of the work of this architect) included in Unesco's list of World Heritage Sites since 1994.

The heart of this city is the **Piazza dei Signori**, overlooked by its 82-m-high, 12th-century clock tower, the Torre di Piazza, which, in the 1300s, boasted the first clockwork clock in public use. The main attraction in this central urban area is the **Palladian Basilica**. This is an imposing building designed for civic use (not religious, as the name tends to suggest), started in the 1400s and completed in 1546 by the young Palladio, who was undertaking his first public appointment. Today it is the municipal headquarters. The brilliant architect maintained

the preexisting Gothic layout, but enclosed it within a double loggia, where arches and short architraves alternate. The classical white-stone exterior is contrasted by the green copper sheeting used on the roof vaulting.

The next stop that is not to be missed on the Palladian tour is the **Teatro Olimpico**, which is reached by walking along Corso Andrea Palladio, the main artery of the city. This theater is still an active venue and was erected in wood and plaster between 1580 and 1583, as commissioned by the Olympic Academy, a secret meeting of ambassadors, artists, and cardinals who wanted suitable premises for classical recitals and other cultural events. Inspiration for the project came from the great Roman theaters, but it was completed by Vicenzo Scamozzi, one of the most capable pupils of Palladio, who takes credit for its lavish scenic area.

Next to Teatro Olimpico stands yet another famous Palladian building, the Palazzo Chiericati, which currently houses the Civic Art Gallery and contains important works by Van Dyck, Tiepolo, and Veronese.

A tour of the city is much more than just an outdoor museum of classical architecture and should not fail to include the **church of Santa Corona**. This 13th-century

Vicenza is the Italian city with the largest number of historic buildings in relationship to its population. Its surroundings are no less valuable, where the admirable architecture stands in a spectacular frame of alpine foothills.

brick building hosts an invaluable religious relic—a piece of Christ's crown of thorns—and masterpieces from the Venetian Renaissance, including the *Baptism of Christ* by Giovanni Bellini.

It's also worth stopping at the **basilica di Monte Berico**, a Baroque sanctuary erected on the spot at the top of a hill where Virgin Mary has twice appeared. The 1,500 m of processional colonnade lead up to the basilica, from where there is a panoramic view of the city, to be enjoyed by looking out from the courtyard, or Piazzale della Vittoria.

From Vicenza to the White House

"There's something divine in his designs," is what Goethe wrote about Andrea Palladio, who gave rise to a unique style that was destined to last over the centuries. His inventions—which were inspired by antiquity and yet, at the same time, highly functional—today still present a landmark as an architectural model. Perhaps not everyone knows that the White House, in Washington, DC, was built in

The scaenae frons of Teatro Olimpico, one of Andrea Palladio's masterpieces, is adorned with 95 statues.

a Palladian style, to achieve an effect of majestic harmony.

The stately home was Palladio's favorite type of building: he designed a very rich repertory of these for the families of the Venetian aristocracy. The best known is the Villa Almerigo Capra, the **Rotonda**, in the city suburbs: a building with a cu-

Baccalà alla Vicentina

The best-known recipe from the city of Palladio is a delicate cream made of cod, a fish that comes from the colder seas and whose presence on Venetian tables reminds us today of the strong trading links the Venetian republic enjoyed in the past with the whole world. Originally, cod was brought to Italy only after being freshly air dried on the shores. Caught in the North Sea, it came from the cities of the Hanseatic League, particularly Bergen, which is considered the capital of stockfish ("stick fish"). Later on, a cheaper variant became

available: baccalà, which was the same fish but that was preserved by salting.

The recipe, named after the city of Vicenza, is prepared with stockfish, not baccalà. The fish has to be beaten, left to soak for a long time, then boiled and boned. After all that, it is heated and sautèed with onions, anchovies, and parsley. Next it has to be sprinkled with grated Parmesan and covered with milk and olive oil. This produces a very soft cream, which is served with fresh or toasted polenta, which, should in any case, be white, following the tradition of this area of northern Italy.

bic structure, a domed roof, and opened by pronaos on every side; reminiscent of an antique temple. Another residence not to be missed is **Villa Barbaro** in **Maser**, where the bond between the Palladian architecture and the paintings of Veronese (Renaissance Old Master) bring about a genuinely unique overall result.

CITY1TAP, THE CITY IN YOUR HAND

ty1Tap is the app for mobile devices
leased by Corriere della Sera and Vivi
ilano that offers news and informa-
on on Milan in an innovative "all in one"
odel to enjoy the city and keep your
allet happy.

ee for Android and iPhone, this app lets
u live Milan in all its aspects, offering a
riety of opportunities selected thanks
the precious know-how of the ViviMi-
no team of editors.

ty1Tap also offers a customized ser-
ce, acting as a personal assistant in
lation to user profiles and top informa-
on searches.

regard to transportation, the app of-
rs the detailed Milan transport ser-
ces (ATM) travel planner that includes
al-time stops, itineraries, and sched-
les of public transport and bike sharing.

Also, you can book a cab using the Taxi-
blu app.

Make restaurant reservations (with
app partner Restopolis) using City1Tap,
or buy event tickets (with Ticketone),
take advantage of all sorts of coupons
(with Yoodeal) and find a cinema with
the chance to take in movie trailers.

The deals map has a slew of offers with
discounts in every area: beauty care,
restaurants, gyms, supermarkets,
(the latter with the partner Risparmio
Super), etc. Receive notices on flash
deals that last only a few hours and offer great savings.

Content is presented through appeal-
ing graphical design largely based on
photographic content that is integrated with Facebook, Twitter and G+.

ITY1TAP IN ROUNDUP

orriere.it Milano news
ublic transport schedules in real-time
axi service that can be booked via app
ike sharing, with bike stations and availability
eviews by Vivimilano.it on the best venues,
staurants, city events, also for children
eals around the city, from coupons to supermarket discounts

SHOPPING AND MORE

DOWN THE WATERWAYS

Discovering Garda, Verbano, and Lario among ancient villas, lush gardens, and tucked-away corners—a day of pure relaxation.

The best way to enjoy the beauty of the mountain landscapes that surround the three major Italian lakes is to leave the car behind and embark on one of the many boats that navigate these waters. **Gestione Navigazione Laghi** (www.navigazionelaghi.it) offers cruises to suit all tastes and of varying duration, even with stops at major tourist attractions, to blend pure and simple entertainment with moments of cultural enrichment.

Tourists can choose the route best suited for them among the many offered by the company and maybe delight in an onboard lunch. The more independent travelers can plan their town itineraries, taking advantage of the free circulation ticket, which allows unlimited travel on ferries and boats throughout an entire day.

What better location for a party with friends or a business convention than a boat (a historic steamer or a modern motor vessel), chartered for the occasion? Make it a special day- or a nighttime cruise.

In the company of sailing and windsurfing on the largest lake in Italy

In addition to the regular boat service, during the summer, Gestione Navigazione Laghi gives you the opportunity to travel the waters of **Lake Garda**, admiring the coasts from a privileged point of view, where you alternate between their extremely varied landscapes and impressive beaches. Take in the gentle coves or inlets in the southern part and craggy peaks to the north, where strong winds blow. The tours provide the opportunity to walk along the Sirmione peninsula, which, as we recall from ancient history, were really the famous caves of Catullo. Stop off at sites of great historical value, such as Gardone, where you can

visit the Vittoriale, home of the poet D'Annunzio, or the medieval town of Salò, reaching the high grounds of the lake in Riva del Garda.

Waves and valleys of Verbano

A dense network of connections links the main towns along the Verbano, better known as **Lake Maggiore**, whether they are on the shore of Piedmont and Lombardy or on Swiss soil. For those arriving by train from Milan, Laveno may serve as a good starting

There is no better way to discover the treasures that the Prealps offer than to sail the waters upon gentle summer breezes.

point, reached either by trains run by Ferrovie Nord Milan or Trenitalia. Otherwise, head toward Arona and Stresa, connected with Milan by Trenitalia.

A visit to the Borromean Islands (located in front of Stresa) is a must. Boats also touch less-known attractions that are of great interest, such as the sanctuary of Santa Caterina del Sasso or la Rocca do Angera.

Particularly striking is a trip on **Lake Maggiore Express**, a circular route that combines a boat and a train ride. The tour begins by embarking from one of the main towns of the lake and, once Locarno has been reached by boat, the journey continues with the panoramic Centovalli and Val Vigezzo train. Trenitalia rails from Domodossola get travelers back to the original place of departure.

Sailing on the lake, among historical villas and gardens

Navigation on **Lake Como** is hustle-free for visitors coming from Milan. The landing point for ferries and tourist boats is right in front of the Como Lago station of the Trenord line, which touches many quaint towns, rich in historical testimonials as to where luxurious villas reside, such as Villa d'Este in Cernobbio, Villa Monastero in Varenna, Villa Serbelloni in Menaggio , Villa Carlotta in Tremezzo, and Villa Balbianello in Lenno, to mention a few of the most renown.

During the weekend, Navigazione Laghi offers **cruises throughout the day,** giving you the chance to make a stop at Piona to visit the ancient abbey of the 12th century—an

Boats, ferries, and steamers— they have gone to every length to offer tourists minicruises that fall short of nothing in comparison to similar seafaring experiences.

architectural gem and privileged vantage point on the northern part of the lake. Of course, opportunities to hike along the best-known central territory of the Lario can also be taken, with a stop at the 18th-century Villa Carlotta to visit important works of art in the museum and for the extraordinary botanical garden, famous for its azalea blooms and rhododendrons. From here, the tour continues to Menaggio, brushing the towns of Bellagio and Varenna.

SHOPPING AND MORE

SHOPPING TOWN PARADISE

At about only one hour by car from Milan, these locations attract a crowd of both Italian and foreign shoppers.

Foxtown

A large mall offering fashion wear and accessories, with 250 different brand names, mostly in the medium- to high- quality range, at affordable prices. Eating facilities include a wooden chalet selling Swiss food. Next door, there is a casino.

Although it's in Switzerland, it's the nearest outlet to Milan, only 50 km on the A9/A2 highway heading north. Daily intercity bus connections leave at 12:00 p.m. from Orio al Serio airport and pass through Milan (Piazza Cairoli). This service is operated by Zani Travel Agency (tickets can be bought from Foro Buonaparte 76).

Fidenza Village

Top-fashion and casual clothing, accessories, and gastronomy, all at low cost. It's more ergonomically laid out than other malls, with all the shops facing on to one walkway. It includes a very popular restaurant.

It's 107 km southeast of Milan and 26 km northwest of Parma. You take the A1 highway to the Fidenza–Salsomaggiore exit. On Wednesdays and Fridays, a shuttle bus goes there from Milan (Piazza Castello). There is also a shuttle bus service from the train station in Fidenza.

Franciacorta Outlet

This is a reference point for low-cost shopping for those going east from Milan. Lots of sports fashion names and accessories, and few high-fashion designer brands.

Follow the A4 highway toward Venice and tthen ake the Ospitaletto exit. It's 90 km from Milan.

Serravalle Outlet

With 150 stores offering a range of goods, from clothing to footwear, accessories, furniture, and jewelry; all the top Italian brand names and more. Prices are 30 percent lower than regular stores, but you can find up to 70 percent discounts.

It's 100 km from Milan (and 48 km from Genoa), right next to the Serravalle Scrivia exit on the A7 Milan-Genoa highway. It's also close to the Novi Ligure exit on the A26/A7 link highway. Intercity buses leave daily at 10:00 a.m. (during the high tourist season, a second bus leaves at 2:00 p.m.) from Milan (Piazzale Cairoli). Buy tickets from Zani Travel Agency, at Foro Buonaparte 76.

Vicolungo Outlet

Goes under the heading of casual, but there are also some top brands. Besides clothing and accessories, you can also find what you need for the home, perfumes and cosmetics, and delicatessens, all at prices a lot lower than the stores downtown.

It's in view from the Biandrate–Vicolungo exit from the A4 highway, 60 km from Milan and 80 km from Turin. It's also close to the interchange with the A26 Genoa Voltri–Gravellona Toce highway. Intercity buses leave daily at 10:30 a.m. from Milan (Piazzale Cairoli). Buy tickets from Zani Travel Agency, at Foro Buonaparte 76.

Foxtown
Via Angelo Maspoli 15,
Mendrisio, Switzerland
Tel: 41848828888
Hours: 11:00 a.m.–7:00 p.m.
Dec. 24–31: Closes at 5:00 p.m.
Closed: Jan. 1, Easter,
Aug. 1, Dec. 25–26
www.foxtown.ch

Fidenza Village
Via San Michele Campagna
Fidenza; Tel: 052433551
Hours: 10:00 a.m.–8:00 p.m.
www.fidenzavillage.com

Franciacorta Outlet
Piazza Cascina Moie 1/2
Rodengo Saiano (Brescia)
Tel: 0306810364
Hours: 10:00 a.m.–8:00 p.m.
www.franciacortaoutlet.it

Serravalle Outlet
Via della Moda 1, Serravalle
Scrivia, Tel: 0143609000
Hours: 10:00 a.m.–8:00 p.m.
www.macarthurglen.com

Vicolungo Outlet
Piazza Santa Caterina
Vicolungo, Tel: 0321875967
Hours: 10:00 a.m.–8:00 p.m.,
except Jan. 1, Easter,
and Dec. 25
vicolungo.thestyleoutlets.it

Printed in Italy
Print completed in November 2013 at Cartoedit - Città di Castello (Perugia)